SUMMIT

150 YEARS OF THE ALPINE CLUB

GEORGE BAND

First published in 2006 by Collins, an imprint of
HarperCollins Publishers Ltd.
77–85 Fulham Palace Road
London
W6 8JB

www.collins.co.uk
Collins is a registered trademark of HarperCollins Publishers Ltd.

7   6   5   4   3   2   1
12 11 10 09 08 07 06

A catalogue record for this book is available from the British Library.

ISBN-13: 978 0 00 720364 2
ISBN-10: 0 00 720364 0

Designed by: Martin Brown

Commissioned by: Myles Archibald
Editorial Director: Helen Brocklehurst
Editor: Emily Pitcher
Production: Graham Cook

Editor and Indexer: Maggie Body
Proofreader: Kathy Gill
Printed in Great Britain by Butler and Tanner, Frome
Colour origination by Dot Gradation, Essex

Future challenges? The endpapers show 16, virgin, 6,000-metre peaks, east of
the Himalaya, researched by Tomatsu Nakamura of the Japanese Alpine Club
(see page 204). They are, from top left to right: Kongga 6,488 m, Nanang
6,870 m, Jalong I 6,292 m, Goyon I 6,252 m (left) and II 6,140 m (right), Kona I
6,378 m (right) and II 6,334m (left), Chuchapo 6,550 m, Lumboganzegabo
6,542 m, Jiongmudazhi 6,590 m, Miancimu 6,054 m, Kawagebo 6,740 m, Ruoni
6,882 m, Tashilanglung 6,170 m, Damyon 6,324 m, Yangmolong 6,060 m,
'Matterhorn of Tibet' Chakucho 6,264 m, Xiannairi 6,032 m.

Collins

CONTENTS

FOREWORD
BY HRH THE DUKE OF EDINBURGH, KG, KT

Anglo-Saxons seem to have a particular desire, and a remarkable talent, for forming clubs. This may be partly due to the wish of like-minded people to add a social dimension to their enthusiasm. It may also be due to a feeling that any activity needs some sort of guidance and management. Whatever the case, the Alpine Club – the first of its kind in the world – has been in existence for 150 years, and it has played a very significant part in the development and evolution of mountaineering.

It is one thing to record the historic mountaineering achievements, the challenge for the club historian is to track the influence of its leaders and to show how the sport of mountaineering has developed through the interaction of practical experience, the clash of opinions and the development of equipment, techniques and technology.

George Band writes with a background of practical experience, and a particular talent for telling a good story. I believe that this volume is a worthy tribute to the Alpine Club's 150th anniversary.

AUTHOR'S NOTE

Several years ago, Myles Archibald of HarperCollins was taken to visit the premises of the Alpine Club in an unpretentious former warehouse just north of the City and was astonished to discover an Aladdin's Cave of books and memorabilia which had been accumulated during almost 150 years of the Club's existence. There were over 25,000 books about mountains and mountaineering, original accounts of first ascents, personal *Führerbucher* of early alpine guides, photographs and slides going back to the earliest days of mountain photography, paintings by distinguished artists and artefacts of all kinds, from ancient ice-axes and nailed boots to de Saussure's compass and Whymper's tent, carefully renovated by the Royal School of Needlework.

Myles felt that there was abundant material here for a richly illustrated book and suggested a meeting. As chairman of the Club's Library, which had charitable status, and scenting possible advance royalties for the Club, I made an immediate appointment. In the course of our discussion, we realised that the fiftieth anniversary of the first ascent of Everest, occurring in May 2003, deserved to be celebrated first, so I left the meeting slightly dazed and charged with writing yet another Everest book. Fortunately, it proved very successful, briefly entering the bestseller lists, and was even classed as a 'fast Climber' together with Michael Schumacher's motor-racing autobiography!

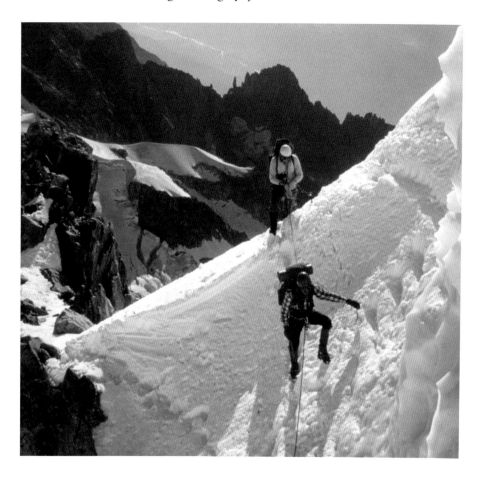

right: Alpine Club Veterans, on the Old Brenva route, Italian side of Mont Blanc, 23 August 1991.

Once Everest was out of the way, I was reminded that the Club's 150th anniversary was due in 2007, and another celebratory book was required. No other Club member volunteered for the task, so here it is, and thanks again to HarperCollins for agreeing to publish it.

There is a slight complication in telling the story. In the 1920s, 1930s and 1950s, the Alpine Club played a major role in the successive attempts to climb Everest, which are already chronicled in my previous book, so I did not feel it was sensible to repeat it all again here. If readers wish to be reminded of the history of climbing Everest, then I can only invite them to beg, borrow or steal a copy of the original hardback edition, which is now out of print, or even buy a copy of the updated paperback *Everest Exposed*, published in 2005, which hopefully is still available.

A further complication was to differentiate between a total history of mountaineering and just a history of the Alpine Club itself. One had to place the latter within the historical development of the sport, before moving on to the early days of the Club and its members. We are also fortunate that, since its inception, many distinguished foreign climbers have also joined the Club or accepted honorary membership, so it is appropriate to include some of their achievements.

This current work was a daunting task to complete in a few months, but it was made much easier by reference to the *Alpine Journals* published annually and, in particular, by the special centenary number of the *Alpine Journal*, together with Sir Arnold Lunn's *Centenary of Mountaineering,* which was generously sponsored by the Swiss Foundation for Alpine Research. For the last 50 years, I have my own set of *Alpine Journals* and library of mountaineering books to consult and a fund of precious memories of my own involvement with the Club, with my climbing friends and with the sport worldwide. I am conscious that there are some omissions, or topics and regions that are treated too superficially, but to amend them would only increase the length and scope of this work and I have already exceeded my publisher's brief. If the result is too personal for some tastes, then I can only apologise for my self-indulgence but it was more enjoyable for me to write this way!

I was keen to use as many illustrations as possible from the Alpine Club's own historical archives and am very grateful to Anna Lawford and Rachael Swann for helping me to select them. Club members have also generously contributed their own recent superb photographs as listed in the photo credits. I also thank several friends who have reviewed all or part of the text or helped in research: Jerry Lovatt, Bill Norton, Peter Berg, Chris Russell, Ken Wilson, Lindsay Griffin, Yvonne Sibbald, Maggie Body and all the staff concerned at HarperCollins, particularly Myles Archibald, Helen Brocklehurst and Emily Pitcher, who have become personal friends. I don't know what I would have done without my personal assistant, June Perry, for her computing skills, proof reading and for keeping me abreast of my work plan. Finally, thanks to my dear wife, Susan, for allowing me to postpone or avoid so many of the household tasks of dog-walking, car-washing, grass-mowing, leaf-raking, gutter-cleaning and bonfire-burning so that I could get on with the book!

Hartley Wintney, January 2006

PERSPECTIVE

I snuggle deeply into my sleeping bag after an ample supper of bread, cheese, saucisson and fruitcake, with a hot drink melted from the surrounding ice and snow. Rob Collister, Jerry Lovatt and I are perched on a rocky eyrie halfway up the stupendous Brenva face on the Italian side of Mont Blanc. It's a fine night with two-thirds of a moon, and the lights of Courmayeur 8,500 feet below. The only sound is the occasional whir of a falling stone and the collapse of an ice sérac in the direction of the rarely climbed Grand Pilier d'Angle. The date is 22 August 1991. You may well ask what on earth is a 62-year-old pensioner doing here? The answer goes back nearly 40 years.

'How did you get on Everest in 1953?' I am occasionally asked. 'Had you done much climbing?' In fact, after only three Alpine seasons, the third in 1952 being particularly successful, I was lucky to be in the right place at the right time to be chosen by John Hunt as the youngest member of the climbing team. But my interrogators were often sceptical. 'Had I climbed Mont Blanc or the Matterhorn?' No, I had to admit. The Matterhorn by the Zmutt ridge was duly accomplished with Mike and Sally Westmacott in 1969 and as a complete surprise on my return home my wife, Susan, marked our tenth wedding anniversary by presenting me with a splendid oil painting of the mountain by the Everest climber and surgeon Howard Somervell. But Mont Blanc still eluded me. Then, fortuitously, I was invited to speak at a Wordsworth Trust weekend in Grasmere,

below: An ice-cliff on the Old Brenva, 23 August 1991, remarkably almost identical to a photograph by Frank Smythe in August 1939.

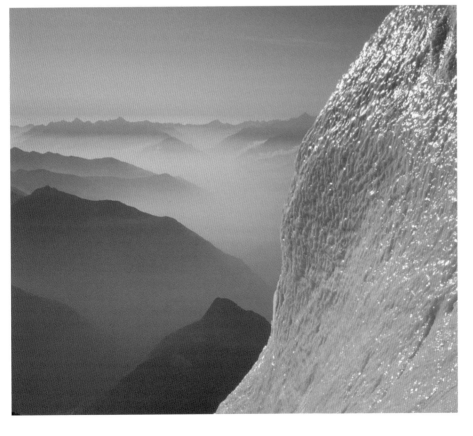

commemorating the poet's epic walk from Cambridge to the Alps 200 years previously. Another contributor, the Alpine Club Librarian Jerry Lovatt, was speaking on the history of the climbing of Mont Blanc, but he had to admit rather shamefacedly that he had never completed the climb himself. We thereupon resolved to do it together that summer.

We wanted to choose a route that would both challenge us and be worthy of the mountain. At our mature age, we would be safer with a guide, a luxury that I would never have considered or been able to afford in my youth, so we were delighted when Rob Collister said he was free to join us. We decided to try the classic Old Brenva route, which was first climbed in 1865. Professor T Graham Brown described it in the 1930s as follows: 'The climb was far in advance of the standard of the time … It is still to be classed amongst the great climbs of the Alps.'

A special feature of the route is a buttress halfway up whose crest forms a horizontal ridge of ice, described by A W Moore after the first ascent: 'Before us lay a narrow, but not steep arête of rock and snow combined, which appeared to terminate some distance in front in a sharp peak … On reaching it, the apparent peak proved not to be a peak at all, but the extremity of the narrowest and most formidable ice arête I ever saw, which extended on a level for an uncomfortably long distance. Looking back by the light of our subsequent success, I have always considered it a providential circumstance that at this moment Jakob and not Melchior, was leading the party.'

Melchior had earlier described the route as 'Eine miserable Dummheit' – 'A wretched piece of folly' but his equally bold but less prudent younger cousin, Jakob, pressed on regardless. The arête became a knife-edge of pure blue ice with steep drops on either side. Jakob cut holes for the feet or simply sliced off the top to make a slippery pathway, but the clients mostly proceeded à cheval, with a leg on either side – safer but considerably more uncomfortable. There were five in the roped party; Jakob Anderegg in the lead at that moment, followed by Frank Walker (aged 59), Horace Walker, George Mathews, Melchior Anderegg with Moore bringing up the rear. It was a very daring expedition for those days; the consequences of a slip were unthinkable. It was customary for the guides alone to carry ice-axes and cut all the steps, the amateurs using a simple pole or alpenstock to keep in balance, although Moore had used an ice-axe on other expeditions.

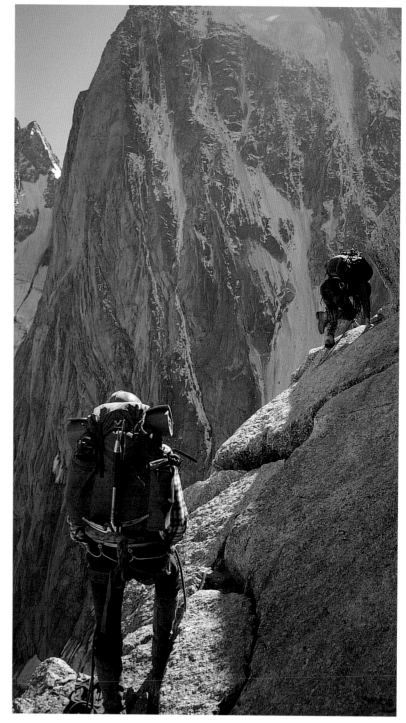

above: Jerry Lovatt rounds a rocky corner on the Old Brenva, with the Grand Pilier d'Angle in the background.

For our attempt, rather than spending the previous night in a stuffy mountain hut – the normal Trident refuge was fully booked anyway – Rob suggested we set our own timetable and bivouacked on the ridge itself. I had wanted a day's rest first, being tired from two training climbs, but Rob was insistent we started early next morning as the present fair weather was forecast to end in two days.

Thanks possibly to global warming, the ice ridge did not hold such terrors for us – it was hard snow and well trodden. The upper ice cliffs also yielded more easily to front-pointed crampons and an ice-axe or hammer-axe in each hand, although in my rush to leave I had only taken the one axe. At one particularly glistening ice cliff, I stopped for a photograph and had a strange sense of having been here before. Later I discovered my snapshot was almost identical to one taken 42 years previously by Frank Smythe and published in his book *A Camera in the Hills*. The ice cliff was remarkably unchanged. Soon the clouds descended and the last 1,000 feet to the summit was an exhausting trudge in a white-out, but,

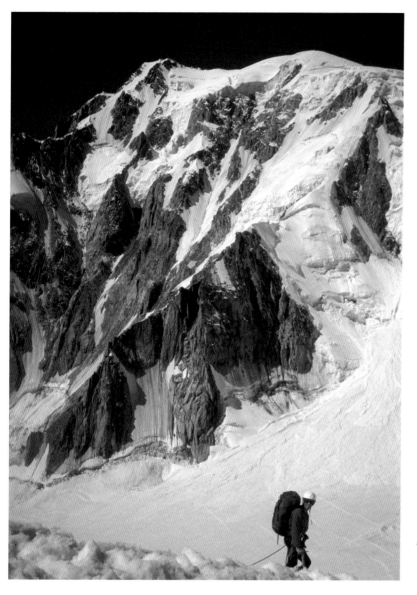

thanks to Rob, we had achieved our objective and climbed Mont Blanc. A storm broke that night. The Met forecast had been accurate; how lucky we were.

Just before we left the valley for our climb, Jerry had heard on the radio that Gorbachev had been deposed. Now on our return, a newspaper headline announced he was back in power. I had totally missed the second Russian revolution!

Reflecting on our successful climb, I thought how much we owed to the vision and daring of those early members of the Alpine Club in the 1860s, together with their Swiss guides; a tradition maintained in the 1930s by their successors such as Frank Smythe and Graham Brown on the Brenva face. In Isaac Newton's famous phrase we were 'standing on the shoulders of giants'.

As the Club approached its 150th Anniversary in 2007, it was time for somebody to accept the daunting task of researching and writing the history of the oldest mountaineering club in the world. I do not feel at all well equipped for the task, but fortunately, over the years the sport has also produced some fine writing, from the first publications in 1859 of the three volumes of *Peaks, Passes and Glaciers* edited by John Ball, to their successor, the *Alpine Journal*, which first appeared in 1863 and regularly ever since. There is a mass of material to draw upon, fully justifying John Ball's prediction in his original preface: 'The degree of success that may

above: Rob Collister and the Brenva Face of Mont Blanc. The Old Brenva is the foreground ridge from lower left to top right.

attend the present volume, and the extent and value of the new materials that may be accumulated in the course of fresh expeditions, will probably decide whether a new collection of Alpine adventures shall at some future time be presented to the Public.'

So, in the words from Ecclesiasticus: 'Let us now praise famous men, and our fathers that begat us.' But let us also look to the future and the continuing success and prosperity of the Alpine Club.

1 In The Beginning

THE FOUNDING OF THE CLUB

On 1 February 1857, William Mathews wrote to his friend the Revd Fenton John Anthony Hort, a distinguished theologian and Fellow of Trinity College, Cambridge: 'I want you to consider whether it would not be possible to establish an Alpine Club, the members of which might dine together once a year, say in London, and give each other what information they could. Each member, at the close of any Alpine tour in Switzerland or elsewhere, should be required to furnish, to the President, a short account of all the undescribed excursions he had made, with a view to the publication of an annual or bi-annual volume. We should thus get a good deal of useful information in a form available to the members.'

Hort agreed but urged that the dining bills be kept within bounds.

Later that summer, Mathews met Edward Shirley Kennedy in the Alps and discussed two projects, an ascent of the Finsteraarhorn and the formation of a mountaineering club. On 13 August in a party with William's cousin, St. John Mathews, Revd John Hardy and J C W Ellis, they successfully made the first British ascent of the Finsteraarhorn and this strengthened their resolve to form a club.

On 6 November, William Mathews senior gave a dinner party at his home, The Leasowes (now the clubhouse of the Halesowen Golf Club), near Birmingham, for Kennedy and various members of the Mathews family at which a list of potential founding members was compiled. Those who accepted met on 22 December at Ashley's Hotel, Covent Garden, with Kennedy as chairman, and founded the first of the Alpine Clubs. Those attending were Messrs Kennedy, Ames, Anderson, Blomfield, Cabell, Coleman, Hawkins, Hinchliff, Shepherd, Walters and Watson.

The first circular in the Club's possession is undated but was sent out by Kennedy earlier in December with invitations to this event. It contained a list of twelve original members: Ainslie, Ames, Hinchcliff, Kennedy, Longman, B St. John Mathews, Edward Mathews, William Mathews, Revd E J Shepherd, Revd Isaac Taylor, Henry Trower and Alfred Wills.

A second similar circular added eight more names: Anderson, Birkbeck, Revd J D Davies, Hawkins, Hort, Albert Smith, Revd H W Watson and George Yool.

A third circular issued in January 1858 added another eight: Blomfield, Cabell, Coleman, Hardy, Hayward, Lightfoot, M'Calmont and Walters.

These circulars listed the objects of the Club and the proposed Rules with various modifications with an opening statement:

left: On the glacier below Mont Blanc. An 1862 photograph by Auguste-Rosalie Bisson (1826–1900).

below: Edward Shirley Kennedy (c. 1880) 1817–98. A prime mover and original member of the Club. President 1861–63.

The Alpine Club invites the membership of all who have explored high mountainous ranges. It facilitates association among those who, in their admiration of natural grandeur, possess similarity of taste … and will enable its members to make arrangements for meeting at some suitable locality whence they may in common undertake any of the more difficult mountain excursions. It will also give to all an opportunity of interchanging information, of recording the results of novel expeditions, and of consulting the maps and books to be placed in the rooms which it is expected the Club will eventually possess. The members will occasionally dine together at their own expense, but the funds of the Club will be made available when on suitable occasions the Club is favoured by the presence of geographical explorers, or by that of other guests of celebrity.

An initial Rule VII stipulated that 'a candidate shall not be eligible unless he shall have ascended to the top of a mountain 13,000 feet in height'. A number of applicants replied that this would exclude them and needlessly restrict the membership so it was dropped and technical qualifications left to the committee's discretion. Those approved were then submitted to a ballot of the members. One blackball in five led to the application being rejected – later altered to one in ten – making it easier for small cliques to bar such distinguished mountaineers as Mummery. I don't know when this practice was discontinued, but the 'blackballing machine' still exists as an historic relic in the Club's archives!

The first formal dinner of the Club was held on 3 February 1858 in the Thatched House Tavern, 85 St James's Street; less than a dozen attended. In those days, a number of such organisations (for example the Royal Geographical Society) started as a dining club only. In the Alpine Club's case, the 'Alpine Dining Club' was formed subsequently, mainly from past and present officers of the Club, to dine together before the monthly meetings. It was still in existence in the 1950s when, although not a member of the Club, I was kindly invited to it during the Everest celebrations in 1953. I automatically arrived in black tie and to my chagrin found everyone else in suits!

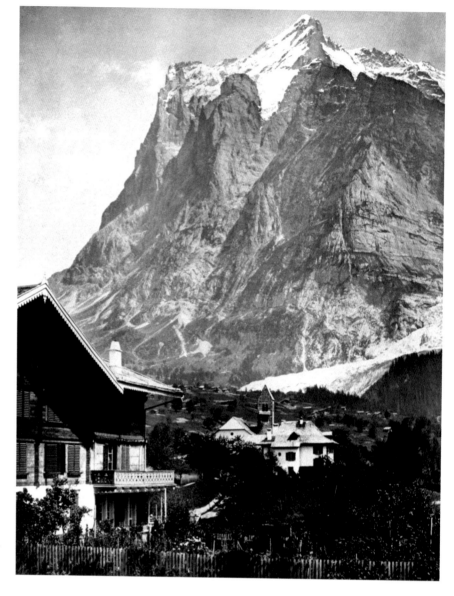

THIS PAGE:

above: Grindelwald and the Wetterhorn. An early photograph by Martens c. 1853.

OPPOSITE PAGE:

above right: Sunrise on Mont Aiguille (2,086 m) in the Vercors, near Grenoble. The first genuine mountaineering challenge? Climbed in 1492.

below right: John Ball, the Club's first President, 1856–60, and Editor of the first volume of *Peaks, Passes and Glaciers* published in 1859.

PEAKS, PASSES AND GLACIERS

The first president of the Club, John Ball, was elected at the March meeting of the Club in 1858. He seemed the perfect choice; having private means he was able to pursue numerous activities: a member of the Irish Bar, he entered parliament and became Under-Secretary for the Colonies, but was also greatly interested in science. He first saw the Alps at the age of nine and became fascinated by everything connected with the mountains. That autumn, he suggested to William Longman, one of the original twelve members and later president of the Club, that members' accounts of Alpine ascents would interest a larger public, so his firm, Longmans Green and Company, published not only *Peaks, Passes and Glaciers* and the *Alpine Journal* but also many of the earlier Alpine classics. The *Journal* was subtitled *A Record of Mountain Adventure and Scientific Observation*.

Ball's *Alpine Guides* were also of great influence in the development of mountaineering, the first volume, *The Guide to the Western Alps* appearing in 1863, by which time Ball himself had already crossed the main Alpine chain by thirty-two different passes and traversed a hundred lateral ones.

The first number of the *Alpine Journal* – the oldest mountaineering journal – appeared in 1863, under the editorship of the Revd Hereford Brooke George, a Fellow of New College. This was the founding year of the Swiss Alpine Club, just a year after that of the Austrian Alpine Club.

I have described the founding of the Alpine Club in some detail, as its history is the subject of this book. Ronald Clark, in his *Victorian Mountaineers*, comments on its naming: 'The result was the Alpine Club – the Alpine Club and not the London Alpine Club or the British Alpine Club. There was no need for any geographical location for this, the first organisation of its kind; in any case, the calm clear assumption of superiority fitted well into the spirit of the age. It had, after all, been the Great Exhibition, unqualified by any adjective. The Alpine Club therefore assumed, at its inception, a certain curatorial rightness – in which it had, after all, it must be admitted, almost every possible claim.' In the same way that our postage stamps are recognised, not by the name of the country, but by our sovereign's head, there may be a tendency to think that the sport, just like the postage stamp, was an English invention. Indeed the beginning of 'sporting' mountaineering and the Golden Age in the Alps is often dated from Alfred Wills' ascent of the Wetterhorn in 1854.

THE APPRECIATION OF MOUNTAINS

17. „Draco Montanus 1660"

Aus „Itinera par Helvetiae alpinas regiones"
von J. J. Scheuchzer

If we go back much farther in time, the Greeks had little interest in mountains and no appreciation of mountain beauty. Homer described them all 'covered in mists which are bad for shepherds but better than night for thieves'. Only Mount Olympus – the home of the gods – had been suitably refurbished for them. 'It is not shaken by winds nor wet with rain. The snow does not come near to it, but mist-clear air is spread above it cloudless, and the white light floats over it. There the blessed gods are happy for all their days.'

In contrast, to the Hebrews, the majesty of the mountains revealed the glory of God. Moses gave thanks 'for the chief things of the ancient mountains and for the precious things of the lasting hills'. And the psalmist proclaimed: 'I will lift up mine eyes unto the hills from whence cometh my help.'

In medieval times we read occasional accounts of mountaineering for enjoyment. Francesco Petrarch (1304–74), the patron saint of mountaineers, ascended Mont Ventoux in Provence on 26 April 1335, revelling in the glorious panorama from the summit, which he described in an enthusiastic letter to his father.

Professor Conrad Gesner of Zurich, born in 1516, made it a rule to climb one mountain a year. He enjoyed the discipline of hardship, the remembered toil and danger and the silence of the heights in which 'one catches echoes of the harmony of the celestial spheres'. It was his friend Professor Marti of Berne who discovered on the summit of the Stockhorn a Greek inscription, cut into a stone: 'The love of mountains is best'.

But these accounts were exceptions to the widespread view that mountains, and especially the Alps, were ugly and fearful places haunted by demons and dragons. It took the romantic movement in the early nineteenth century, and the influence of poets such as Byron and Wordsworth, to discern their beauty. Arnold Lunn regards Byron's visits to the Oberland in 1816, which provided the setting for his dramatic poem *Manfred*, as perhaps the greatest single influence in popularising the Oberland in general and the Kleine Scheidegg in particular.

John Ruskin was unrivalled as a word-painter of mountain scenery, and a fine artist as well. He became a member of the Alpine Club in 1869 – elected on a literary rather than a mountaineering qualification – having presumably been forgiven for his earlier intemperate attack on the Alpine Club in *Sesame and Lilies* when he criticised the early pioneers for looking on the Alps 'as soaped poles in a bear-garden, which you set yourselves to climb and slide down again, with shrieks of delight'. He was rather more perceptive in summing up the ascetic nature of mountaineering in a letter to his father from Chamonix in 1863:

That question of the moral effect of danger is a very curious one; but this I know and find, practically, that if you come to a dangerous place, and turn back from it, though it may have been perfectly right and wise to do so, still your character has suffered some slight deterioration; you are to that extent weaker, more life-less, more effeminate, more liable to passion and error in future; whereas if you go through with the danger though it may have been apparently wrong and fool-ish to encounter it, you come out of the encounter a stronger and better man, fitter for every sort of work and trial, and *nothing but danger* produces this effect.

top left: 'The Alps were ugly and fearful places haunted by demons and dragons.'

bottom left: A Tyrolese hunter (c. 1830). Note his snow shoes; crampons at his waist; and ice-axe.

THIS PAGE:

below: The Club Room of Zermatt 1864; an engraving by Whymper. In the group are, left: Grove, Foster, Robertson, Morshead, F. Walker, Stephen, Moore, MacDonald. Centre: Ball, W. Mathews, Kennedy, Bonney, Lauener, Tyndall, Wills. Right: Lucy Walker, Maquignaz, Perren, Andermatten.

THE BIRTH OF MOUNTAINEERING

The first ascent of Mont Aiguille (6,880 ft/2,096 m) in the Vercors near Grenoble was the scene of the first genuine mountaineering challenge, accepted and achieved. When Charles VIII of France passed by in 1492 he was so struck by its appearance that he ordered his chamberlain, Dompjulien de Beaupré, to make the ascent. Beaupré wisely delegated the task to Antoine de Ville, aged 40, Captain of Montelimar, commander of 450 men, and one of the king's most suc-cessful campaigners. De Ville chose a team of seven including Noble Raymond Jubie, siege-ladder builder to the king, Pierre Arnaud, master carpenter, and Cathalin Servet, master stone-mason. Spiritual support was provided by Sebastian de Caret, royal master of theology and chaplain to the king, and François de Bosco, de Ville's personal confessor.

On 26 June, after weeks of prepa-ration and with the aid of 'subtle means and engines' and ascending 'half a league of ladders', de Ville success-fully led his men to the top. They remained there for several days until the clerk from Grenoble arrived to verify the ascent. It was not repeated until 1834, nearly 350 years later, by a young Frenchman who found black-ened rocks and debris from the earlier expedition.

Many of the more enterprising pioneers of the eighteenth century were priests, the most distinguished being the Benedictine monk Father Placidus à Spescha. He was not just a one-off climber: between 1788 and 1824 over nine seasons he made a series

of brilliant first ascents of peaks over 11,000 feet in eastern Switzerland, such as the Stockgron, Piz Urlaun and the Rheinwaldhorn. Graham Brown, in his introduction to the Londsdale Library volume on mountaineering, described him as 'perhaps the first of the true mountaineers'.

It was in 1760 that a distinguished scientist from Geneva, Horace Bénédict de Saussure, visited Chamonix and offered a reward of two guineas to whoever first climbed Mont Blanc (15,782 ft/4,807 m), the highest peak in the Alps, although not in Europe if you include Elbruz (18,481 ft/5,633 m) in the Caucasus. The prize was claimed controversially in 1786 by Jacques Balmat, a crystal gatherer, who accompanied the local doctor Michel Paccard, although surely both shared in the success. One year later on 9 August, Colonel Mark Beaufoy made the fourth ascent, becoming the first Englishman to do so. The Club has his manuscript account of the climb.

From then until the 1850s, many of the higher Alpine peaks were climbed for the first time by continental mountaineers: the Gross Glockner by the Bishop of Gurk; the Ortler, the highest in the Tirol, by Joseph Pichler, an Austrian chamois hunter; the Jungfrau by members of the Meyer family of Aarau; the Finsteraarhorn, the monarch of the Oberland, by the two guides Jakob Lenthold and Johann Währen, employed by a Swiss scientist, F J Hugi.

During this period another Swiss scientist, Professor Louis Agassiz, carried out research on glacial movement on the Unteraar glacier, sleeping under an overhanging boulder called 'Hotel de Neuchâtelois'. Two of his companions, Edouard Desor, a German, and Dollfus Ausset, from Alsace, meanwhile climbed the Lauteraarhorn, the Galenstock and the Rosenhorn. The various summits of the Monte Rosa massif were climbed mostly by Italians or Valaisians who had

above: Mur de la Côte, one of four colour prints by George Baxter (1804–67) from *The Ascent of Mont Blanc*, 1853.

OPPOSITE PAGE:

above right: Albert Smith lectured to capacity audiences for six years at the Egyptian Hall, Piccadilly.

right: Albert Smith, consummate showman and a founder member of the Club..

migrated to Macugnaga or Gressoney, notably J Zumstein, who gave his name to the Zumstein Spitze (15,004 ft/4,563 m), climbed in 1820. Three more notable climbs were the Mittelhorn (12,166 ft/3,708 m), the highest point of the Wetterhorner, in 1845 by a Scotsman, Stanhope Templeman Speer; the Pelvoux (12,973 ft/3,954 m) in the Dauphiné in 1848 by a Frenchman, Victor Piuseux, and the Piz Bernina (13,295 ft/4,152 m), highest in the Engadine, in 1850 by Coaz of Switzerland. These brilliant early exploits were characteristic of an era of isolated ascents. After 1850, mountaineering became more of an organised sport in which British climbers, with their guides who were mostly Swiss, were to play a major part.

THE PHENOMENON OF ALBERT SMITH

Albert Smith (1816–60) was given a book about Mont Blanc at the age of ten, which fired his imagination, and he determined to reach the summit. He earned a living as a writer for *Punch* and the *Illustrated London News* and travelled to Constantinople and the Nile. He turned his eastern travels into very popular illustrated lectures which earned him enough to try Mont Blanc in August 1851. With three companions, he made the fortieth ascent accompanied by at least 16 guides and 18 porters, carrying 46 fowls, 20 loaves, 91 bottles of wine and 3 of cognac. Smith wore high leggings tied with scarlet gaiters, Scots tartan trousers, a worsted helmet, green veil and blue spectacles. The ascent went off without incident but lost nothing in the telling in his book *The Story of Mont Blanc*. He was a consummate showman and taking advice from Phineas T Barnum, originator of the Greatest Show on Earth, he hired the Egyptian Hall, Piccadilly, for a series of illustrated lectures which were an instant success – clearly outshining those for the first ascent of Everest a century later. The show ran from 1852 for six years. In the first two seasons alone more than 200,000 people saw it, earning him £17,000 or over £1.2 million in today's money. There were three royal command performances, including a visit by Queen Victoria. Someone invented the Game of Mont Blanc, a board game like Snakes and Ladders, of which the Alpine Club has an original copy.

Although Smith became a founder member of the Club, he was not much liked by his contemporaries. A *Punch* colleague said his initials ARS were only two-thirds of the truth. Who cared if Smith wasn't a real mountaineer? He gave the public what they wanted, and there is no doubt he made many converts to mountaineering.

ALBERT SMITH.

THE ALPINE CLUB PIONEERS

Alfred Wills (1828–1912) was a more conventional mountaineer, among the first to visit the Alps regularly, driven by a love of the natural environment. He came first as a law student in 1846 and, with few interruptions, celebrated his Golden Jubilee as an Alpine traveller and mountaineer at Chamonix in 1896. He became the Club's third President in 1864.

In 1857, after climbing Mont Buet in the Haute Savoie, he descended to the Plateau des Fonds – an isolated meadow surrounded by luxurious forests above the village of Sixt. He resolved to build a chalet there. His wife, Lucy, designed it, and his guide, Auguste Balmat (a great-nephew of Jacques Balmat of Mont Blanc), took charge of the construction. Sadly, his wife died before it was completed, and Wills dedicated his book, *The Eagle's Nest in the Valley of Sixt: a summer home among the Alps*, 'To the memory of a gentle, loving and most accomplished wife …' Their eldest daughter, Edith, became Mrs Edward Norton and was given the Eagle's Nest by her father in 1902. Wills died in 1912 and thereafter the history of the chalet belongs to the Norton family until they sold it in 1958. Wills' great-grandson, Bill Norton, is a fellow member of the Alpine Club, his father being Lieut-General E F Norton, leader of the 1924 Everest Expedition.

Alfred Wills was a leading British climber in the early 1850s even though the ascent of the Wetterhorn on 17 September 1854, his first major peak, described in his book *Wandering among the High Alps*, was probably the second or third rather than the first, for which the credit must go to Speer on 9 July 1845, with his guides Jaun, Abplanalp and Michel. It seems that Wills' guide, Peter Bohren, had climbed it previously but was reluctant to disillusion his client from believing he was making a first ascent. One should not doubt Wills' integrity. He became a judge, being appointed after his predecessor had died of heart failure in a brothel. Queen Victoria was so shocked that she insisted to the prime minister that the personal character, religion and home life of the successor should be exemplary. Wills later presided over the trial that led to the conviction of Oscar Wilde.

below: Alfred Wills, eminent lawyer, judge, and Club President 1864–5 at his chalet, The Eagles' Nest, above Sixt.

Graham Brown, discussing the relative importance of Speer's and Wills' ascents of the Wetterhorn, concluded that Speer's well publicised narrative soon after his climb probably played a greater part in the beginnings of mountaineering as a sport than the part attributed to Sir Alfred Wills, whose account did not appear until 1856. Wills brought in early recruits to the young sport; Speer's service was to prepare the way for the sport itself.

In its initial years, the members of the Alpine Club were predominantly middle- or upper-class, and mostly from the towns and cities, happy to get away from the smoke and grime of the industrial revolution to rediscover fresh air and the countryside. From the data recorded in Mumm's Alpine Club Register, Arnold Lunn analysed the professions of the first 281 members elected between 1857 and 1863: 57 were barristers and 23 solicitors; 34 were clergymen, 15 dons and 7 schoolmasters. There were 5 scientists, 4 authors, 4 artists, 2 architects, 2 librarians and 1 lecturer. The Civil Service was represented by 12, the Army by 7, and the Royal Navy by 2 members, medicine by 4 and surgery by 4 members. There were 2 publishers, 5 engineers, 6 printers, stationers and engravers, 8 bankers, 4 insurance agents, 2 railway directors, 2 estate agents, 5 stockbrokers, 18 merchants. The club included 3 professional politicians, 13 rentiers, 19 landed gentry, 4 foreign members and 7 whose professions cannot be ascertained.

below: Leslie Stephen, President 1866–8, Editor of the *Alpine Journal* 1868–72, and first editor of *The Dictionary of National Biography*, dressed for the City.

below right: Leslie Stephen, dressed for the mountains, with his favourite guide, Melchior Anderegg.

left: The Walker family with friends and guides:
back row: Jacob Anderegg, M J Moore, Lucy
Walker, Melchior Anderegg,
middle row: Miss Hughes, Horace Walker,
(Lucy's brother), Mrs F Walker, A W Moore,
front row: Frank Walker (Lucy's father),
Johann Jaun.

below: Mr and Mrs E P Jackson c.1870s.
The best-dressed couple on the crags?

OPPOSITE PAGE:

right: A memento of Edward Whymper's
handwriting supplied by Emlyn Jones.

below right: W A B Coolidge, the 'Sage of
Grindelwald', by Granville, 1922.

One of the scientists was undoubtedly Professor J D
Forbes, who was elected a Fellow of the Royal Society at the
age of 23 and appointed to the Chair of Natural Philosophy at
Edinburgh University a year later. Between 1832 and 1844,
he travelled extensively in the Alps as a pioneer explorer and
glaciologist, crossing numerous glacier passes. He visited
Agassiz on the Unteraar glacier and in 1842 he pioneered a
systematic study of glaciers, carrying out detailed observations
on the Mer de Glace.

Forbes' explorations formed a link between the scientific
investigations of de Saussure and the climbers of the Golden
Age, for many of whom his writings had been an inspiration.
Arnold Lunn noted: 'Agassiz accused Forbes of stealing his
ideas, and thus forged the first link in a daisy chain of alpine
quarrels, for Tyndall quarrelled with Forbes after which the
torch of strife was passed on from the scientific mountaineers
to the unscientific; Tyndall quarrelling with Whymper,
Whymper with Coolidge and Coolidge, the Lord of Battles,
with almost every contemporary mountaineer who put pen to
paper and with many who did not.'

Forbes' book *Travels Through the Alps of Savoy* (1843) was the
first in English to describe a series of Alpine climbs. He
became known as the Father of British Mountaineering and in
1859 the Alpine Club made him its first honorary member.

29 Ludgate Hill, E.C.
Dec. 23, 1904.

My dear Walker,

The LIST OF MEMBERS of the *Alpine Club* that was issued in 1859 is believed to be the first one which was printed. It has become extremely scarce. The Club itself does not possess a copy of it, and from enquiries which have been made amongst the older Members of the Club, I am led to suppose that the copy in my possession is very likely the only one in existence. It was given to me in 1860 by Mr. William Longman.

The List has been re-printed by Messrs. Spottiswoode in the same form and as nearly as possible exactly like the original. I have much pleasure in offering the enclosed copy for your acceptance.

Faithfully yours,
Edward Whymper.

Professor John Tyndall also occupied an important place as a scientist and mountaineer in the period succeeding Forbes between 1856 and 1871. He and Forbes were involved in a bitter controversy, disagreeing over the manner of glacial motion. Forbes' careful investigations confirmed the plasticity and viscous nature of ice, whereas Tyndall believed in the rigid composition and sliding motion of glaciers. In 1853, he was appointed Professor of Natural Philosophy at the Royal Institution.

He was the son of an Irish shoemaker, but such was the prestige of science in the class-conscious Victorian age that the Duke of Abercorn's sister was delighted when he married her daughter.

Tyndall was also an outstanding mountaineer, making the first ascent of the Weisshorn, a solitary ascent of Monte Rosa and in 1868 the first complete traverse of the Matterhorn from Italy to Switzerland. Later in life, to relax from the stress of his professional work, he loved to stay in the house he built at Belalp, a green balcony perched above a forest belt overlooking Brig and the wide sweep of the lower Aletsch glacier. At the Alpine Club winter dinner in 1862, Tyndall could not stomach some jocular remarks by Leslie Stephen satirising science as an adjunct to mountaineering. He resigned in a huff from the Club which had elected him vice-president only six weeks earlier.

Stephen reproduced the jest in his book *The Playground of Europe*: '"And what philosophical observations did you make?" will be the enquiry of one of those fanatics who, by a reasoning process to me utterly inscrutable, have somehow irrevocably associated alpine travelling with science. To them I answer that the temperature on the summit of the Zinal Rothorn was approximately (I had no thermometer) 212 (Fahrenheit) below freezing point. As for ozone, if any existed in the atmosphere, it was a greater fool than I take it for.'

Few of the pioneers had a longer list of first ascents than Leslie Stephen: the Schreckhorn, Blümlisalphorn, Bietschorn, Rimpfischhorn, Zinal Rothorn, Monte della Disgrazia and Mont Mallet. Most of these were climbed with his favourite guide, Melchior Anderegg. Stephen was quite ready to give all the credit to his guides: 'The true way at least to describe all my alpine ascents is that Michel or Anderegg or Lauener succeeded in performing a feat requiring skill, strength and courage, the difficulty of which was much increased by the difficulty of taking with him his knapsack and his employer.'

He became president of the Alpine Club in 1866 after Alfred Wills and Editor of the *Alpine Journal* in 1868. By birth a member of the intellectual aristocracy of Victorian England, he married first a daughter of Thackeray and, secondly, Julia Jackson. One of their daughters was the writer Virginia Woolf. Stephen went to Eton and Trinity Hall, Cambridge, where he was elected a fellow in 1854 provided, as the rules required, he took Holy Orders. But in 1862, he abandoned Christianity, becoming an agnostic, so was forced to resign his fellowship. He was able to supplement a small private income with literary work and criticism. He launched, and was first editor of *The Dictionary of National Biography*, which continues to this day. His biographer, Noel Annan, said of him: 'Revenge or malice were beneath him; he despised personal gain and all devious ways of influence or persuasion; and if this magnanimity took him a pace or two out of the world, it invested his character with a noble simplicity.'

These Alpine Club pioneers have left a visible reminder of British achievement during the Golden Age of mountaineering if you view the ring of peaks in the wonderful panorama from the Gornergrat above Zermatt: the Dom, Täschhorn, Alphubel, Allalinhorn, Rimpfischhorn and Strahlhorn were all climbed by the British, as were also the Nord End of Monte Rosa, Lyskamm and Castor. Pollux and the Breithorn fell to Swiss and French climbers but, thereafter, the Matterhorn, Gabelhorn, Zinal Rothorn and Weisshorn were British successes. The Swiss had a better record in the Bernese Oberland where they claimed the Wetterhorn, Jungfrau and Finsteraarhorn. According to Coolidge, of the 39 major peaks climbed during the Golden Age, 31 were first ascended by British amateurs with their guides, who were mostly Swiss.

above: The Young Coolidge with his aunt, Miss Meta Brevoort, flanked by their guides, Christian and Ulrich Almer. The beagle bitch Tschingel accompanied them on numerous climbs, c. 1870.

OPPOSITE PAGE:

above right: Drawn by G S Holland, formerly Chief Cartographer of the Royal Geographical Society. Note the great ring of peaks around the Matterhorn in the Pennine Alps.

right: 'Ascent of the Rothorn'. Whymper's engraving formed the frontispiece to Leslie Stephen's classic *The Playground of Europe*.

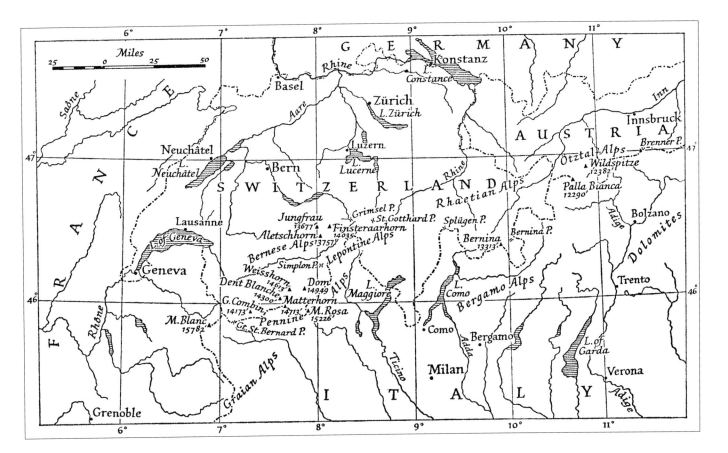

The guides began as shepherds, chamois hunters, crystal gatherers or smugglers and learned as much from their employers as they taught them. The relations between the best of the amateurs and the greatest of the guides became a genuine partnership, gradually developing and perfecting the technique of mountaineering. It took some years before the guides mastered the proper use of the rope – possibly evincing a lack of confidence in their client. It was not uncommon for a good guide to remove the rope in dangerous places and hold a coil in one hand. These were the difficulties the pioneers had to overcome and led Lord Schuster to reflect 'but for those men in whiskers, long trousers and gigantic ice-axes, climbing for Englishmen would, if it had ever existed, have been long delayed'. In the next chapter, I recall some of the greatest Alpine guides in the two decades 1860–80.

The first half of the 1860s may fairly be claimed as the greatest period in alpine history. Leslie Stephen was in full stride, although eclipsed by Whymper in 1864–5. Adams Reilly, the Walkers (not forgetting Lucy) and A W Moore are other giants, with 'Hornby-and-Philpott' just behind them.

The following list of the principal climbing events of 1864 and 1865, taken from the Alpine Club's *Centenary Journal*, shows how great were the accomplishments during those two vintage years. For simplicity, the guides' names are omitted; the names of non-members of the Club are in italics. Asterisks indicate a first ascent, or crossing of a pass.

1864

June

21	*Col des Aiguilles d'Arves	A W Moore, Horace Walker, and E Whymper
23	*Brèche de la Meije crossed	(as above)
25	*Barre de Ecrins, asc. N. face, desc W arête	(as above)
27	*Col de la Pilatte crossed	(as above, with J Reynaud)

July

5	Grand Combin	Lucy Walker, F and H Walker
8	*Bouquetin	A W Moore
8	*Col de Triolet crossed	A Adams Reilly and E Whymper
9	*Mont Dolent by S face and SE arête	(as above)
12	*Aig de Trélatête	(as above)
15	*Aig d'Argentière, W face and NW arête	(as above)
18	*Morning Pass crossed	W Moore and E Whymper
21	*Balmhorn by SW arête	Lucy Walker, F and H Walker
22	*Wetterlücke crossed	A W Moore
24	Lysjoch crossed	Miss Lewis Lloyd and the Misses Straton
27	*Col de la Dent Blanche crossed	J J Hornby and T H Philpott
28	*Ochsenhorn from SE	E von Fellenberg
30	Bruneggjoch crossed, possibly first time	J J Hornby and T H Philpott

August

1	Laquinjoch (first known tourist crossing)	J Robertson and C G Heathcote
1	*Pollux from the Schwarztor	Jules Jacot
3	*Konigsspitze	F F Tuckett, E N and H E Buxton
3	*Dent Parrachée	T Blanford and R M Cuthbert
4	Schreckhorn (2nd asc.)	E von Fellenbert, Chr Aeby and Pastor Gerber
5	*Grande Motte	T Blanford and R M Cuthbert
6	*Gr Wannehorn	R Lindt, G Studer
9	Jungfrau from Lauterbrunnen (1st asc. from Rothtal side)	L Stephen, F C Grove, R J S Macdonald
10	*Schallijoch cr. Zinal to Zermatt	J J Hornby and T H Philpott
10	*Monte Sissone from N	D W Freshfield, J D Walker and R M Beachcroft
13	Aletschhorn, 1st trav.	J J Hornby and T H Philpott
16	Lyskamm from Felikjoch (SW arête; 1st trav. of two summits)	L Stephen and E N Buxton
16	Jungfraujoch, 1st passage from S to N	J J Hornby and T H Philpott
17	*Aig Du Tour from E	C G Heathcote
22	*Zinal Rothorn by N arête	L Stephen and F C Grove
25	*Presanella	R M Beachcroft, D W Freshfield and J D Walker
25	*Col Tournanche crossed	F. W Jacomb and J A Hudson
28	*Col de Trélatête crossed	C E and G S Mathews

September

6	Col des Gr Jorasses from French side	F Taylor, A Milman, Alfred and A W Wills
26	*Berglistock	Chr Aeby

1865

June

16	*Gr Cornier by E. arête	E Whymper
17	Dent Blanche, 3rd asc.	(as above)
24	Gr Jorasses, 1st asc lower summit	(as above)
26	*Col du Mont Dolent crossed	(as above)
28	*Piz Roseg	A W Moore and H Walker
28	*Unter Gabelhorn	Lord Francis Douglas
29	*Aig Verte from SE	E Whymper

July

1	*Wellenkuppe	Lord Francis Douglas
3	*Col de Talèfre crossed	E Whymper
5	Aig Verte by Moine ridge	C Hudson, T S Kennedy and G C Hodgkinson
6	*Ruinette by SW arête	E Whymper
6	*Ober Gabelhorn from Zermatt	A W Moore and H Walker
7	Ober Gabelhorn from Zinal	Lord Francis Douglas
9	*Pigne d'Arolla	A W Moore and H. Walker
14	*Matterhorn from Zermatt	E. Whymper, C Hudson, Lord Francis Douglas and D H Hadow
15	Mont Blanc by Brenva arête	A W Moore, F and H Walker, and G S Mathews
17	Matterhorn from Breuil	J A Carrel and J B Bich
28	*Aig De Bionnassay from NW	E N Buxton, F C Grove and R J S Macdonald
29	Triftjoch (guideless)	A, C and S Parker
31	*Lauterbrunnen Breithorn, W. arête	E von Fellenberg (followed by J J Hornby and T H Philpott a few minutes later)

August

10	Finsteraahorn (guideless)	A, C and S Parker
10	Silberhorn, 1st asc by NW face	J J Hornby and T H Philpott
29	Jungfrau from Guggi Gl	H B George and Sir Geo Young

September

11	*Mont Blanc de Seilon	F F Weilenmann
18	*Nesthorn, W arête	H B George and A. Mortimer
19	Brunegghorn by SW.arête	G F Cobb, W D Rawlins, and R B. Townsend
20	*Aig du Chardonnet from W	R Fowler

2 THE MATTERHORN AND AFTER
(1865–1882)

The Golden Age of mountaineering conventionally extends from Wills' ascent of the Wetterhorn in 1854 until the historic ascent of the Matterhorn in 1865. Then follows the Silver Age until the ascent of the Dent du Géant in 1882 – the last great Alpine peak which was named and well-known before it was climbed. Thereafter pioneers in search of new routes had to seek out virgin ridges or faces or the minor pinnacles and satellites of the major peaks.

EDWARD WHYMPER (1840–1911)

left: A superb image of the Matterhorn north face by John Cleare, with the Hornli ridge on left and the ice slope on right forming the base of the Zmutt ridge.

below: Edward Whymper in 1865 at 24 years of age.

Edward Whymper was identified so strongly with the Matterhorn that it is appropriate to introduce him here. He was born in 1840, the second of eleven children, and at 14 years of age left school to be apprenticed to his father, Josiah, a talented wood engraver and painter. Learning quickly, he was commissioned by William Longman to illustrate *Peaks, Passes and Glaciers* – the precursor to the *Alpine Journal* – and made his first trip to the Alps in 1860, visiting Kanderstag, Saas Fee and Zermatt. Returning next year with a further commission and also starting to climb, he made the first British ascent of the Pelvoux which then encouraged him to try the Matterhorn, the most spectacular Alpine peak and one of the few big ones still unclimbed. He became hooked. His seven unsuccessful attempts over four years were all from the Italian side, many with the great Italian guide Jean Antoine Carrel.

But Carrel, an ardent patriot, wanted leading Italian mountaineers to claim the first ascent, so when Whymper arrived in Breuil (now called Cervinia) on 8 July 1865, Carrel said he was already engaged. Frustrated, Whymper decided to cross the Théodule pass to Zermatt, engage the best available guide, and tackle the mountain from the Swiss side, which had not been seriously tried because it looked so impregnable from this aspect. Meeting first with Lord Francis Douglas, who had been climbing with the Taugwalders, who should they meet in Zermatt but Michel Croz, with whom Whymper had climbed the previous summer. Years later, Whymper confessed: 'Of all the guides with whom I ever travelled, Croz was the one who was most after my own heart.' Croz had unexpectedly become free and had linked up with the Revd Charles Hudson and Douglas Hadow for an attempt on the Matterhorn. That evening they agreed to join forces – seven was rather too large a party and the 19-year-old Hadow had little experience, but that was how it was.

THE TRAGEDY

They left Zermatt on 13 July, camping at about 11,000 feet: 'Long after dusk the cliffs above echoed with our laughter and with the songs of our guides; for we were happy that night in camp, and feared no evil'. Next day they were delighted to find how easy it was up the east face to the shoulder. Even turning onto the north face the 'solitary difficult part was of no great extent' and by 1.40 pm they were on the summit. There were no footsteps to be seen. The fight for the Matterhorn was over! Peering over the ridge, with great satisfaction, Whymper could see Carrel's Italian party far below. They shouted and hurled stones to attract their attention. On the descent came the accident about which so much has been written. Briefly, Hadow slipped, pulling off three others, and the rope broke between Taugwalder and Douglas. Only Whymper and the two Taugwalders, father and son, survived. The frayed end of the broken rope is displayed in the little museum in Zermatt – little more than a washing line – when they had better rope available.

The accident received sensational publicity. 'Why,' thundered *The Times*, 'is the best blood of England to waste itself in scaling hitherto inaccessible peaks; in staining the eternal snow and reaching the unfathomable abyss never to return?' Whymper's reluctant account of it appeared in *The Times* of 8 August. Only 25 years old at the time, he emerged from the disaster with increased stature. Although engraving was gradually being overtaken by photography, it still provided his main income, which he later supplemented by lecturing and writing. The Club holds his set of original lecture slides and his classic *Scrambles Amongst the Alps,* written over six years, made many converts to mountaineering.

above: The Ascent of the Matterhorn, 14 July 1865: Arrival at the Summit.

His subsequent expeditions were mostly exploratory: two trips to Greenland in 1867 and 1872; with the two cousins Carrel of Val Tournanche he climbed Chimborazo and Cotopaxi in the Andes, the former at 20,498 feet (6,247 metres) being the highest peak climbed at that time. He wrote *Travels Amongst the Great Andes of the Equator*, and two guide books to Zermatt and Chamonix which he regularly updated. Despite his reputation as a great climber, Whymper was not normally considered a very sociable or likeable man; few men climbed with him regularly and with the exception perhaps of Croz and Almer, guides did not care for him: 'He was a hard taskmaster to himself and his guides', wrote Smythe. 'And the gulf between them was absolute'.

ASCENTS OF THE SILVER AGE

The Matterhorn accident may temporarily have discouraged new recruits to the sport. Coolidge even wrote: 'There was a sort of palsy that fell on the good cause, particularly amongst English climbers'. But the core members of the Club were reluctant to forego their annual month or two with their favourite guides. The *Alpine Journals* of the late 1860s soon began to record a good list of new climbs associated with familiar names: Tuckett, Freshfield, Moore, the Walker and Mathews families. Coincidentally, the great route up the Brenva Face, involving Moore and the Walkers, with the Anderegg, was climbed the very day after the Matterhorn accident. In December 1866, unable to curb their enthusiasm, Moore and Horace Walker initiated winter mountaineering by crossing the Strahlegg and Finsteraarjoch. Others soon followed the trend: Coolidge with Christian Almer, James Eccles and Gabriel Loppé. Writing in the *Centenary Alpine Journal*, Harold Porter (vice-president 1953–4) gives an excellent summary of the outstanding climbs of this period:

THIS PAGE:

above: The Fall, 14 July 1865. A pair of dramatic images by Gustave Doré (1832–83). Lithograph by Eugene Ciceri. Douglas, Hudson, Hadow and Croz fell to their deaths.

OPPOSITE PAGE:

far left: Michel Croz, the guide closest to Whymper's heart, killed on the descent. From a portrait by Lance Calkin, 1893.

near left: One of the Club's treasures: Whymper's tent, before renovation by the Royal School of Needlework!

In the Dauphiné, still primitive and neglected despite some brave efforts in the sixties by Whymper, Tuckett and Moore to elucidate its mysteries, Coolidge and Christian Almer now began a systematic exploration, though the greatest prize of the district, the highest peak of the Meije, the last of the giants, eluded them, and fell to the Frenchman, Boileau de Castelnau, guided by Pierre Gaspard and his son in 1877. In 1873 Clinton Dent began the long series of attacks on the Dru, which he brought to a final successful conclusion at the 18th attempt in 1878 in the grand company of J. Walker Hartley, 'the best and most skilful amateur of his time', Alexander Burgener and Kaspar Maurer. In 1879, G. A. Passingham, one of the toughest men of all the climbing fraternity of the 'seventies, whose predilection it was to climb his peaks from the valley without bivouac, crowned a career of vigorous achievement by the ascent of the West face of the Weisshorn with Louis

Zurbrücken and Ferdinand Imseng. In 1872 R. and W. M. Pendlebury and the Rev. C Taylor followed the same brilliant and meteoric Imseng up the fearsome Macugnaga face of Monte Rosa. Thomas Middlemore, a strenuous figure who aroused feelings of violent opposition in the breasts of the orthodox, shone like a comet from 1871 to 1876, his career culminating in that glorious week when with J.O. Maund, Henri Cordier, Jakob Anderegg, Hans Jaun and Andreas Maurer, he conquered Aiguille Verte and Les Courtes from the Argentière glacier and Les Droites from the Talèfre. Two great routes from Italy to the top of Mont Blanc must not be omitted; T. S. Kennedy's route via the Glacier du Mont Blanc with Johann Fisher and J. A. Carrel in 1872, and 1877 the classic route, not to be repeated for forty-four years, by which James Eccles, Michel and Alphonse Payot, from a bivouac on Pic Eccles, forced their way via the Brouillard and Fresnay glaciers and the Peuterey ridge to the summit in 8 1/4 hours. As for the Matterhorn itself, once the evil spell on the Hornli ridge had been broken by the ascent of the Rev. Julius Elliott with Peter Knubel and J. M. Lochmatter in 1868, the route became so popular that by 1880 one hundred and thirty-two ascents had been recorded as against only twenty-seven from Breuil. It was, in fact, becoming an 'easy day for a lady'. Now in 1879 the reputedly impregnable Zmutt arête succumbed to the friendly rivalry of two superb parties on the same day, A. F. Mummery with Alexander Burgener, Augustin Gentinetta, and Johann Petrus who arrived first, and W. Penhall with Ferdinand Imseng and Louis Zurbrücken.

I feel that Albert Frederick Mummery (1855–95) had more in common with the modern rock climber than any other of the early pioneers. Anyone who has struggled up the Mummery Crack on the Grépon develops a deep respect for him (including Chris Bonington in clinker-nailed boots, recreating the role in 1990 for a television programme). He made first ascents of the Charmoz (1880), the Grépon (1881) and the Dent du Requin (1883) in the Chamonix Aiguilles, and in 1880 left on the Géant the card found by Alexander Sella two years' later and inscribed: 'Absolutely inaccessible by fair means'. Slingsby, Collie and Hastings were his favourite climbing companions. His classic book, *My Climbs in the Alps and Caucasus*, published in 1895, ends on a prophetic note: 'It is true the great ridges sometimes demand their sacrifice, but the mountaineer would hardly forego his worship though he knew himself to be the destined victim. But happily to most of us the great brown slabs bending over into immeasurable space, the line and curves of the wind-moulded cornice, the delicate undulations of the fissured snow, are old and trusted friends, ever luring us to health and fun and laughter, and enabling us to bid a sturdy defiance to all the ills that time and life oppose.'

THE GREAT GUIDES

The great guides who made so many of those climbs possible were the descendants of the earlier shepherds and chamois hunters. Of 22 chosen by the best amateurs, ten came from the Oberland, five from Chamonix, four from the Valais, and three from Italy. Again quoting from Harold Porter:

> Of the Oberlanders the oldest was the picturesque giant, Ulrich Lauener, 'the very picture of a true mountaineer', while it is generally agreed that Christian Almer and Melchior Anderegg were in a class by themselves, dominating the Alpine world from 1860 to 1880. Christian Almer has to his credit the longest and most splendid list of first ascents ever recorded. Melchior Anderegg has been called the headmaster of the great school of Oberland guides: his one failing seems to have been an excess of caution, which might perhaps be deduced from his famous remark on the summit of the Dent Blanche in a discussion of the feasibility of the Zmutt arête: 'Ja, es geht, aber ich gehe nicht.' St Niklaus produced Peter Knubel, 'the earliest of the modern specialist guides', Josef Imboden, a man of substance and of great influence among his fellows, and Alois Pollinger, great founder of a great family. From Saas Fee came Alexander Burgener, immortalised by Dent and Mummery, surely the most colourful of all guides. Italy could pride herself on J. A. Carrel, magnificent in achievement, on the superbly gifted Emile Rey, and on J. J. Maquignaz who succeeded on the Dent du Géant. Chamonix was redeemed by a few great men: François Devouassoud, equally at home on mountain or in a great city; and Michel Payot, pupil and successor of Michel Croz, who travelled with Eccles for forty years!

These were the exceptional guides, the vast majority were not enterprising enough to seek out or lead new routes and were often exorbitant in their demands. The Chamonix guides produced an iniquitous rota system, despite protests from the Alpine and other clubs. It was an invitation to encourage guide-less climbing, despite ingrained opposition to the practice from most Alpine Club members. It was up to the confident Pilkington brothers and Frederick Gardiner to usher in a new era by their first guideless ascent of the Meije in 1879.

OPPOSITE PAGE:

above left: A F Mummery 1855–95, forerunner to the modern rock climber.

below left: Mummery climbing his eponymous Crack during a traverse of the Grépon, 1893, photographed by the spirited Lily Bristow carrying a heavy plate camera.

THIS PAGE:

below: Crossing a crevasse on the Bossons glacier, photographed by Charnaux 1886.

below right: Mathews and Zurbriggen at their overnight bivouac, 1893.

ENTER THE LADIES

In those days, there were very few women climbers, and the Club was an entirely male preserve. The most striking early lady climbers were the Pigeon sisters, Anna and Ellen who, in eight years, climbed 63 peaks and crossed 72 passes. Their crossing of the Sesiájoch from Riffel to Alagna on 12 August 1869 was a daring expedition in bad weather. They had intended to cross the easier Lysjoch to Grassoney but their young guide, Jean Martin, lost his way. Anna, the elder, took control, acting as anchor during the steep 62-degree descent of the south-east precipices of Monte Rosa. She became a vice-president of the Ladies' Alpine Club in 1910.

Another outstanding Victorian lady climber was Elizabeth Jackson (1843–1906) with some 140 major climbs to her credit. Climbing mainly with her husband until he died in 1881, she still carried on, in 1884 with Dr K Shultz descending the Ferpècle arête of the Dent Blanche five years before its first ascent. Then in 1888, with guides Ulrich Almer and Emil Boss, she made the first winter ascents of the Gross Lauteraarhorn, Pfaffenstöckli, Gross Fiescherhorn and a first winter traverse of the Jungfrau, all within 16 days. Both she and Almer suffered frostbite from an unplanned bivouac on the Guggi glacier but this was not mentioned in her subsequent *Alpine Journal* article, 'A Winter Quartette', for fear of adverse public reaction.

The best known lady climber, Lucy Walker, climbed frequently with her father and brother and was the first lady to climb the Matterhorn, just ahead of Coolidge's aunt, Miss Brevoort, in July 1871. In 1859, Lucy first climbed with Melchior Anderegg, the beginning of a 21-year partnership with the Walker

below: Ladies and their guides on the Mer de Glace above Montenvers, another 1886 photograph by Charnaux.

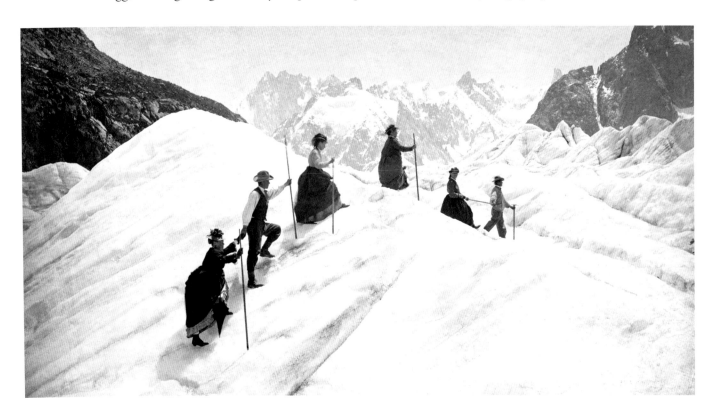

family, during which she made 98 expeditions, climbing most of the major Swiss and French peaks. Asked why she never married, she reputedly replied: 'I love mountains and Melchior, and Melchior already has a wife.' At 76, she became the second president of the Ladies' Alpine Club in 1912.

Another spirited young lady was Lily Bristow, a close friend of Mary Petherick who in 1883 married Mummery. In 1892, Lily joined a mass assault on the Charmoz and in 1893 traversed the Grépon, taking a heavy plate camera to record the events. It was this climb that led Mummery to remark how the hardest climb in the Alps soon becomes 'an easy day for a lady', although it was Leslie Stephen who originally coined the phrase. She then went on to climb the Petit Dru and the Zinal Rothorn with Mummery, and in 1894 her final serious climb, but not with Mummery, was the first descent of the Zmutt ridge with the guides Zurbriggen and Pollinger.

Another English lady, Beatrice Tomasson, climbed in the Dolomites, making the first route up the south face of the Marmolada di Penia (10,965 ft / 3,343 m) with her guides Michele Bettega and Bortolo Zagonel on 1 July 1901. This was a huge undertaking for its day, for such a long and demanding route, which Beatrice had initiated the previous year by hiring another guide, Luigi Rizzi, to reconnoitre the lower section of the climb.

Women had to be very determined to persevere against male disapproval. Mrs Aubrey Le Blond says of this period: 'I had to struggle hard for my freedom. My great-aunt, Lady Bentinck, wrote to my mother: "Stop her climbing mountains; she is scandalising all London and looks like a Red Indian".'

Mrs Le Blond, born Elizabeth Hawkins-Whitshed, outlasted three husbands, F C Burnaby, D F Main, and Aubrey Le Blond, writing nine books published variously under her three married names, including an autobiography. She made numerous classic ascents, and some remarkable winter climbs including traverses of Piz Palu and Piz Bernina, her favourite guides being Edouard Cupelin and Joseph Imboden. She became the first president of the Ladies' Alpine Club in 1907.

I have already mentioned Coolidge's aunt, the formidable Miss Meta Brevoort, both from the United States. It was her enthusiasm for mountain travel and exploration that led the 15-year-old Coolidge to devote his life to the Alps as a climber, explorer and historian, outliving her by 50 years, and becoming known as the 'Sage of Grindelwald', dying in 1896 at the age of 76. In 1868, they engaged Christian Almer, by then a well-established guide, and in 1870 for six seasons turned their attention to the Dauphiné, which was then very little explored. They made the first ascent of the Pic Centrale de la Meije (the highest Grand Pic eluding them) and the second ascent of the Écrins. A new route on the Bietschorn in 1871 was described in the *Alpine Journal*, but appeared under her nephew's name. She died suddenly when only 51.

below: Mrs Aubrey Le Blond (1861–1934), first president of the Ladies Alpine Club, 1907–12, avoids sunburn using a face mask. Self-portrait on Durmaalstind, Norway, c.1900.

An unusual companion on their climbs was a beagle bitch called Tschingel, a consolation present from Almer to Coolidge after having to abandon a climb on the Eiger. Tschingel became a passionate mountaineer, climbing 30 peaks and crossing 36 passes in an eleven-year career. She enjoyed red wine and warm, weak tea. Her first big climb was the Blümlisalphorn (12,020 ft / 3,664 m). 'She seemed to like it very much,' wrote Coolidge, 'running on ahead of us to the summit, and then running back to encourage us by showing how near we were to the wished for goal.'

ARE THE ALPS EXHAUSTED?

With the major peaks all climbed, some mountaineers proclaimed the Alps to be exhausted. Leslie Stephen famously asserted: 'The number of unaccomplished feats may be reckoned on the fingers.' It was time to look further afield to what we now term the Greater Ranges. An early choice was the Caucasus, and Moore, Freshfield and Tucker were the first to venture there in 1868, succeeding on the slightly lower of the twin peaks of Elbruz. The highest peak, at 18,481 feet (5,633 metres), is a straightforward climb but 2,700 feet higher than Mont Blanc. They also climbed Kasbek at the other end of the range. Moore, Walker, Gardiner and Grove followed in 1874 when the higher Elbruz peak was climbed. They started the practice of taking their Alpine guides with them, which paid dividends on the more challenging climbs. W C Slingsby made his name in Norway making the first ascent of Skagastølstind in 1876, completing the last 500 feet on his own. Pioneers in the Pyrenees were the Leicestershire squire Charles Packe and the eccentric Franco-Irish Count Henri Russell, who developed a passion for the Vignemale. He climbed it 33 times and spent weekends in grottoes hacked out of the rock where he would celebrate mass and entertain friends to dinner in full evening dress.

below left: Mont Blanc from the Grands Mulets refuge by Garcin 1890s.

below: The Dent du Geant, first climbed in 1882, and Glacier des Périades from the Aiguille du Tacul, photographed by W F Donkin, also in 1882.

But the unsung heroine of the Pyrenees was a certain Anne Lister from Halifax. With her guide Henri Cazaux, who had already made the first ascent of the Vignemale, she repeated the ascent on 11 August 1838 by a new route from the south up a long rock and snow coulour which is still graded '*assez difficile*' in the modern French guidebook. This preceded Russell's and Packe's explorations by 20 years.

Further afield, the Himalaya had not yet been opened up to recreational climbers, if one excludes the incredible exploits of the pundits, such as the first circuit of the Everest group by Hari Ram in 1871, and the map-makers of the Survey of India who set up their plane tables at heights well over 20,000 feet.

In 1873, Sir George Bowen, the Governor of New Zealand, officially invited Alpine Club members to explore the Southern Alps, but it was eight years before the Revd W S Green, with Boss and Kaufman of Grindelwald, came and very nearly succeeded on Mount Cook, which was not actually climbed until Christmas Eve 1894 by three young enterprising New Zealanders, Fyfe, Graham and Clark.

In the United States, 32 prominent peaks were climbed between 1866 and 1879, of which 14 exceeded 14,000 feet, the best known, Mount Rainier, falling to General Stevens and P B Van Trump 1870. In 1878, Eccles explored the Rockies in Wyoming and Idaho with his inseparable guide, Michel Payot. Meanwhile, as already mentioned, Whymper visited Greenland and climbed in 1880 Chimborazo in the Andes of Ecuador.

below: Lending a shoulder; early 'bouldering' on the Matterhorn 1893.

THE ALPINE CLUB AND THE CONTINENTAL CLUBS

By 1865, the membership of the Alpine Club had risen from its original 29 members to 290, where it remained for a while until the tact and energy of A W Moore, secretary from 1872 to 1874, helped to boost numbers to 432 by 1879. The Club found its first home in St Martin's Place, and with its specific climbing and social qualifications for membership, it became the accepted authority on mountain matters.

In contrast the continental clubs – the Austrians, Swiss, Italians, Germans and French – all founded between 1862 and 1874, adopted a different policy, accepting anybody with an interest in mountains. This so increased their numerical and financial strength – the Swiss setting up eleven original sections – that they were able to embark on building mountain huts and improving maps and pathways, which, in turn, attracted even greater growth. A first International Congress was held in 1878 in Paris and a second in 1879 at Geneva, where 480 guests attended a banquet presided over by M Henri de Saussure, the Alpine Club being represented by its president C E Mathews.

The Alpine Club with its slenderer resources financed the production of Adams Reilly's meticulous map of Mont Blanc and a revised edition of John Ball's Western Alps. Best of all, it produced the *Alpine Journal*, edited in succession by the Revd H B George, Leslie Stephen and Douglas Freshfield. Five classic books of this period were Whymper's *Scrambles amongst the Alps*, Stephen's *Playground of Europe*, Tyndall's *Hours of Exercise in the Alps*, Moore's *The Alps in 1864* and Crauford Grove's *The Frosty Caucasus*, the forerunner of numerous books in which Britons have recorded their mountain adventures in the Greater Ranges.

Martin Conway gives a delightful contemporary account of Zermatt in the Silver Age:

> The Zermatt of the Seventies was in every way very different from what it afterwards became. It was quite a small place. There were only two hotels that counted, the Mont Cervin for tourists and the Monte Rosa for climbers. Year after year the same group assembled. They were more like a family than a club. A common interest united them. Most were English of one class. The two Seilers were their father and mother. In fine weather we climbed and in bad weather we played billiards on an unlevel table and talked without end. Year by year old members dropped off and were replaced by new: thus the group was continuous with the early pioneers. It remembered Hudson, Whymper, Tyndall and the rest as belonging to themselves. The atmosphere of *Scrambles* lingered on. We regarded the high peaks with a respect now long banished.

above: The North Face of the Grand Charmoz by C Douglas Milner, one of the Club's keenest photographers before and after World War II.

above left: Avoiding stonefall during a hurried descent of the Aiguille du Midi, a drawing by Edward Whymper.

C E Mathews, reviewing the growth of mountaineering in 1881, could say: 'We look forward with confidence to the future. Whatever is doubtful, one thing is certain, that mountaineering will never cease to be a genuine sport for Englishmen. Men of wealth or of leisure, or in pursuit of some scientific object, will as the years go on investigate great mountain ranges as yet unknown or unexplored. We have created a new sport for Englishmen.'

It could also be a perilous sport. On 11 August 1882, J S Anderson and G P Baker, with guides Alois Pollinger and Ulrich Almer, made the first ascent of the east ridge of the Dent Blanche. It proved to be much more difficult and sustained than they had expected and they reached the summit with great relief, whereupon Almer solemnly declared, '*Wir sind vier esel*' (We are four asses). Ever since, the ridge has been called the Viereselsgrat. They descended by the south ridge to the Schonbiel hut, meeting W E Gabbett and his guides J M Lochmatter and his son Alexander. Sadly, the very next day these three fell while climbing the Dent Blanche and were all killed.

There were more accidents in that summer of 1882 (to Professor Balfour and to William Penhall and their guides), which prompted Queen Victoria to write on 24 August (through her private secretary Sir Henry Ponsonby) to the prime minister, William Gladstone, asking whether she should publicly mark her disapproval of dangerous Alpine excursions. Fortunately Gladstone was able to dissuade her from doing so.

below & below right: Two contrasting views of the Aiguille du Petit Dru. *Left*: a drawing by Edward Whymper. *Right*: tourists on the Mer de Glace.

3 Evolving an Exclusive Alpine Tradition (1882–1914)

FREE OR ARTIFICIAL?

The ascent of the Dent du Géant in 1882 is deemed to mark the end of the Silver Age of mountaineering in the Alps. Did it also usher in the Iron Age? Whymper had used his grapnel on the Matterhorn, but on the Géant the brothers Maquignaz had spent four days hammering pitons into the rocks and fixing ropes on the more difficult passages before the Sellas made the ascent. No previous route had required such artificial aids. Indeed one of the Sella brothers admitted a tinge of guilt in encouraging their guides to do so. It marked the beginning of a controversy between 'free' and 'artificial' climbing which continues even to this day.

The British on their own crags have continued to endorse free climbing so that the quality and difficulty of a route is not downgraded by permanent fixtures left in the rock. This policy encouraged the invention and development of 'nuts', special wedges and cams which could be slotted into cracks to provide both fixed belays and intermediate protection for the leading climber, but which could be taken out by the last man on the rope without damaging or defacing the rock.

On the Continent where the use of pegs or pitons was condoned – particularly on types of rock where there is a scarcity of natural belays – the variant of 'sport climbing' has become popular because the climber can test his ability and technique to the limit without risking life and limb. Before the invention of 'nuts', if you couldn't do a climb without using pitons, the ideal attitude on British crags – although often disregarded – was not to attempt it, but to leave it to a better man or woman who could! However, if one were keen to attempt the harder Alpine climbs, which had only been achieved by using pitons, it was necessary to learn and practise artificial climbing – as did Joe Brown discreetly on the limestone cliffs of Dovedale, and Tom Bourdillon by driving six-inch nails into the trunk of a tall tree in his garden.

But I am getting 50 years ahead of my narrative. Josef Knubel told Arnold Lunn that in all his climbs with Geoffrey Winthrop Young he only ever used two pitons – as safety belays on the first descent of the east ridge of the Grandes Jorasses to the Col des Hirondelles. If we look for any mountaineer to symbolise this period before the World War I, it is Geoffrey Young – comparable to Whymper at the end of the Golden Age and to Mummery in the Silver Age of mountaineering.

left: Mist on Crib Goch, an outlier of Snowdon, by Basil Goodfellow, Hon Secretary, 1950–54, and a very talented photographer.

below: W E Davidson, President 1911–13, with his guide, Christian Almer at Grindelwald, in 1896.

THE ALPINE TRADITION

In writing about this period in the *Centenary Journal*, Geoffrey Young points out how the surviving pioneers, such as Ball and Tuckett, and their successors, like Conway and Slingsby, enhanced the reputation of the Club by their climbs in the more distant ranges, but those members who did not have the time or taste to travel afar tended to form a conservative core of the Club, happy to be guided up traditional Alpine routes, and to enjoy its social amenities without any organising or representative responsibilities. So the premier mountaineering Club in the world became fixed in its exclusively Alpine tradition, reflecting also the social structure of the day. It took an Italian, Guido Rey, a member of the Sella family, and later an honorary member of the Club to see ourselves as other see us. I quote from his book, *El Cervino*, translated by J E C Eaton, which Lunn considered was one of the few Alpine classics to rival the best of the English authors.

The instant a climber, on his return from a difficult expedition, sets his foot on the threshold of his hotel, he begins to be his guides' superior. They leave him shortly before, discreetly disappearing without saying good-bye. They go modestly in by the servants' door and hide themselves in their underground room, while their Herr enters triumphantly by the front door, and is received with distinction by the landlord and his attentive waiters; and when he is nice and clean after his bath, he shows himself to the guests of the hotel, pretending he is not tired, and relates in his own way, and without inconvenient witnesses, the feats he has performed.

He estimates with calm superiority the difficulties he has met; he does not exaggerate them, but an occasional word he lets fall during his discourse sufficiently indicates that the situation must have been serious in places.

And he allows it to transpire that the guides were exhausted, that during the descent he held one of them who slipped – but he does not say how often he himself was held by the guide. At the *table-d'hôte*, near the end of a good dinner, the climber's neighbours, who mostly know nothing at all about Alpine expeditions, but who are nevertheless eager for sensation, are filled with wonder at the description he has given them; they unite in praising his courage, his coolness and his modesty, while no one thinks of the guides supping humbly by themselves in a dark room on the floor below. It is a severe lesson in modesty that the guides give us.

But these innocent triumphs on the small stage of the hotel are denied to a climber's vanity when he has failed. The mountaineer who returns empty handed must digest his defeat by himself. He avoids talking about what has occurred, and tries to baffle the importunate curiosity of the friends who have been waiting for him, and who cannot bring themselves to believe that so great a climber can have spent two nights and a day on the mountain and then have nothing to tell. These are unpleasant moments, and he is sick at heart; he feels so very small, and fancies himself unworthy to belong to an Alpine Club.

Guido Rey is best known for his bold exploration of the Furggen ridge of the Matterhorn. On 24 August 1899, he and his guides, Aimé and Ange Maquignaz, were stopped at the immense vertical prow not far below the summit. They descended and four days later climbed by the Italian ridge to the summit where Rey was lowered by a rope ladder to the point where they had been stopped, thus completing his knowledge of the entire ridge. That would have been a good story to tell at the table-d'hôte! It was not until 23 September 1941 that an Italian party achieved a direct ascent, using some 43 pitons, leaving 14 in place, and taking seven hours over the 500-feet (150-metre) vertical section. My friend, the late Alfred Tissières, repeated the route with Georges de Rham on 2 August 1946. I remember Alfred telling me the rock was so rotten he could just pull out the pitons with his hands!

RYAN AND THE LOCHMATTERS

OPPOSITE PAGE:

top left: Another way into the Club premises at 23 Savile Row!

bottom left: The souvenir cover of the Club's Jubilee Dinner Menu

THIS PAGE:

right: A picnic beside Loch Maree, from left to right: Travers, W.C. Slingsby, J. N. Collie, T. S. Priestley and W.P. Haskett-Smith.

The only British climbers in the Alps during this period, 1882–1914, who achieved an international reputation were V J E Ryan and Geoffrey Winthrop Young. Ryan (1883–1947) was an Irish landowner who later settled in Jersey. He began climbing at the age of 15, but 1903 was his first great season, developing a partnership with the brothers Franz and Joseph Lochmatter. Their best known route was the Ryan-Lochmatter ridge of the Plan, the east ridge; a superb rock climb and one of the finest classic routes in the whole of the Chamonix Aiguilles. They climbed it in an astonishing eleven hours from Montenvers, a good time even today. Their other famous route was the south face of the Täschhorn which I shall describe later, where they joined forces with Young and Knubel.

Ryan was obviously an excellent rock climber, but he left all the route-finding, step-cutting and rucksack-carrying to the Lochmatters. Unusually for those days, he never wrote about his climbs. He had an aloof, frosty nature and was actually black-balled by the Alpine Club, allegedly for being rude to a fellow member. Roger Chorley contributed an essay on Ryan to *Les Alpinistes Célèbres*. When, in 1952, we were staying together at the Monte Rosa hut, working on a glacier tunnelling project, on a 'rest' day we sought out another rarely climbed Ryan-Lochmatter route, the Cresta di Santa Caterina of the Nordend, forming the frontier ridge between Switzerland and Italy. It was another fine rock climb with great views overlooking the spectacular east face of Monte Rosa.

GEOFFREY WINTHROP YOUNG

In contrast to Ryan, Geoffrey Young (1876–1958) was a prolific and brilliant writer and poet. 'Here for the first time,' wrote Lunn, 'a member of our own brotherhood had translated into noble poetry the aspirations and ardours of mountaineering.'

The Cragsman

In this short span
between my finger-tips on the smooth edge
and these tense feet cramped to the crystal ledge
I hold the life of man.
Consciously I embrace
arched from the mountain rock on which I stand
to the firm limit of my lifted hand
the front of time and space:-
For what is there in all the world for me
but what I know and see?
And what remains of all I see and know,
if I let go?

above: An excerpt from the Führerbuch of Franz Lochmatter, 1878–1933, describing his epic lead on the Täschhorn climb, 11 August 1906.

left: Geoffrey Winthrop Young, this 1934 portrait from the Presidents' Gallery, 1941–3.

Young had a great influence on young climbers, including myself. As a Cambridge undergraduate he invented the sport of roof climbing and wrote the *Roof Climbers Guide to Trinity*. One of his most important books was *Mountain Craft,* which he edited although writing two-thirds himself. This updated and replaced the classic 1892 Badminton volume on mountaineering, being completed in 1914 but not published until after the war in 1920. Then came *On High Hills,* published in 1927, the ultimate panegyric to mountaineering. To me, the climax is the first ascent of the south face of the Täschhorn where I quote four separate passages:

THE TÄSCHHORN

I have confessed to a period when it seemed that the early romance of alpine climbing could best be recaptured by inventing novel routes up the great peaks; and have mentioned that this occasionally brought me across the path of that comet of the Alps, V.J.E. Ryan, and Josef and Franz Lochmatter. Into their tail – if they had one – little Josef Knubel and I were willingly swept, in somewhat irregular conjunction. So long as there was no danger, in the mountain sense, we all climbed unroped. In a danger-zone we grouped as a trio and a duet working independently. But where, as sometimes happened, there was no safe holding for any member of the party of three or the party of two, we joined up our ropes. There are few mountain passages which do not allow of good holds for at least one member of a party of five spaced out along four hundred feet of rope. Since upon this plan it was usually possible for several of us to be moving simultaneously, we gained the extra security which a span of five men can give, and climbed almost as quickly as a rope of three.

We had decided from the top of the Weisshorn opposite that the Täschhorn from the south could be climbed. I based my opinion on what I used flippantly to call *prima facie* evidence; every south 'face' must have a route up it, and all the better if we were the 'first'. Ryan had sounder advice: he had looked down the wall itself from above. There are two couloirs up the face, which, as they approach the pyramidal summit, fork out to left and right on to the western and south-eastern ridges. The final diamond of precipice which they thus enclose we thought, as we examined it from Zermatt, might prove the ace of trumps against us. But we could possibly cut out, by the couloirs, on to either ridge, and as it lay with us to lead off, we were safe in opening the game with a high heart ...

Josef, and other great guides, on slabs moved with the free poise of an athlete and the foot-cling of a chamois. Franz, in such case, had the habit and something of the appearance of a spider or crustacean. His curled head disappeared altogether. His body and square shoulders split and elongated into four steely tentacles, radiating from a small central core or hub of intelligence, which transmitted the messages between his tiny hands and boots as they clung attached and writhing at phenomenal angles and distances...

below: The South Face of the Täschhorn, an aerial photograph by the daring Alpine pilot E Gyger, 1943.

Suddenly I heard that unmistakable scrape and grit of sliding boot-nails and clothes. Above my head, over the edge of the roof to the right, I saw Franz' legs shoot out into space. Time stopped. A shiver, like expectancy, trembled across the feeling of unseen grey wings behind me, from end to end of the cliff. I realized impassively that the swirl of the rope must sweep me from my holds before it tightened on the doubtful belay of the blister. But fate was playing out the game in regions curiously remote …

Franz' boots again disappeared above the edge. No one in the recess had known of the slip, out of their sight and lost in the gusts. He had stopped himself miraculously on the rim by crushing his hands on to ice-dimples in the slab.

Has Lochmatter's lead up the final overhang ever been surpassed? Georges de Rham, one of the best Swiss climbers of his time who led the third ascent on 8 August 1943, said: 'Even with all the recourses of modern technique, pitons, clasp rings and rubber shoes, I thought the place which was so brilliantly climbed by Franz Lochmatter in nailed boots, without pitons, exceptionally severe.'

YOUNG AND KNUBEL

No mountaineer of that period, not even Ryan, had a record of first ascents comparable to Young's. Lunn gives a succinct list:

These included a route up the Weisshorn from Zinal which bears his name, the first direct ascent of the east face of the Weisshorn, the first ascents of the east face of the Zinal Rothorn, the Younggrat on the Zermatt Breithorn, the south face of the Täschhorn with Ryan, and the following climbs in the great year of 1911 with H.O. Jones; the Jorasses from the Col des Grandes Jorasses and the first descent to the Col des Hirondelles, the first complete ascent of the Brouillard Ridge of Mont Blanc from the Col Emile Rey, the ridge itself having been climbed by the Gugliermina brothers, and the first ascent of the Mer de Glace face to the actual summit of the Grépon in which Todhunter joined the party. Ryan had made the first ascent of the Grépon from the Mer de Glace but he had struck the Grépon-Charmoz Ridge some distance below the summit.

above top: André Roch leads Alfred Tissières (AC), Gabriel Chevalley and Georges de Rham on only the third ascent of the Täschhorn south face, 8 August 1943.

above: The crowd at the inauguration of the Britannia Hut above Saas Fée, 17 August 1912, supported by British contributions.

Finally, Young and Siegfried Herford made the first ascent by the grim Red Teeth Ridge of the Gspaltenhorn in 1914.

Young had often climbed without guides in his early years and made with Mallory and Donald Robertson one of the very few all British guideless first ascents, the first ascent of the south-east ridge of the Nesthorn, but once he had met the incomparable Joseph Knubel the partnership between the greatest amateur and the greatest professional of that particular decade was never again broken.

above: George Leigh Mallory (right) of Everest and Siegfried Wedgewood Herford (killed in World War I) were both brilliant rock climbers; an iconic photograph by Geoffrey Winthrop Young taken at one of his Pen-y-Pass Easter Parties, December 1913.

right: Basil Goodfellow on the East Ridge of the Weisshorn, with the Dom and Täschhorn behind, taken by John Hunt.

Another exceptional climbing feat described by Young was Knubel's ascent of the final crack on the first direct ascent of the Mer de Glace face to the actual summit of the Grépon.

> Josef was in the throes of a last daring inspiration. He whipped his axe upward, balanced himself audaciously outward, and with lightning speed wedged the point of the axe-shaft into the crack above the bulge of the canopy, so that the axe-head projected horizontally and fraily into space, between our heads and the sky … Using the wedged shaft as a horizontal bar, Josef dangled clear of the niche, and swung himself up on it as adroitly as a Japanese juggler, until he was standing upon it – over us and nothingness.

top left: Josef Kuubel, G W Young, H O Jones in Chamonix, 20 August 1911, the day after their epic climb on the Grépon, with Todhunter and Brocherel.

top right: André Roch strides along the path below the Mer de Glace face of the Grépon.

Being much the hardest pitch on the climb and still graded 'V superior' in the French guidebook of the 1950s, it was given a page to itself, including a drawing with numbered holds and instructions how to use them! I have special memories of repeating the climb with a Cambridge party in 1952 including Roger Chorley, Ted Wrangham and Chris Simpson. Unusually, all three were Alpine Club members while still undergraduates. Fortunately, I was rather taller than Knubel so I didn't have to use my ice-axe as a horizontal bar, although I remember doing something similar on an ice climb four years later in Peru.

I was able to repeat another of Young's routes during the Club's centenary celebrations in Zermatt in 1957; the so-called Younggrat on the Breithorn. Chris Brasher and I were climbing together and managed to get away first from the Monte Rosa hut, as we had to drive back to London overnight for Chris to get to a meeting at *The Observer* office next morning.

Our climbing party was most prestigious: John Hunt with Albert Eggler (both leaders of Everest expeditions), Fritz Luchsinger (first up Lhotse in 1956), Fritz Gansser, John Tyson, John Hobhouse, Chris Brasher and myself. I committed an early *faux pas* by asking the leader of a Swiss pair, who had started earlier from the Gandegg hut, whether he knew the route and would he like me to take over to give him a rest from step-cutting? He turned out to be a Zermatt guide

above: Ted Wrangham leads the formidable Knubel crack on the Grépon in 1952.

and retaliated by cutting faster and most excellent steps. I had expected the middle part of the ridge to be straightforward, but it proved quite challenging on mixed ground in crampons with scarce belays.

We knew the real crux was where the ridge merged into the face shortly below the transverse summit ridge, where there was normally a sheer face of hard ice. This was where a rope of four young Frenchmen fell while attempting only the second ascent in 1928: '*elle fut precipitée sur le glacier ou l'on ne releva que des cadavres*', warned the Valais guidebook. To avoid the same fate (before the development of ice screws, of which I brought back an early example from the Russian Caucasus in 1958) we decided to link up as one large caravan of eight which I had the privilege of leading. At 2 pm Chris Brasher and I breasted the cornice and after hurried farewells, began the long slog down. In Zermatt we drank a litre of milk between us, caught the train to Visp, retrieved his Triumph sports car and took turns at the wheel across France, Brasher chewing Benzedrine tablets to keep himself awake. We breakfasted in Champagne country and reached his office only a few hours late!

A few weeks later, I was geologising in Yorkshire when I heard that Geoffrey Young would be staying at the Old Dungeon Ghyll in Langdale next weekend. What a chance to meet the grand old man. I brought with me the colour slides I had taken on the Younggrat and he was thrilled to see them. 'Young man,' he enthused, 'You have come all this way across England to show me these; I am delighted.' He died the following year.

GUIDELESS CLIMBING

While these remarkable guided climbs were being made, guideless parties were also raising their standard. Two unguided ascents in the 1870s were exceptional: Cust, Colgrove and Cawood on the Matterhorn in 1876 and the two Pilkington brothers and Gardiner on the Meije in 1879. But in the 1890s, particularly in the Chamonix district, men such as Mummery, Collie, Hastings and Cecil Slingsby were more often dispensing with guides. The development of rock climbing in Britain was giving them and other climbers the confidence to do so, once they had learned from their guides how to deal with snow and ice in the Alps. Three climbers, Wilson, Wicks and Bradby, did many routes together. Of Claude Wilson's 360 main expeditions, 238 were without guides. They liked to avoid the club huts, starting from an inn in the valley and descending to another on the far side. Another pair, W T Kirkpatrick and R P Hope paid great attention to saving weight, with silk shirt and shorts, a 6-ounce sweater, 11-ounce crampons, and an aluminium collar stud! The Scottish climbers W N Ling and Harold Raeburn were another strong partnership making first British guideless ascents of the Zmutt ridge of the Matterhorn and the north face of the Disgrazia.

But Charles Pilkington in his presidential address in 1898 felt he still had to apologise to some extent to the conservative core of the Club: 'Guideless climbing came to be recognised as a necessary evil, and the older members of the Club slowly yielded their assent.' Young observed that one classic element in the Club continued to maintain that the Alps were exhausted; another and official element that the Club existed only to climb the Alps; a paralysing contradiction! But the adventure of climbing for its own sake was slowly substituting itself for the adventure of the Alps.

CLIMBING IN BRITAIN

In Britain local clubs began to form: the Scottish Mountaineering Club in 1889; the Climbers' Club in 1898 focused on North Wales; the Yorkshire Ramblers in 1899; the Wayfarers' Club in Liverpool in 1906; the Rucksack Club in Manchester in 1907; the Fell and Rock Climbing Club of the English Lake District also in 1907. These were spontaneous developments where individual Alpine Club members often formed the initial core of the local clubs.

OPPOSITE PAGE:

top right: The classic Red Wall on Lliwedd, an outlier of Snowdon.

bottom right: Mont Blanc and the Aiguilles, by W F Donkin 1883.

THIS PAGE:

below: Ed Webster and Nick Kekus on the Napes Needle, Great Gable, in 1991. It was first climbed solo by W.P. Haskett-Smith in 1886.

Guidebooks were beginning to appear for British rock climbs: W P Haskett-Smith (famous for his solitary first ascent of the Napes Needle on Great Gable in 1886) wrote *Climbing in the British Isles, Volume I, England* in 1894; O G Jones *Rock Climbing in the English Lake District* in 1897; the Abraham brothers covered North Wales and Skye in 1906 and 1908 respectively, and there were more detailed

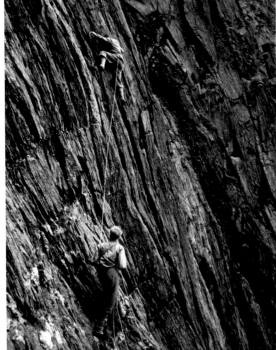

descriptions by A W Andrews and J M Archer Thomson for climbs on Lliwedd and in the Ogwen District in 1909 and 1910. The pioneers had felt safer in the enclosed gullies and chimneys which they climbed using back and foot, but as technique improved, so did their confidence to launch out onto the more exposed open faces. It was around this time that Pen-y-Pass developed into a climbing hostelry where Geoffrey Young organised his popular Easter gatherings.

LOOKING BEYOND THE ALPS

The year 1907 marked the Golden Jubilee of the Club. The standard of achievement had risen significantly since 1857. At the anniversary dinner, Alfred Wills described himself as 'one of that little band who braved the scorn of Ruskin and the sarcasms of the Press, and were held up as lunatics and madmen, if not something worse'. And Douglas Freshfield asked: 'Will the company which dines here fifty years hence include the conqueror of Mount Everest?'

In the *Alpine Journal* of 1900, Martin Conway, who was one of the few who had the means to travel and climb widely, surveyed possible future

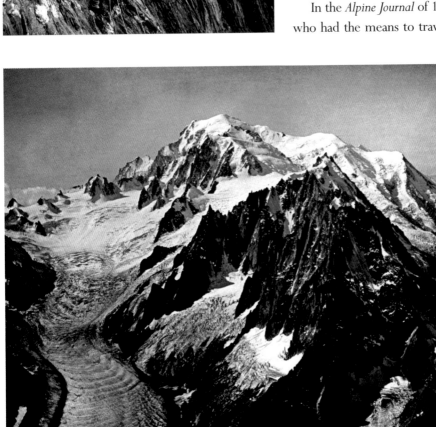

activity: 'The exploration of the Alps is nearly complete ... By accident, not by design, the exploration of the mountains of the world has become a characteristic work of our Club, and the first record of such explorations is the noteworthy feature of our Journal. I maintain that the time has now come when this spontaneous development should be adopted as the Club policy, when the Club should frankly look beyond the Alps, and constitute itself the centre and chief home of mountain exploration in general.'

In the next chapter, let us look at what some of the more enterprising and better-off members of the Club, who had not been constrained by the 'conservative core', had been doing in the Greater Ranges.

4 THE FREEDOM OF THE GREATER RANGES
(1868–1914)

The Club members who had the means and leisure to explore the Greater Ranges had a greater freedom to climb as they wished. They were able to shake off the shackles of Alpine convention, created by the less enterprising members who restricted their activities to the Alps. Tom Longstaff, in the *Centenary Journal*, recalling 50 years earlier, wrote that 'guideless climbers were still looked at askance by many members, while going only two on the rope was definitely reprehensible. I believe that Hope and Kirkpatrick, with Rolleston and myself, were the first to get away with it'. Longstaff continued:

Good Victorian as I am I must admit that fifty years ago the traditions of the Club were exclusive to the point of snobbery. All those distinguished clerics, doctors, dons, schoolmasters and lawyers were quick to close their ranks against 'outsiders'. Elections were by ballot, and blackballs frequent, though I cannot actually remember casting one myself. Mummery was rejected on the allegation that he was a boot-maker. Ryan, acknowledged the finest climber of my early days, was blackballed on the grounds of incivility in the Alps to some older members: he was Irish and always a difficult character. But a few years later I was present at a very different scene. The elders of the Committee proposed a titled financial magnate as the new president: the younger supported Hermann Woolley, because of his superior mountain record and also for his personal charm of character. The head of one of the big London banks objected that Woolley was only a Midland manufacturer. Instantly Douglas Freshfield retorted, 'That's a queer thing for *you* to say; you're only "something in the city" yourself.' There was no answer and Woolley was proposed and duly elected in 1908!

left: Vittorio Sella's classic photograph of K2 from the east.

below: The second Caucasus expedition of 1874, F C Grove, H Walker, A W Moore and F Gardiner, taken at Odessa.

Following Leslie Stephen's urging that it was time to look farther afield, the most enterprising Club members of the 1860s and 1870s responded with new routes in the Caucasus, Norway, Pyrenees, United States and the Andes of Ecuador. These have already been mentioned in Chapter 2, and I now continue the story into the 1880s up until the temporary hiatus of World War I.

THE CAUCASUS

The Caucasus is a wonderfully challenging range, with peaks like Ushba (15,453 ft/4,710 m), the 'Matterhorn' of the Caucasus, and those in the Bezingi area: Dych-tau (17,054 ft/5,198 m), the second highest, and its close rival Shkhara (17,060 ft/5,200 m). Freshfield, who compiled the monumental two-volume work *The Exploration of the Caucasus* (1896) with Sella's photographs, had this to say: 'For unearthly magnificence in mountain architecture, for sheer height of cliffs, enriched with frozen incrustations and with slabs and bosses of veined snow and crystal ice, with cornices of pendent icicles – there is not scenery in the Alps or Caucasus to compare with the amphitheatres of the Bezingi and Mishirgi Glaciers.'

I am happy to agree with him, having been a member in 1958 of the first foreign party to be allowed to climb there after World War II, led by John Hunt.

After the initial exploration in 1868 and 1874, there was a period of local unrest, followed by the Russo-Turkish war of 1877–78 so it was some years before further expeditions were possible. In 1886, the English attack began, and in the next ten years most of the great peaks fell. Dent and Donkin, with Alexander Burgener and Basil Andenmatten, accounted for Gestola (15,946 ft/4,860 m), and in 1887 Freshfield, climbing with M de Dechy of Budapest and their guides, climbed Tetnuld (15,923 ft/4,852 m), both in the Bezingi area.

The following year, 1888, was a great one in Caucasus climbing history. Three British parties were in the field. Dych-tau fell to A F Mummery and Heinrich Zurfluh from the south-west side, and a few weeks later, Holder, Woolley and Cockin, with Ulrich Almer and Christian Roth, climbed it by the north ridge, believing it was still virgin. They also climbed Katuin-tau (16,356 ft/4,985 m) by the Bezingi face. Then Cockin, with Almer and Roth, climbed Shkhara (17,060 ft/5,200 m) by the north-east ridge, the east peak of Jangi-tau (16,350 ft/4,984 m) and, finally, at the third attempt under exceptionally favourable snow and ice conditions, the north peak of Ushba (15,407 ft/4,696 m) from the Gul glacier. This route is rarely repeated, and the south peak was not climbed until 1903 by a German-Swiss party.

It was noteworthy that all these climbs were done in a single day from high camps. They were clearly strong fast movers and their guides great ice-men. Modern Russian parties allow two to three days, even with the benefit of crampons.

below: Dych-tau from the south, the higher west peak 5198 m first climbed by A F Mummery and H Zurfluh in 1888; the sunlit rib leading to the east peak 70 years later by M Harris and G Band.

above: Ushba from a camp at Betshoi by W F Donkin 1888.

above right: Shkhara, forming the east end of the intimidating Bezingi Wall, photographed from the summit of Dych-tau. In 1888 Cockin, with Almer and Roth, climbed the curving north-east ridge, and in 1958 Harris, Bull, Kutsovski and Band made the third ascent of the north buttress (Muller route).

The third party consisted of Dent, the current Alpine Club president, William F Donkin, who was a brilliant photographer, and Harry Fox, from a respected Somerset family, with Kaspar Streich and Johann Fischer. Dent became ill and had to return to England. Donkin and Fox then set off to attempt Koshtan-tau but they never returned. The following year, therefore, a strong search expedition was sent out from England and they discovered Donkin and Fox's last bivouac high up under the east ridge, concluding that they must have fallen to their deaths. This finding was greeted with great relief by the local villagers who had been under suspicion of foul play. In 1958, we were befriended by an aged shepherd who remembered that, when he was a small boy, his father had assisted the search party. As a gesture of solidarity, our liaison officer and close friend Eugene Gippenreiter secretly purchased the old man's *bourka* (a heavy homespun cloak), and eleven years' later formally presented it to John Hunt at an international climbers' assembly, still smelling pungently!

After concluding the search, several more climbs were accomplished. Woolley succeeded in climbing Koshtan-tau (16,881 ft/5,145 m) from the Tiutiun glacier on the south-east side, and also the east peak of Mishirgi (16,136 ft/4,918 m). The Italian photographer and climber Vittorio Sella also visited the Caucasus that year, and again in 1890 and 1896. There were further British parties in the 1890s but by 1896 the main initial exploration in the Central Caucasus was largely complete. Future new ascents would be of greater technical difficulty and, with few exceptions, the work passed into continental hands.

Notably, the German mountaineer W R Rickmers came with a strong party in 1903 and climbed the south peak of Ushba (15,453 ft/4,710 m), one of the greatest achievements before World War I. A British pair, Tom Longstaff and L W Rolleston, climbing guideless, had hoped to try this but were forestalled. Rickmers described them as 'two semi-attached English freebooters'! Nevertheless, they succeeded in climbing the west peak of Shkhara (16,592 ft/5,057 m) by a complicated new route from the south. They were benighted high up without today's comforts of down jackets and lightweight cagoules. Longstaff describes his experience:

> The rocks were too difficult to explore by candle-light, and we had to be content with an uncomfortable narrow ledge. We could not hitch the rope anywhere, and were too insecure to think of trying to sleep – the height of our bivouac was at least 14,500 feet. Neither of us had been benighted before, and up till midnight we endured the experience fairly well; afterwards we found it horribly cold while clouds gathered and a little rain fell. We kept our feet from frost-bite by putting them in the rucksacks together with the lighted lantern but when we tried to improve matters by adding our aluminium stove, we had more heat than we had bargained for, and destroyed a rucksack and a pair of stockings.

In his absorbing autobiography *This My Voyage*, Longstaff counted this as the finest climb he ever made. 'The peak itself and every foot of the way was all new, and it was a good ending to a great season of seven peaks in twenty-nine days climbing, five of them first ascents.'

Here are two other glimpses of his Caucasian venture:

> Gem-like amid the austerity of the scene a wall-creeper, crimson and plum-coloured, with half-open wings and fanned tail, clung to the final rocks of the summit. It sang a tenuous song of happy repetition as it crept mouse-like across the slabs. The wall-creeper (Tichodroma Muraria) is my favourite bird, an old friend of the Alps and afterwards of the Himalaya, yet this was the only time I have heard the wild beauty of its song.
>
> Off with our sodden clothes and into our sleeping-bags, where Nestor fed us with my own special Caucasian dish. It has great merits. A chicken is boiled in plenty of water with a cupful of rice. The diners start with as many cups of soup as they can drink. Then comes the chicken, which may literally be a pièce de résistance: but no matter if you are hungry. Finally, at the bottom there is the rice pudding. A complete three-course dinner in one cooking-pot.

below: Imposing 5,000 m peaks surround the Bezingi glacier in the central Caucasus

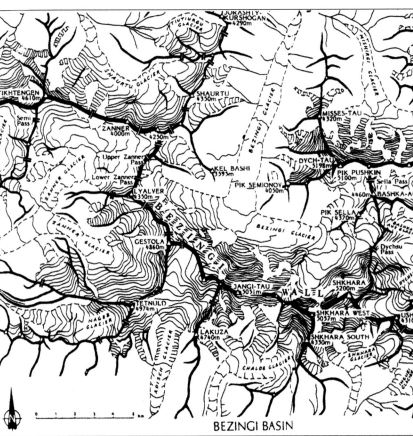

BEZINGI BASIN

The last visits to the Caucasus by British mountaineers for many years were in 1913 and 1914 before the outbreak of World War I, which put a stop to further activity. They were Scottish parties including Harold Raeburn, already one of the great pioneers of Scottish mountaineering, and W N Ling, after whom the Ling hut in Torridon was named.

NORWAY

A few years after the first venture to the Caucasus, William Cecil Slingsby (1849–1929) began his exploration of the mountains of Norway where he became known as the 'father of Norwegian mountaineering'. He is particularly known for his success on Skagastolstind (7,887 ft/2,404 m) in the Jotunheim ('Home of Giants'), which he first saw in 1872 and resolved 'to make it my own'. He made three attempts on the mountain – one with his sister – until in 1876 he reached the summit after his two Norwegian companions deserted him at what is now known as Mohn's Skar, some 500 feet from the top.

below: Cecil Slingsby was the first to climb Skagastolstind in 1876, seen here from the south.

I certainly should not have attempted rocks such as those when alone upon any other mountain than Skagastolstind; but it was the particular peak on which I had concentrated my energies, and that solitary climb I shall always look back upon with a feeling of veneration, as it formed an event in my life which can never be forgotten, and although I have climbed a greater number of the higher Norsk mountains than any other person, yet the ascent of none can leave such a vivid impression in my mind as this.

Slingsby made a pioneer crossing of the Jostedalsbre, the largest icefield (340 square miles) on the European mainland, with the Norwegian schoolmaster Johannes Vigdal. He also introduced ski touring, crossing the Keiser pass in 1880, which might have been crossed on ski by native reindeer hunters, but certainly not by amateur mountaineers or tourists.

In 1903, Slingsby and his son Will joined Norman Collie in the Lofoten Islands, where they climbed the west and east peaks of Rulten. Two years previously, Collie had been there with Woolley, Hastings and Priestman: 'rock climbing as good as any one could wish to get … where the wondrous summer skies slowly change their exquisitely rich colouring of long-drawn-out evening for the more delicate tints of early dawn, and where the restless waves of the great Arctic Ocean are for ever washing against the precipitous sides of the bare, rock-girt mountains.'

Although spending far more time in Norway, Slingsby did some fine Alpine climbs, notably the guideless first ascent of the Dent du Requin with Mummery, Collie and Hastings. He also participated in the first ascents of the Lakeland classics, the north face of Pillar Rock (1891) with Haskett-Smith and Hastings, and Eagle's Nest ridge on Great Gable (1892) with Baker, Brigg and Solly. He was a founder member of the Climbers' Club in 1898 and his daughter married Geoffrey Young.

I never succumbed to the delights of climbing in Norway myself, despite an advertisement placed annually in the *Cambridge Mountaineering Journals* of the 1950s, drafted by an enthusiastic copywriter for the Norway Travel Association:

> It is an astonishing fact that the Nordmöre mountains have only seen one solitary British expedition – as far back as in 1906. And, what is more interesting, there is still scope for further exploring in this area. One of the most outstanding tasks, still awaiting its completion, is the W. wall of Kalken, which has never been climbed. Slingsby has described it as follows in the *Alpine Journal*:

>> 'The precipices of Kalken which rise to such an enormous height out of the grim canyon, are of a sort rarely seen in this planet. In Norway there are but few real mountain walls over a mile in vertical height. In the Alps there are none. About a couple of miles up the Lilledal valley, there is an awful crack on the face of Kalken, a chimney nearly 6,000 feet in height.'

> This giant still awaits its conquerors, and Norwegian experts say it can be done.

To conquer this and other stupendous wall climbs one had to wait for the advanced techniques and skills of the 1970s and 1980s.

ANDES

Exploration of the Andes began in Ecuador in 1736 by a French scientific expedition, followed in 1802 by the German naturalist Alexander von Humboldt, and in 1872 by the German geologist Wilhelm Reiss, with A M Escobar, making the first ascent of Cotapaxi (19,335 ft/5,893 m). But Whymper, with the two Carrels, was the first Alpine Club member to put in an appearance, in 1880, making the fifth ascent of Cotapaxi and the first of Chimborazo (20,550 ft/6,247 m). It was not until 1897 that a British party tackled the highest Andean peak, Aconcagua (22,835 ft/6,960 m), in Argentina close to the border with Chile: Alpine Club member E A Fitzgerald, who had already made a name for himself in New Zealand, a younger Englishman, Stuart Vines, and several guides headed by

right: A superb drawing by Edward Wymper of Chimborazo, climbed with the two Carrels in 1880.

Matthias Zurbriggen. Although it is not technically difficult, the party was severely affected by altitude sickness. After three failures, Fitzgerald reached 22,000 feet but could go no further. 'I sent Zurbriggen on at once to complete, if possible, the ascent, although myself obliged to turn back. I had the greatest difficulty in crawling down; my knees were so weak that I repeatedly fell, cutting myself with the sharp stones that covered the mountainside.'

But Zurbriggen made it! He planted his ice-axe on top and built a summit cairn; possibly a world height record at the time. A month later, Vines made the second ascent with an Italian porter guide, Nicolas Lanti. The Club Library recently acquired Vines' manuscript diary of the climb. Not to be outdone, the ubiquitous Martin Conway repeated the ascent the following year, and also made the first ascent of Illimani (21,200 ft/6,462 m), which towers above La Paz, Bolivia.

CANADIAN ROCKIES

After his Andean adventures, in 1901 Whymper took a strong party of Alpine guides to the Rockies for the Canadian Pacific Railway Company. Although he did not accomplish much himself on this trip, two of the guides, with Sir James Outram, made the first ascent of the striking isolated pyramid of Mount Assiniboine (11,870 ft/3,618 m). The following year, Norman Collie, with Woolley and Stutfield, went there also and was impressed with the scope for the mountaineer: 'For should he climb to the summit of any peak, even near

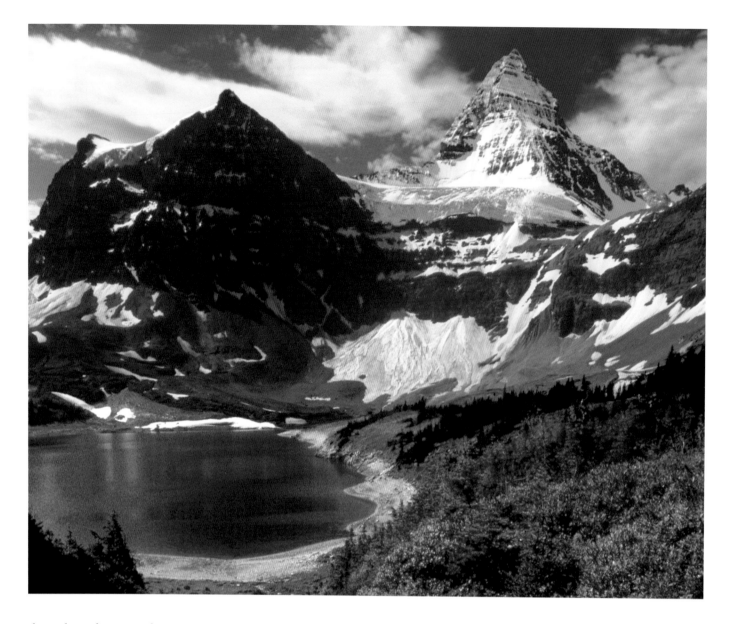

the railway, big enough to give an extensive view, by far the greater number of the mountains and peaks that can be seen stretching in every direction, as far as the eye can see to the horizon, are as yet untrodden by human feet.'

In 1909, the Canadian Alpine Club had a camp at Lake O'Hara from which V A Fynn and E O Wheeler (later Sir Oliver Wheeler) ascended Hungabee. They both became Alpine Club members in 1911. Also from the camp Hastings, Amery and Mumm, with their guide Moritz Inderbinen, made a fine attempt to climb Mount Robson (12,972 ft/3.954 m) from the east, but it was not until 1913 that the first ascent was achieved by the brilliant Canadian climber A H MacCarthy and W W Foster with the famous Austrian guide Conrad Kain. Amery was thrilled with the area and vowed to return. When he retired as Secretary of State for Dominion Affairs in 1929, he did indeed return and made the first ascent of the eponymous Mount Amery! Tom Longstaff was another visitor to the Canadian Rockies during this period, climbing the north-west face of Assiniboine with Rudolf Aemmer in 1910.

above: The striking isolated pyramid of Assiniboine in the Canadian Rockies climbed by Sir James Outram, with two guides, in 1901.

JAPAN

On the other side of the Pacific, the Revd Walter Weston had been discovering the mountains of Japan. Although the three most famous mountains: Fujiyama, Tateyama and Hakusan, had been ascended long ago, before the development of mountaineering in the European Alps, they were looked upon primarily as objects of religious devotion, and climbing them was more in the nature of a pilgrimage than a recreation. Climbing in its modern sense came only after the introduction of western culture following the Meiji restoration of 1868. Walter Weston, a missionary, was the most influential foreign climber in those early days, writing *Mountaineering and Exploration in the Japanese Alps* (1896) and *The Playground of the Far East* (1918), both published by John Murray. He inspired the young climbers of the day to found the Japanese Alpine Club in 1906 which in turn did a great deal to encourage the Japanese to take a wide and deep interest in mountaineering. He arrived in Japan in 1888 and returned to England in 1915. Another missionary, the Revd Murray Walton, extended Weston's work with *Scrambles in Japan and Formosa*, published by Arnold in 1934. Contributing a foreword, the president of the Japanese Alpine Club at that time, Mr Usui Kohima, concluded: 'The joy of us Japanese mountaineers at its appearance is great. We send it forth on its way with a hearty cheer from the Far East.'

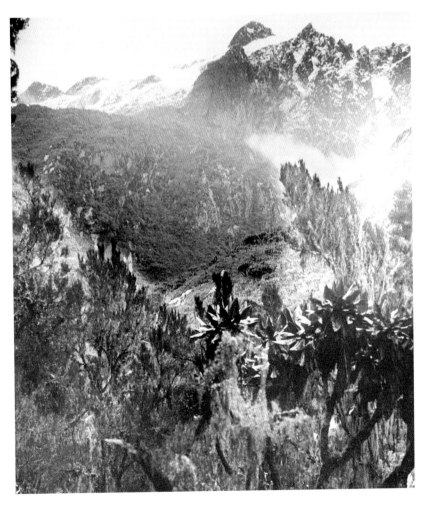

below: Mountains and moorland in the Ruwenzori group, photographed during the Mumm–Freshfield expedition of 1905.

RUWENZORI

Turning now to the African continent, Ruwenzori is the great mountain group on the Congo–Uganda border rising to 16,795 feet (5,120 metres). Seen from afar, it was known to the ancients as the 'Mountains of the Moon' and thought to be the source of the Nile. The explorer Henry Stanley was the first white man to see the range in 1888, and the first Alpine Club members to visit were Freshfield and Mumm, with Moritz Inderbinen in 1905. They reached the snowline above 14,000 feet but vile weather defeated them. For most of the year the summits, down to 9,000 feet or lower, are clothed in mist and you may never see them.

In April the following year, 1906, the Duke of Abruzzi, who had been a Club member since 1894, had better luck. He led a well-equipped expedition, including the photographer Vittorio Sella, and four guides, with the aim of climbing every summit and mapping the whole range. Despite variable weather they successfully climbed the two highest peaks and christened them Queen Alexandra (16,750 ft/5,105 m) and Queen Margherita (16,795 ft/5,120 m), after members of the British and Italian royal families. A Belgian expedition in 1932 carried on the royal tradition by naming a peak they climbed in the Stanley group after King Albert, who was not only a keen mountaineer but founded a series of National Parks in the Congo. So when the diplomat and Alpine Club member Douglas Busk went there with Arthur Firmin in 1952, he was able to identify two more unnamed peaks in the Stanley group for which he proposed the names of Elizabeth and Philip. These were formally accepted by the queen, after approval of the competent authorities, in the year 1953 and the glacier between the two peaks was appropriately named Coronation.

My wife and I became good friends with the Busks when he was appointed ambassador to Venezuela in Caracas and I arrived there in 1961 as a young petroleum engineer with Shell, confined to salt flats beside Lake Maracaibo. In no time he had lured me up into the Venezuelan Andes for a week's climbing.

THE HIMALAYA – EARLY EXPLORATION

After reviewing most of the rest of the world's mountains, it is time to move to the highest range of all, the Greater Himalaya and its adjacent ranges. The recreational mountaineers were long preceded by the early explorers; the naturalists, such as Joseph Hooker, who travelled in Sikkim and Nepal in 1848–9, and the staff of the Great Trigonometrical Survey. As recorded by Kenneth Mason in his *Abode of Snow*, W W Graham was the first traveller to come out from England with the main object of climbing mountains 'more for sport and adventure than for

OPPOSITE PAGE:

right: The Gurkha Rhagobir in camp with Charles Bruce and A F Mummery during the ill-fated expedition to Nanga Parbat in 1895.

maps left & right: The major peaks of the Karakoram in Pakistan (left) and the Indian Himalaya, from Rimo to Nanda Devi (right).

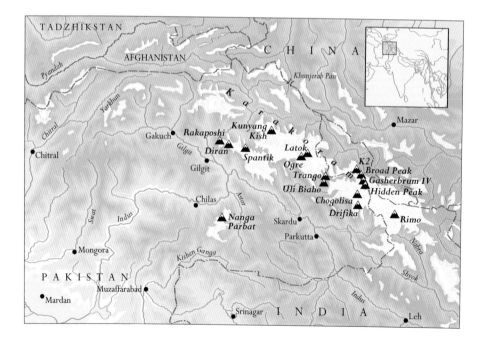

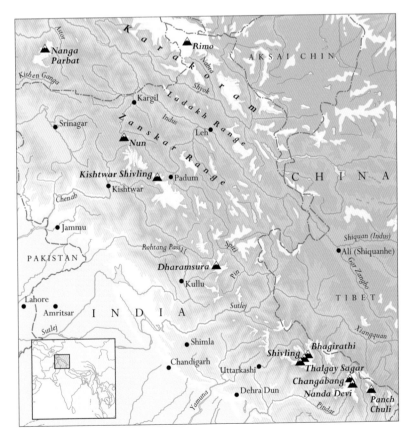

the advancement of scientific knowledge', as he admitted on his return to the Royal Geographical Society in 1884. He took with him Joseph Imboden from St Niklaus and tackled peaks in Sikkim, just across the border in Nepal, and in Kumaun near Nanda Devi. From a camp at 18,500 feet in Sikkim he claimed to have climbed Kabru (24,000 ft/7,315 m) on 8 October 1883. The climbing world was divided on his claim; it was probably a lower peak. Not carrying any instruments for accurate positioning he may well have been genuinely mistaken.

By 1885, roads were being improved and the mountains becoming more accessible. The valleys were known reasonably well and the higher peaks correctly located, but hardly anyone climbed for pleasure. It was a period of ascending passes rather than peaks. The glaciers and general topography of the high peaks and their satellites were unknown and ripe for exploration, providing wonderful opportunities for both sporting and scientifically minded mountaineers.

One of the most adventurous feats of pass-crossing was that by Francis Younghusband in 1887, as a young lieutenant in the King's Dragoon Guards, travelling by land from Manchuria by the shortest route across the Gobi desert to India. He made a daring crossing of the Karakoram by the 19,000 feet (5,790 metres) Muztagh Pass to the Baltoro glacier. On the way, he discovered the Aghil mountains, the Shaksgam, which flows into the Yarkand river, and the Sarpo Laggo glacier, the first of the northern glaciers of the Karakoram to be encountered. He was also the first white man to see the northern flanks of K2. I was thrilled to cover the same ground in 2003 on a trek with David Hamilton, Clare Marvin and several other Alpine Club members. We used camels for load-carrying to cross the Aghil pass and ford the Shaksgam, instead of the more normal porters or yaks employed in Nepal. The camels carried 100 kg each but had no objection to my extra 90 kg on top when we came to a river crossing which was too deep and swift for me to want to get my feet wet! It was the same stark country surveyed by Eric Shipton in his *Blank on the Map* expedition of 1937.

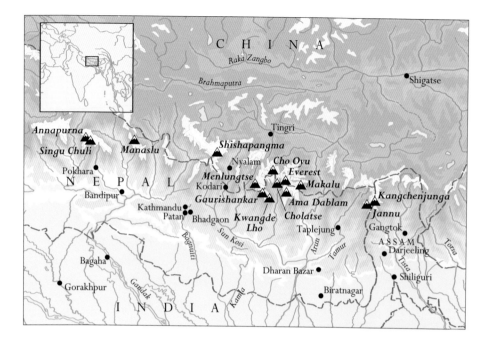

above left : The major peaks of Nepal.

left: The original caption to this photo of Charles Bruce rock climbing stated: 'General Bruce should go home and lead a quiet, regular life'. Extract from proceedings of Medical Board, held in Rawalpindi, 4 August 1919.

above: Sir Martin Conway, later Lord Conway of Allington, President 1902–04, the first man to be knighted for his services to mountaineering.

above right: Charles Bruce in Chitral 1904, trying more gentle pursuits?

PAVING THE WAY FOR CONWAY'S 1892 EXPEDITION

On a second mission to the same area in 1889 to investigate other passes and recent raids on caravans by Hunzukuts, Younghusband had a small escort of soldiers from the 5th Gurkha Rifles, perhaps the first occasion Gurkhas were used in mountain exploration. Charles Bruce was already training his riflemen to be mountaineers. Following the Hunza-Nagir campaign of 1891, and the pacification of this borderland area, Lieutenant George Cockerell was deputed to explore and map the western Karakoram and Hindu Kush, an area of some 12,000 square miles. This prepared the way for the first major expedition organised from England to the Himalaya in 1892, the first such venture to receive financial support from the Royal Society and Royal Geographical Society.

It was organised and led by Martin Conway and included, amongst others, Oscar Eckenstein, Charles Bruce and four of his Gurkhas, and the guide Matthias Zurbriggen of Macugnaga. They did a great deal of general exploration, including the first crossing of the Hispar pass on 18 July and exploration of the Biafo. In the course of attempting Baltoro Kangri ('Golden Throne') (23,390 ft/7,129 m), they climbed Pioneer Peak (22,600 ft/6,888 m). Conway kept detailed records and a reconnaissance map, published by the Royal Geographical Society, which provided the basis for the Duke of Abruzzi's great expedition in 1909.

above: Sunrise over Kangchenjunga. A water-colour by T Howard Somervell, reproduced as the Club's Christmas card for 2004.

Martin Conway, later Lord Conway of Allington (1856–1937), made his name as an art critic, becoming Professor of Art in Liverpool, then Slade Professor at Cambridge, and a Trustee of both the National Portrait Gallery and the Wallace Collection. He was elected to the Alpine Club in 1877, and president in 1902. As with many of the early pioneers, he was better on snow and ice than on rock, but was primarily an explorer, his reputation resting on his expeditions to the Greater Ranges: Karakoram 1892, Spitsbergen (now Svalbard) 1896 and 1897, the Andes and Tierra del Fuego 1898, and his great journey described in *The Alps from End to End*. He also initiated the first *Climbers' Guides*: to Zermatt 1881; the Pennines; and then jointly with Coolidge to other parts of the Alps.

He was the first man to be knighted in connection with mountaineering, principally for his map of the Karakoram, and one of the few prominent mountaineers not to quarrel with Coolidge! Geoffrey Young summed him up: 'Martin Conway was a personality appropriate to a renaissance, of scintillating contrasts, a romantic, a sociologist, an art connoisseur, a wordling, an omniscient lecturer and compiler, a busy public character, and a completely casual will-o'-the-wisp.'

THE LOSS OF MUMMERY

Next after Conway, in 1895 Mummery, Collie and Hastings came out to reconnoitre Nanga Parbat (26,660 ft/8,125 m), one of the 14 8,000-m peaks. They were joined in India by Charles Bruce (later General Bruce) and two of his Gurkhas. With Rhagobir, the more experienced Ghurkha, Mummery climbed a rock rib on the Diamir face and spent three days examining the ground above before Rhagobir was taken ill and they had to come down. They then decided to move round to look at the Rakhiot face. While Collie and Hastings moved base camp, Mummery and the Gurkhas planned to cross a high ridge between Nanga Parbat and Ganalo at over 20,000 feet. Mummery's party were never seen again, almost certainly swept away by an avalanche.

Charles Bruce continued to climb and travel in the Himalaya; with Mumm and Longstaff he had hoped to explore Everest in 1907 from the Tibetan side but the proposal was vetoed by the British government. In his obituary of Bruce, Longstaff wrote:

> His greatest contribution to mountaineering came through his wide knowledge of the tribes of the Himalaya. It was he who first trained Gurkhas for serious mountain work. He started the Baltis of Kashmir and the Bhotias of Garhwal on the upward path, a lead which Kellas so ably followed. But his great discovery was the value of the Sherpa, a Tibetan tribe long settled in Nepal. These, with their purer Tibetan cousins, have long been the mainstay of every Himalayan expedition of recent years.

below: Douglas Freshfield, the first person to be elected president of both the Alpine Club 1893–95 and the Royal Geographical Society 1914–17.

FRESHFIELD AND KANGCHENJUNGA

The next expedition of real note was Douglas Freshfield's celebrated circuit of Kangchenjunga (28,169 ft/8,586 m), the world's third highest peak, on the border between Nepal and Sikkim which took him seven weeks from 5 September to 24 October 1899. He was accompanied by Vittorio Sella, who, as usual, took wonderful photographs including the telephoto of the crest of Siniolchu (22,570 ft/6,879 m), which makes this relatively modest peak look like one of the Himalayan giants. Also in the party was Sella's brother Erminio, a guide, Angelo Maquignaz, and the geologist Professor Edmund J Garwood, who had been with Conway in Spitsbergen and who produced an excellent sketch map of the massif. Freshfield's account certainly helped to create the mountain's aura of invincibility. Here is his opinion of the north-west face: 'The whole face of the mountain might be imagined

to have been constructed by the Demon of Kangchenjunga for the express purpose of defence against human assault, so skilfully is each comparatively weak
spot raked by the ice and snow batteries.'

The circuit has been completed very few times: first by one of the incredible
pundits, Rinsing, in 1884; secondly by Freshfield in 1899; and thirdly in 1930 by
Frank Smythe's party, while returning from an unsuccessful attempt on the
north-west face by Professor G O Dyhrenfurth's International Expedition; then
in 1991 by an Indian team led by Dorjee Lhatoo from the Himalayan
Mountaineering Institute in Darjeeling. To mark the centenary of Freshfield's circuit I had hoped it might be possible to undertake a fifth round. We did indeed
manage to get permission from the Indians in 2002 to visit the Lhonak Valley in
north-west Sikhim, which had been closed to Europeans since the 1930s, but getting formal permission to cross the frontier from there over the Jonsong La into
Nepal proved another matter. I was told that there was a treaty between India and
Nepal recognising some 17 official crossing places. To add another one or two
would require renegotiation of the treaty, so I gave up!

Douglas William Freshfield (1845–1934) had a privileged upbringing. His
father had been solicitor to the Bank of England. He was called to the Bar but
never needed to practise because of his inherited wealth. His parents introduced
him to the mountains, and he had climbed the Titlis and Mont Blanc before he left
Eton. Combining his interest in mountaineering with geography, he was the first
person to be elected president of both the Alpine Club and the Royal
Geographical Society. As T S Blakeney notes in his three-part article 'The *Alpine
Journal* and its Editors', spread over the 1974, 1975 and 1976 *Alpine Journals*: 'It is
difficult, indeed, to say which was the greater; his service
to the AC or to the RGS. He was RGS Hon. Sec.
1881–94; a Gold Medallist (1903), Vice-President
1906–13, and President 1914–17. In the AC, he was
Editor 1872–80, Vice-President 1878–80 and President
1893–95. He was a member of the AC for seventy years,
being an Hon. Member for the last ten.'

Freshfield's particular forte was in clarifying the
topography of lesser known mountain ranges and giving
clear and objective accounts of his explorations. He
headed the strong expedition to the Caucasus in 1889 to
search for Donkin and Fox and their guides Streich and
Fischer lost on Koshtan-tau. Geoffrey Young describes an
encounter with Freshfield in the Club's hall at Savile
Row: 'I watched him on the platform steps, tall and head-
tossing, and overlooking us with his genial, aquiline
sneer. He hurried down, caught me by the elbow and
said "Let's sit at the back – there's only those bald and
white heads to the fore!" He himself was then well over
eighty; but he still revelled in all the intolerant privileges
of youth.'

below: Oscar Eckenstein, an innovative
engineer and mountaineer, designed more
efficient crampons and a shorter axe for
climbing steep ice.

CROWLEY AND ECKENSTEIN

Freshfield's book *Round Kangchenjunga*, published in 1903, may have inspired the next expedition to the mountain in 1905 to try the south-west face approached by the Yalung glacier. It was led by the Swiss Dr J Jacot Guillarmod and included the infamous Aleister Crowley, self-styled 'Great Beast 666', who later gained a reputation as the 'wickedest man in the world', practising black magic in his abbey at Cefalu, Sicily. Sadly, before the expedition had got much above 20,000 feet an avalanche killed the 31-year-old Alexis Pache, a lieutenant in the Swiss Cavalry, and four porters. Crowley had no sympathy: 'I was not over anxious in the circumstances to help. A mountain accident of this sort is one of the things for which I have no sympathy whatever.' Crowley had already climbed in Mexico and the Karakoram with Oscar Eckenstein, for whom he had great affection and admiration as a climber.

'Eckenstein, provided he could get three fingers on something that could be described by a man far advanced in hashish as a ledge, would be smoking his pipe on that ledge a few seconds later, and none of us could tell how he had done it.' It was Eckenstein who, by 1899, had devised a new type of crampon or climbing irons derived from those used by generations of Bavarian and Tyrolean chamois hunters, which enabled mountaineers to dispense with much of the laborious work of cutting steps in ice. It was a significant invention but only caught on slowly amongst the conservative British mountaineering fraternity. Even in the 1930s some senior Club members would advocate that a novice should gain one or two seasons' experience before trying crampons. The introduction of rubber Vibram-soled boots instead of clinker nails or tricounis after World War II probably helped to accelerate their adoption. Longstaff recalls 'an off day at Montenvers in 1899 when, with the assistance of the peculiar Crowley, already notorious and in full Highland kit, Oscar gave me a most valuable lesson in their use. Squatting on very steep ice above a crevasse he insisted on my sitting on his shoulder to prove the security they gave. This was a new artificial aid which gained early popularity, although stalwarts like my old friend Bill Strutt continued to abuse them mercilessly.'

Eckenstein's father was a German Jew who, after the failure of the 1848 revolution, deemed it prudent to retire to England, where he married an Englishwoman. Eckenstein was a considerable innovator. A railway engineer by profession, he applied his mechanical knowledge to solving climbing problems. He also designed an ice-axe for use in conjunction with crampons on more difficult ice, some 5 inches shorter than the average 39-inch and with a smaller head, so that it could be effectively plied with one hand.

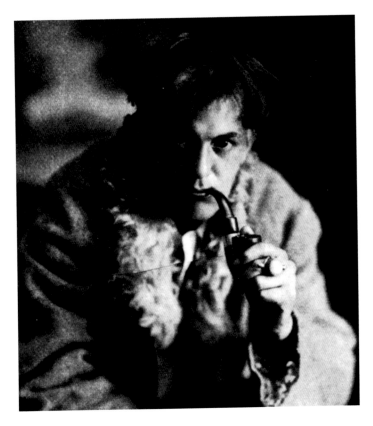

below: The infamous Aleister Crowley, who, just as well, was never a member of the Alpine Club.

left: Gabriel Loppé's evocative painting of sunrise on the Grandes Jorasses seen from Mont Blanc, 1896. Loppé (1825–1913) a close friend of Leslie Stephen, was elected an honorary member of the Club on 12 January 1864.

I had always thought that both Crowley and Eckenstein were Alpine Club members, but searching the members' list during that period, I could find no record of their election. This comment by Crowley in his *Confessions* could well explain why: 'The policy of boycotting Eckenstein and his school, of deliberately ignoring the achievements of Continental climbers, to say nothing of my own expeditions, has preserved the privilege and prestige of the English Alpine Club, Ignorance and incompetence are unassailable. Ridicule does not reach the realms of secure snobbery.'

LONGSTAFF, THE WANDERER

Longstaff had a great time in 1905 during his six months of wandering in the Himalaya. First, with Alexis and Henri Brocherel he tried to penetrate the ring of peaks – more than 30 over 21,000 feet high – surrounding Nanda Devi (25,660 ft/7,851 m) in Garhwal, the highest peak in the British Empire. The most determined previous effort had been by W W Graham in 1883 accompanied by two top guides, Emil Boss, a captain in the Swiss army, and Ulrich Kaufmann. They had tried to force a route up the Rishi Ganga gorge on the western side. The terrain was so difficult that their porters deserted them and they had to turn back. Longstaff reached a 19,000-feet saddle on the eastern rim on 8 June, now known as Longstaff's col, and came back again in 1907 with the two Brocherels, Charles Bruce, with some of his Gurkhas, A L Mumm and his guide Moritz Inderbinen. This time they reached the Bagini col (20,100 ft/6,127 m) on the

above: Mount Gurla Mandhata 7,727 m from the sacred lake of Rakas Tal. Longstaff tried the long west ridge.

north side on 22 May and forced a crossing but eventually found themselves in the Rishi Nala, barely beyond the point Graham had reached in 1883, before they too were defeated.

Continuing in 1905, Longstaff journeyed into Tibet to the totally unexplored isolated mass of Gurla Mandhata (25,350 ft/7,727 m), ten miles south of the Manasarowar and Rakas Tal lakes. They tried the main western ridge. From a snowy shoulder at about 23,000 feet they descended to seek the shelter of a rock outcrop for a bivouac. But before reaching it, they were avalanched:

Just as I turned to take in the slack of Henri's rope I heard a sharp, hissing sound above me: Henri laying flat and trying to stop himself, came down on top of me and swept me from my hold. As I shot past Alexis I felt his hand close on the back of my coat, and we went down together … I could do nothing but try and keep on the surface of the avalanche. Then somehow I got turned round with my head downwards … I seemed to rise on a wave of snow and dropped over a low cliff, with Henri mixed up in my part of the rope … On we went with the rope round my neck this time; but it was easy to untwist it. Then came a longer drop, which I thought must be the last from my point of view. The next thing I remember was that suddenly, to my intense surprise, the rope tightened round my chest, stopping me with a jerk which squeezed all the breath out of my body.

They had fallen some 3,000 feet in a minute or two. Their rope was of silk for lightness and the knot was so tight around Longstaff's chest that he had to cut it. Astonishingly, after a bivouac they continued the ascent next day. But Alexis collapsed with a severe headache, so they spent another night in a snow hole before retreating, much to the disappointment of Henri, who seemed completely impervious to heat, cold or altitude.

While at Cambridge in 1950, I vividly remember Longstaff speaking to the Mountaineering Club about this adventure. He showed a slide illustrating his high point and then announced: 'We were swept down 3,000 feet by an avalanche to here. Next slide please,' banging the butt of his billiard cue pointer on the ground for emphasis. 'We then spent the night in this snow hole here.' Bang. 'Next slide, please.' He was a little man, still with traces of his original red hair, and I felt he had quite a resemblance, both physically and in character, to Francis Younghusband, 'the Last Great Imperial Adventurer'.

Their ascent of Trisul (23,406 ft/7,165 m) in 1907, the highest peak on the outer ramparts of the Nanda Devi Sanctuary, must have seemed a pushover by comparison. They decided to adopt risk tactics and climb 6,000 feet in one day.

above: Tom Longstaff, President 1947–49, made a record climb on Trisul in 1907, two years after being avalanched on Gurla Mandhata in Tibet.

> Suddenly the slope ended and Alexis turned and shouted back to me: 'The top!' The summit of Trisul is in form like the two humps of a Bactrian camel. Alexis insisted that the one on which we stood was the higher. Excitement made me lose all sense of fatigue, but I had no breath to shout through the gale, so passed through and took the lead. I cut a few steps in ice, up on to the cornice. Henri stood back to hold in case it gave way as I crawled to the top. I craned over on my belly to look down the astounding southern precipice. Spread below were all the middle hills we had marched through: then the foothills: then the plains with rivers winding. To the west all was clear; the whole scarp of the western Himalaya so vast that I expected to see the earth rotating before my eyes.

He had achieved his boyhood dreams. For 23 years it remained the highest summit reached by man.

From the age of 15, Longstaff had declared mountain travel to be his ambition. Luckily there was enough money in the family for him to do so. But his father urged him to take a medical degree first: 'every man, he said, ought to have a profession to fall back on, nor should I enjoy my freedom unless I had gone through some mill or other.'

Here is a final reminiscence from Longstaff:

As a boy I had read an account of Graham's approach to Nanda Devi in 1883, so that my attention was early called to this region. Later I devoured many books on Himalayan travel, yet none of them aroused in me the same feeling of excitement or mystery. Reading led me to map hunting – a fascinating game which later enabled me to meet Whymper. Just before his marriage he wished to sell his Himalayan maps and books of which he had a considerable collection, and some of these I bought. Edward Whymper was at that time a rock-faced lion in appearance, difficult and incalculable. Often when I pounced on some particular item he would decide to keep it for himself. I admired a case of Ecuadorian humming birds in his rooms and on a subsequent visit they had gone: onto his wife's hat he said.

KELLAS, THE SCIENTIST

The same year that Longstaff climbed Trisul, another doctor, Alexander M Kellas, a lecturer in chemistry, made his first visit to Sikkim. Unusually, he climbed on his own, without guides, assisted only by local porters who, as Bruce had realised, had the potential to be trained as mountaineers. This process was not without excitement. Kellas conceded that 'the cloth boots worn by the coolies were not satisfactory on ice. When one of them slipped on Kangchenjau within a few moments of Anderkyow's slip we were whizzing down the ice-slope with the speed of an express train.' Kellas estimated the vertical distance fallen at about 1,000 feet at an average speed of 40–50 miles per hour, though he considers that 'for the inexperienced, computation of time is interfered with during such a rapid descent!' Was he trying to outdo Longstaff on Gurla Mandhata? Nevertheless, in 1911 with his porters he made first ascents in Sikkim of Pauhunri (23,180 ft/7,064 m) and Chomiomo (22,430 ft/6,836 m). Tragically he died on the way to Everest in 1921.

Kellas had become very interested in high-altitude physiology and concluded in a remarkable paper written in 1920 that: 'Mount Everest could be ascended by a man of excellent physical and mental constitution in first rate training without adventitious aids [supplementary oxygen] if the physical difficulties are not too great, and with the use of oxygen, even if the mountain may be classed as difficult from the climbing point of view.' It took 58 years for Reinhold Messner and Peter Habeler to bear out the first part of this prediction.

below: Alexander Kellas made several first ascents in 1911 in Sikkim without guides, but realised the potential of local porters to be trained as mountaineers.

THE DUKE OF ABRUZZI LOOKS AT K2

We have already mentioned the Duke of Abruzzi (1873–1933), who was a member of the royal house of Savoy. In 1894, he climbed the Zmutt ridge of the Matterhorn with Mummery and was elected to the Alpine Club. He made the first winter ascent of Monte Viso in 1897, but was principally known for his three great expeditions: the first ascent of Mount St Elias (18,012 ft/5,462 m) in Alaska on 31 July 1897; to the highest point of the Ruwenzori (16,795 ft/5,120 m) on 18 June 1906, named after his aunt Queen Margherita, and to the Karakoram in 1909 with the two Brocherels where, on the east ridge of Bride Peak, they reached a record height of 24,600 feet (7,500 metres), some 500 feet below the summit. They were stopped not by the effects of altitude but by a dense mist on a corniced ridge in bad snow conditions where the duke prudently considered it was too risky to continue. They had had a serious look at K2, the world's second highest peak (28,250 ft/8,611 m), recorded in Sella's iconic photograph, but after examining all four ridges concluded it was too formidable for those days.

De Filippo in his account wrote: 'After weeks of examination, after hours of contemplation and search for the secret of the mountain, the Duke was finally obliged to yield to the conviction that K2 was not to be climbed.' In actual fact he had, though he did not know it, solved the problem – via the southern so-called Abruzzi ridge by which it was first climbed by the Italians in 1954.

Of these three expeditions, the one to Mount St Elias was the most remarkable, in Arctic conditions lasting five months. 'Though only twenty-four at the time of this expedition he was,' writes Count Aldo Bonacossa, 'already a leader of men, with the power to attract a team whose devotion to the duke was life-long. He was sometimes a little exacting in his demands, and he never ceased to be a prince, but how great was his psychological insight into the souls of men, and above all how striking was his personal example in endurance and in dangers!'

During World War I he commanded allied naval units, but then returned to Africa, settling in Italian Somaliland, where he died in 1933, mourned by his natives 'comme chef et père'. He never married.

VITTORIO SELLA, THE SUPREME PHOTOGRAPHER

The duke was fortunate to be accompanied on these three expeditions by Vittorio Sella (1859–1943), who became the finest mountain photographer of his day and provided all the illustrations for the articles and books about them. His father died when he was young so he was brought up in Biella, in the Italian Piedmont, by his uncle Quintino Sella, a famous statesman and founder of the

right: HRH The Duke of Abruzzi in full regalia. He led three great expeditions: climbing Mount St Elias in Alaska in 1897; to the Ruwenzori in 1906; and to the Karakoram in 1909.

Italian Alpine Club. Vittorio's father was a pioneer photographer so, not surprisingly, Vittorio also took up the pursuit, taking his huge plate camera weighing nearly 40 pound up into the hills. The glass plates measuring 30 x 36 cm (about 12 x 14 in alone weighed two pounds. When I attended a conference in Biella with Lord Hunt and Lord Chorley in the 1980s we were delighted to meet Vittorio's great nephew, Dr Ludovico Sella, who kindly took us to see Vittorio's studio where all his precious plates and equipment are now preserved on display. Using such huge plates, the quality and definition of his enlargements was exceptional. It is difficult to do better with today's 35 mm compact digital or even conventional slide film cameras. With the much slower film of those days, when he wanted a contact print, he would just hold the frame out in the sun for a few moments exposure before taking it indoors to develop!

The great American photographer Ansel Adams paid tribute to Sella's work: 'Knowing the physical pressure of time and energy attendant on ambitious mountain expeditions, we are amazed by the mood of calmness and perfection pervading all of Sella's photographs.'

Sella was also a pioneer of Alpine winter mountaineering: the first winter ascent of the Matterhorn, 16–17 March 1882, traversed from Breuil to Zermatt with J A Louis and Baptiste Carrel; the first winter ascent of Monte Rosa, 26 January 1884; also the Lyskamm, 22 March 1885; and the first winter traverse of Mont Blanc from Courmayeur to Chamonix, 4 January 1888, all with first-class guides, including the brothers J J and Daniel Maquignaz. He was made an honorary member of the Club.

THE WORKMANS, TRAVELLERS EXTRAORDINARY

The American couple Dr William Hunter Workman and Mrs Fanny Bullock Workman were not members of the Alpine Club, but their travels and writing about the Karakoram have always fascinated me, with such wonderful titles as *The Call of the Snowy Hispar* and *Two Summers in the Ice-Wilds of Eastern Karakoram*. One photograph showed them enjoying tiffin at 14,000 feet (4,267 m) on the Chogo Lungma glacier wearing pith helmets and seated formally at a little table, attended gravely by a puggaree-wearing bearer. I am indebted to Dr Michael Plint, who had access to their private papers and spoke about them at the Alpine Club on 12 February 1991.

They mounted seven Himalayan expeditions between 1899 and 1912.

Although they covered a great deal of ground between the Chogo Lungma, Hispar and Biafo glaciers (after Sir Martin Conway's earlier exploration), the maps they produced left much to be desired, and geographers such as Kenneth Mason were not complimentary: 'When they did refer to the work of their predecessors it was in too carping and controversial a manner. Probably from an excess of zeal and enthusiasm the Workmans were, on their journeys, the victims of their own faults. They were too impatient and rarely tried to understand the mentality of their porters and so did not get the best out of them'.

They did seem to redeem themselves on their last 1912 expedition when they secured the services of Captain Grant Peterkin and Sarjan Singh of the Survey of India who between them were responsible, during nine weeks of exceptionally good weather, for the triangulation of the Siachen glacier, which remains the basis of current maps. The high point of the expedition was the ascent to the Indira col (18,950 ft/5,776 m), which they discovered and named after the goddess Laxmi. They were thus the first people ever to see that tremendous view northward towards the remote mountains of Chinese Turkestan. One cannot help envying them.

Finally, to conclude this lengthy Himalayan section up until World War I, C F Meade made three determined attempts on Kamet (25,447 ft/7,756 m) in 1910, 1912 and 1913, reaching a saddle between Abi Gamin and Kamet now known as Meade's col at 23,420 feet, but still with 2,000 feet to go. Being in British India it was relatively accessible so it had been attempted several times previously, as far back as 1855 by the redoubtable pioneers Adolf and Robert Schlagintweit, who reached 22,250 feet. Eventually it was the first of the Himalayan giants over 25,000 feet to be climbed, by Frank Smythe's expedition in 1931.

NEW ZEALAND

I have left the New Zealand Alps to the last which does their wonderful mountains less than justice, but they were too far away to be visited by more than a few British climbers before World War I. Much of the serious mountaineering was done by members of the Alpine Club living in New Zealand. A P Harper founded the New Zealand Alpine Club and with C E Mannering began a series of explorations in the 1880s shortly after the visit in 1881–2 by the Revd W S Green, who, as mentioned earlier, nearly succeeded in climbing Mount Cook (12,349 ft/3,764 m). They were elected to the Alpine Club in 1892 and 1891 respectively and became honorary members, upholding the best traditions of the Club. Other members were Dr E Teichelmann, a very fine photographer elected in 1903, Revd H E Newton in 1908, and R S Low in 1913. Revd W S Green was the first into print with *The High Alps of New Zealand*, followed by E A. FitzGerald's *Climbs in the New Zealand Alps*. He arrived in January 1895, and with Matthias Zurbriggen (who in 1897 was to solo the last part of Aconcagua) made the first ascent of Mount Tasman (11,475 ft/3,498 m), the second highest peak in New Zealand, and the first crossing of Fitzgerald's pass, creating a route from the Hermitage over the main divide to the west coast. Then in 1909, L M Earle, with Jack Clark and the two Grahams, made a new ascent of Mount Cook by the west face above the Hooker glacier, previously thought to be impassable.

below: Camp in the Malte Brun range with views of the Caroline and East Face of Mount Cook. A fine image from Colin Monteath's New Zealand Alpine Calendar 2006.

5 BETWEEN THE WARS
(1919–1939)

THE ALPINE CLUB LOSES ITS LEADERSHIP

The period between the Wars was a strange one for British mountaineering. It lost its pre-eminence. What were the reasons? Jack Longland's essay in the centenary number of the *Alpine Journal* gives a brilliant analysis and I couldn't do better than summarise some of his conclusions. First, we had lost in the war many of the young men who might have envisaged the goals and set the standards of the next decade. Secondly, the numbers of participants from countries with the Alps on their doorsteps: the French, Germans, Austrians and Italians, had increased enormously at all social levels and their best climbers, uninhibited in the use of pitons and artificial climbing techniques, were putting up routes of a higher standard than was possible by traditional methods. Third, the Alpine Club, which conveyed the message through the pages of its august *Alpine Journal*, chose to be obstinately backward-looking during much of this period, decrying the new techniques and newer attitudes of the young climbers of other countries. At the same time, it barely recognised the expanding numbers climbing on home crags and their considerable advances in technical free climbing – such as were being achieved by the weekend climbers quitting the grimy northern cities for the fresh air and the gritstone outcrops of the Pennines.

As a result, concludes Longland, the Alpine Club lost the leadership of the Alpine world. The *Alpine Journal* still spoke with enormous authority, but the trouble was not only that it spoke with dislike of much that was happening, but that many people simply stopped listening.

There were a few dissident voices amongst the members, Longland himself, and he cites Douglas Busk, the most admirable of Etonian revolutionaries, who was fed up with the old fogies that ran the Club and who coined a phrase, the 'Young Shavers', for a ginger group he organised to try to reform it from the inside. 'Thirty years later,' wrote Lord Chorley, 'Douglas had become a pillar of the establishment, he was by then "Sir Douglas", and had been ambassador in all sorts of capital cities. But I am glad to say he still had a radical streak.'

Winding up a symposium on accidents in 1931, Busk declared: 'The Alpine Club is the oldest of all Alpine Clubs. It was founded by young men and it should be its proudest boast that it is the youngest in spirit.'

left: The Aiguille Verte, the Drus and the Mer de Glace from Chamonix, an oil painting by G. Barnard, 1877. Presented to the Alpine Club by the artist.

below: Frank Smythe, on the summit of Mount Hardesty in the Canadian Rockies.

below right: Graham Brown and Alexander Graven on the Midi rocks.

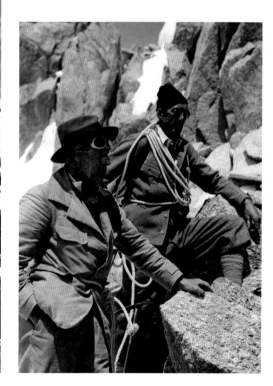

Jack Longland's fourth point raised the considerable preoccupation with the attempts and repeated failures to climb Everest. The British, through their rule of India, had privileged access to the mountain, but the teams of amateurs they sent out were not comparable with the best professional and amateur climbers that the other European countries could have assembled if they had been given the opportunity.

THE BRENVA TRIPTYCH

The above rather depressing introduction to this chapter should not obscure the fact that there were still some splendid achievements by British mountaineers during this period in the Alps and elsewhere. For example, a clutch of first ascents on Mont Blanc: the remarkable Innominata route made by Courtauld and Oliver on 20 August 1919 with their guides Adolphe and Henri Rey and Adolf Aufdenblatten, and the great triptych on the Brenva face – the Red Sentinel in 1927, and Route Major in 1928, by Graham Brown and Frank Smythe, followed in 1933 by the Via Della Pera by Graham Brown with Alexander Graven and Alfred Aufdenblatten. These and other successes will now be discussed in more detail, together with contemporary comments from the *Alpine Journal* and the achievements of continental climbers in opening up the great Alpine north faces on the Matterhorn, the Grandes Jorasses and the Eiger.

OPPOSITE PAGE:

top right: Graham Brown studying the Promontoire Hut Book before traversing the Meije.

bottom right: Josef Knubel, 1881–1961, at Montenvers in July 1931.

THIS PAGE:

below: Mont Blanc – the triptych on the Brenva Face: X Col Moore, XA Red Sentinel, XB Route Major, XC Via Della Pera.

It is not my intention to make more than passing reference to the successive attempts on Everest in the 1920s and 1930s as I have already chronicled these in my previous book, *Everest: 50 years on Top of the World*, published in 2003 to mark the fiftieth anniversary of the first ascent in 1953.

EDITING THE ALPINE JOURNAL

As the role of the *Alpine Journal* between the Wars has come in for considerable criticism, it is perhaps fair to try to understand why the editors during this period thought as they did. There were, in fact, only three: George Yeld, 1896–1926, Edward Strutt, 1927–37, and Henry Tyndale, 1938–48. However, J P Farrar, who was president from 1917 to 1919, also served as assistant editor, 1909–19, and then joint editor to 1926. Between them, Farrar and Strutt were the most influential.

CAPTAIN FARRAR

Captain John Percy Farrar DSO (1857–1919) was educated in Lausanne, fought in the Boer War, and was successful in business in South Africa. This varied background enable him more than anybody to bring mountaineers together again after the World War I. Geoffrey Young paid this tribute:

> I know nothing comparable with the affection and respect in which Farrar was held by the climbers, young and old, of nearly every land. During the troubled interlude following the last war, his tireless work in promoting international understanding through a common mountaineering interest, seemed to me – when engaged upon parallel lines – the most successful undertaking of the kind in Europe. Among ourselves, protesting fierce prejudices, he encouraged or shared in every new form of adventure with vigorous indulgence. His catholic sympathies embraced every age and variety of climber, and his finger was upon the mountaineering pulse of every country.

He had a long and distinguished Alpine climbing career – his list of expeditions taking up seven pages in Mumm's Alpine Club Register, including the second ascent of the Peuterey ridge of Mont Blanc with Daniel and B Maquignaz in 1893. Climbing both with and without guides, at the age of 67, he succeeded on the Piz Badile and the Grépon.

He never wrote a book, but his contributions to the *Alpine Journal* were, in Young's words: 'always in character, virile, brusque, eloquent, strict in censure but all of a sudden aflame with admiration and generous praise'. Few writers have ever summed up as well as Farrar the relationship which binds a great amateur to a great guide, Daniel Maquignaz:

> To some I may seem to have portrayed in too glowing colours a man who in life was a simple Piedmontese peasant. Still, there are many among my contemporaries who will understand the feeling of more than ordinary friendship that binds one to a man like this whom one has learned to know and to judge in that school of stern, though voluntary, discipline and not infrequent danger that is the essence of serious mountaineering. I lose in him one from whom I learned much – from whom I never ceased to learn – my leader on many a glorious day of triumph – one whose memory will in my mind for ever be entwined with some of the most unsullied and serene joys that enter into the life of man.
>
> May you rest in peace, mon Daniel, *sans peur et sans reproche*, in the shadow of your marvellous mountain that none knew – in all its moods and by all its ways – so well as you. You have played the man in your generation. You are not forgotten, in memory you live.

COLONEL STRUTT

Colonel Edward Lisle Strutt CBE, DSO (1874–1948) was a distinguished soldier, decorated for exceptional gallantry in Flanders. He was outspoken in condemning individuals and methods of which he disapproved. But he was not a vindictive person, and he was prepared to revise his views if he felt he had been mistaken. To quote Arnold Lunn: 'Strutt was editor of the *Alpine Journal* for ten critical years, 1927–37, and probably did more than any other man to convince the advance guard of Continental mountaineers that the Alpine Club was hopelessly out of touch with modern developments.' He fought a stubborn rearguard action against the use of crampons, oxygen on Everest, and artificial climbing. A splendid example of his style was his commentary on contrasting ascents of the 5,000 feet north face of the Eiger. The north-east face was first climbed in 1932 by the outstanding Swiss climbers Hans Lauper and Alfred Zürcher, who both became members of the Alpine Club, with the unusual combination of Josef Knubel and Alexander Graven as guides. The ascent proved to be free from objective dangers and was climbed without using a single piton; a route in the classic tradition. The north-west face, on the other hand, is the notorious Eigerwand, subject to stonefall, avalanches and the perils of a retreat if the weather deteriorates. Numerous dramatic attempts were made and several lives lost in the 1930s before it was finally climbed on 24 July 1938.

Of the Lauper route, Strutt wrote: 'We must congratulate our members on a superb expedition, by far the most important problem of the 1932 season. We might add that it is a source of gratification to us that the north face of the Eiger, the last important problem of the Bernese Oberland, should have been solved by this unsurpassed all-Swiss party.' And in his president's valedictory address in 1937: 'The Eigerwand still unscaled, continues to be an obsession for the mentally deranged of almost every nation. He who first succeeds may rest assured that he has accomplished the most imbecile variante since mountaineering first began.'

Comparing Farrar and Strutt, Longland had this to say: 'Farrar, who remained young and adventurous in heart to the end, was more generous about the achievements and more tolerant about the methods and ambitions of the best foreign climbers than any British mountaineer of comparable stature … Strutt had little sympathy for the revolution in continental mountaineering which was taking place before his angry eyes, and little understanding of the causes and purposes of the changes in technique and ethics alike.

During this period the *Journal* too often appeared in the role of a shocked and censorious maiden aunt, appalled by the immoral goings-on of the younger generation.'

Not surprisingly, long before the end of this period young climbers, British as well as continentals, were turning to other journals to find sympathetic understanding of their philosophies and techniques. Strutt believed that crampons were an invention of the devil, and pitons were much worse. An editorial note on the first ascent of the Capucin de la Brenva by two young Italians, in the 1928 *Journal*, read: 'This sort of exploit is quite beyond the pale and is a degradation of mountaineering. Any steeplejack could have done the work better and in a tenth of the time'.

As Lunn observed: 'The general British prejudice against artificial climbing was still strong between the wars, and is at least a partial explanation of the fact that our record in the Alps was less distinguished than that of mountaineers with no such prejudice.' This is illustrated by the story of the strong German party that came to climb in North Wales in July 1936 and were unimpressed with our routes, so they were shown a fresh bit of rock on the south buttress of Tryfan on which they put up the 'Munich Climb' with the aid of three pitons. Troops were mobilised, the pitons removed by Menlove Edwards and the climb done without. The pitons were then sent back with a courteous note saying that we did not want them in our cliffs. This was indeed the overwhelming view of the climbing community at the time and it has thankfully kept British crags generally free from pitons. But it did not help our best climbers to gain practical experience of artificial climbing which was necessary for the hardest Alpine climbs.

Fortunately, the world has moved on and opinions with it. By May 1955, the then editor of the *Alpine Journal*, Francis Keenlyside, was able to include, without carp or comment, an article on the techniques of artificial climbing by Ted Wrangham.

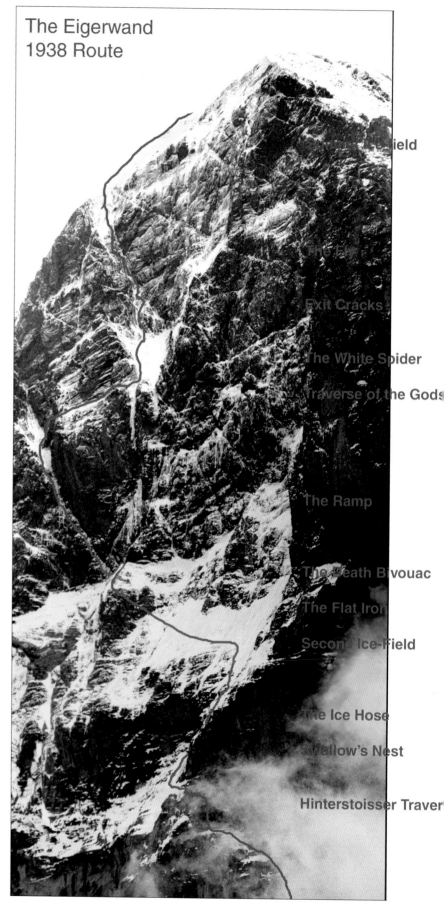

The Eigerwand
1938 Route

...field

The Fly

Exit Cracks

The White Spider

Traverse of the Gods

The Ramp

The Death Bivouac

The Flat Iron

Second Ice-Field

The Ice Hose

Swallow's Nest

Hinterstoisser Traverse

NATIONALISM CREEPS INTO CLIMBING

Where Strutt had a point was in decrying the nationalistic tones behind the outstanding climbs of the period which were achieved by Germans and Italians and then exploited on behalf of the Nazi and Fascist dictatorships. It is difficult for us to appreciate life under such regimes. Ernest Marples MP, a member of the Climbers' Club, had climbed with Bavarians for many years and knew them well and rejected as absurd the theory that the motive which inspired their most desperate climbs was the desire 'to bring prestige to the Nazi party'. 'In my opinion,' he wrote, 'they climbed desperately as a form of escapism from Nazism. Most of them joined the party because they could not obtain employment otherwise.'

What Strutt had difficulty in appreciating were the changes taking place both in Britain and on the Continent: the spread of serious climbing among sections of the population which had not previously discovered the sport, their general lack of money, and their relatively short periods of leisure. If the weather remained bad, the temptation still to try to reach their long-planned objective was very strong.

THE THREE NORTH FACES: MATTERHORN, JORASSES AND EIGER

Toni Schmid and his brother Franz would not have bicycled from Munich to the north face of the Matterhorn and camped among the Hörnli rocks if they had had money for the train fare, hotels and hut fees. They had trained hard and knew they were tackling one of 'the last great unsolved Alpine problems'. The key to the face was the central couloir, a natural channel for falling stones. But the heavy snowfalls of that particular July would help to keep the stones in place, and would diminish its dangers. They climbed the couloir; no stone fell and they reached the summit in a violent storm at 2 pm on 1 August 1931, the Swiss national day.

The north face of the Grandes Jorasses, the second of the Big Three was the next to fall. Martin Meier and Rudolf Peters climbed it on 28/29 June 1935 up to the Pointe Croz, which is not the highest point. The higher Pointe Walker was attained by an Italian group, Ricardo Cassin, G Exposito and U Tizzoni, on 4/6 August 1938.

The last of the Big Three, the Eigerwand, was finally climbed on 20/24 July 1938. On the first attempt, in 1935, two Munich climbers were caught in a storm and died of exposure. On the second, in 1936, two Germans and two Austrians were also caught in a storm and managed to descend close to the Eigerwand Station where a rescue party was summoned. Toni Kurz, the only

left: The north face of the Eiger showing the key features of the original route climbed 20/24 July 1938 by Kasparek and Harrer joining forces with Heckmair and Vorg.

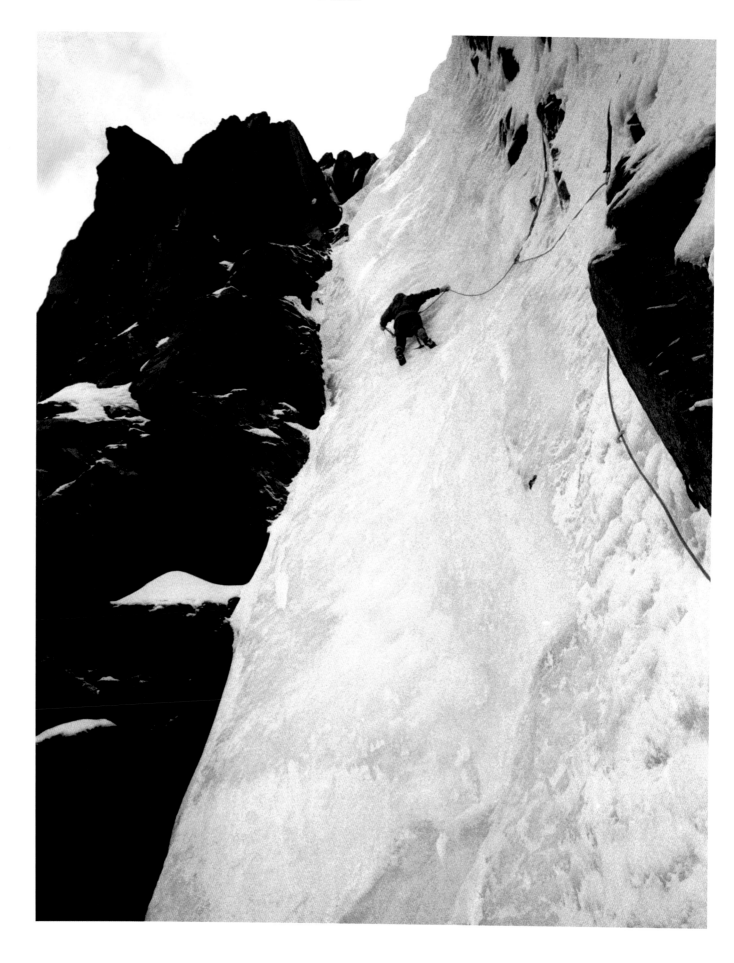

survivor, was found hanging on a rope after his abseil had failed. The other three had perished, frozen, fallen or caught up in the rope and strangled. The guides managed to pass him a 40-metre rope so he could continue his descent. Using up his last reserves of strength he began to lower himself, very slowly, over the overhang until they could almost touch the soles of his boots with their axes. But then all movement ceased. He was dead.

In 1936, two Italians were killed, bringing the death roll up to eight. On 20 July 1938, two Austrians, Kasparek and Harrer, started on the face. Next day two Germans, Heckmair and Vörg, caught them up, using their steps, and they joined forces. They battled their way towards the summit in a blizzard, disregarding the shouts of a potential rescue party, and reached it, almost played out, after three more days on the face.

In 1939, Heinrich Harrer was caught up in India at the outbreak of war, interned, but escaped to Tibet and was befriended by the Dalai Lama. His *Seven Years in Tibet* was a bestseller. In 1998, the sixtieth anniversary of the Eigerwand ascent, he was an honoured guest at the Alpine Club's annual dinner. He died on 7 January 2006, aged 93. Andreas Heckmair died in 2005 and our Club president, Stephen Venables, sent his widow a sincere letter of condolence (p.248). How times change. What would Colonel Strutt have had to say?

In the 1930s, no British climbers had reached the required standard of expertise and all-round experience to be able to tackle any of the Big Three north faces with impunity. We had to wait until the 1950s and 1960s. If I had not been diverted to the Himalaya, perhaps I would have dared to try the Grandes Jorasses by the Walker Spur. It still remains a great and formidable climb, virtually free from objective dangers, as it follows a steep and clean granite spur. It succumbed to two British parties on successive days on 22/23 July 1959, including my friend John Streetly with whom I had climbed the north ridge of the Dent Blanche in 1952 – another 'last great problem' in its day.

The first British ascent of the Eigerwand was made by Christian (Chris) Bonington and Ian Clough in 1962. The ice has receded since the 1930s, pitches that were ice for the pioneers now being polished rock. But it is basically a dangerous climb by reason of stonefall, avalanche and sheer length and complexity. Bonington and Clough were lucky to encounter dry conditions and good weather, so they climbed it fast and very competently with just the one bivouac on the face.

But these outstanding first British ascents by Alpine Club members belong properly to the next chapter where they deserve and will get fuller treatment.

left: An Eiger-like ice-climbing image, but actually taken on an ascent of the Diamond Couloir of Mount Kenya.

below: Heinrich Harrer kindly gave me this autographed postcard celebrating the 60th anniversary of the Eiger ascent, when he came to London in 1998.

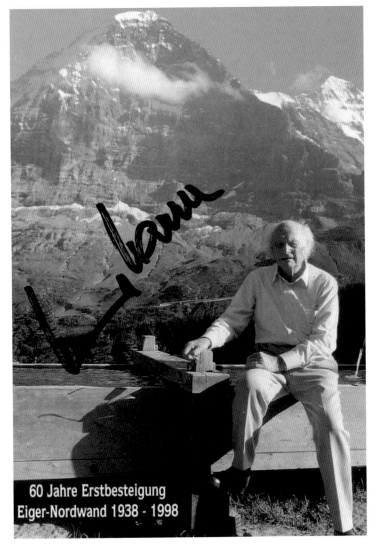

60 Jahre Erstbesteigung
Eiger-Nordwand 1938 - 1998

OTHER BRITISH ASCENTS

Some further fine British ascents in the Alps deserve mention. On 2 August 1923, George Finch (of Australian origin), Forster and Peto made a guideless first ascent of the north face of the Dent d'Hérens, selecting a clever zig-zag route up the face. Finch's book *The Making of a Mountaineer* also includes earlier climbs in Corsica as a way of preparing for the Himalaya and his experience on Everest in 1922.

R W Lloyd, climbing with Joseph and Adolf Pollinger, made a first direct ascent of the north face of the Aiguille de Bionnassay on 18 July 1926. Lloyd was a very successful businessman, became chairman of Christie's and an avid collector of Swiss prints, Turner watercolours, Japanese swords and beetles. He was known as a tight-fisted treasurer of the Joint Himalayan Committee, which organised the 1953 Everest Expedition. However, when I sent him a £90 cheque, being proceeds from lectures I had given (a lot of money for me in those days), he expressed surprise and invited me to visit him at his home, which was a rare invitation. Sadly, he died before I took it up, but later the cheque was found among his effects uncashed, perhaps deliberately? As it was time-expired, to my chagrin, the new treasurer asked me to write out another!

Another climb, which Lunn regarded as perhaps the most difficult British expedition of this period, was the first ascent of the north ridge of the Dent Blanche on 20 July 1928 by Ivor Richards and Dorothy Pilley (on their honeymoon!) with Joseph Georges (*le Skieur*) and his brother Antoine. On one particularly restricted stance where the couple were clutching each other tightly, Antoine appeared from below and exclaimed, '*Ah! Les amoureux!*' This, as with the south face of the Täschhorn, was another of the hard routes where the second ascent was made in wartime by the top Swiss climbers André Roch, Georges de Rham, Alfred Tissières and Gabriel Chevalley; Roch and Tissières being members of the Club.

The Richards/Pilley ascent of the north ridge of the Dent Blanche came as a bitter blow to Dr Maud Cairney and her guide Théophile Theytaz who had a long cherished ambition to do this climb. Nineteen twenty-eight was a very dry year and Theytaz felt his moment had come. Just three weeks later, on 11 August, they successfully completed a variation, deviating left onto the very exposed north face, in normal years dangerously subject to stonefall. It was the culmination of six alpine seasons for Maud Cairney, who then joined the Colonial Service in Malaysia.

below: The north ridge of the Dent Blanche seen from the summit of the Grand Cornier. The Pilley/Richards/Georges route of 20 July 1928 (A) sticks to the ridge, whereas the Cairney/Theytaz route of 11 August (B) deviates left onto the exposed north face.

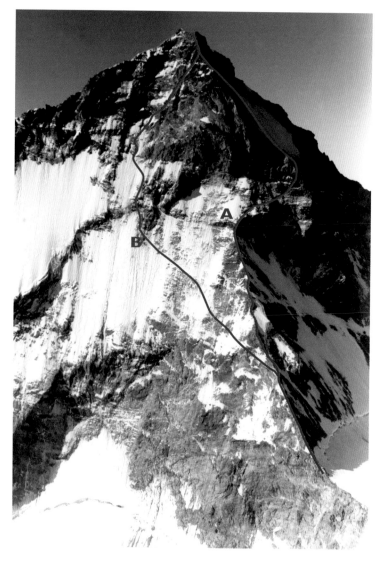

Finally, the Manchester engineer Eustace Thomas took on the continental goal of climbing all then recognised 4,000-metre peaks, which he achieved in just six years in the 1920s with Josef Knubel and in relatively advanced middle age. Depending on how a peak is actually defined, the total tally is in the range of 60 to 75, but the goal then may have been fewer than 60.

BEYOND THE OVER-EXPLOITED ALPS

below: Dorothy Pilley Richards 1893–1986, a passionate climber from the age of 17, was a founder of the Pinnacle Club for lady members only.

In contrast, Frank Smythe, spurning the over-exploited Alps, turned to organising Himalayan expeditions and climbed Kamet (25,447 ft/7,756 m) in 1931, the first 25,000-feet peak to be climbed. He had already participated in Professor Dyhrenfurth's International Expedition to Kangchenjunga in 1930 when, after withdrawing from the main objective, they climbed Jongsong Peak (24,344 ft/7,420 m), the highest summit previously reached. Smythe went on to climb high on Everest.

In Africa, Wyn Harris and Eric Shipton climbed the two peaks of Mount Kenya, Batian (17,040 ft/5,194 m) and the virgin Nelion, just 30 feet lower, named after two Masai chiefs, in January 1929. It was only the second ascent of Batian, following the pioneer climb by Halford Mackinder with two guides, César Ollier and Joseph Brocherel, in 1899. Both Wyn Harris and Shipton went on to Everest.

The seven British Everest expeditions of the 1920s and 1930s were tending to dominate British mountaineering. Although they were not successful in climbing the mountain, they did establish new height records over 28,000 feet (8,535 metres). They were matched by Paul Bauer's Bavarian expeditions to Kangchenjunga in 1929 and 1931 and the succession of German expeditions to Nanga Parbat. Jack Longland recalls: 'The evil shadows of growing national rivalries and of the false doctrine that mountaineering achievement is a proper means of enhancing a national's prestige fall heavily athwart the mountaineering scene of this period, and it is to the honour of Colonel Strutt that in the *Journal* he never ceased to recognise and denounce the evil wherever he saw it.' Even during the Everest fiftieth anniversary events in 2003, German TV companies were resuscitating the idea of British and German rivalry on Everest and Nanga Parbat as the basic theme of their programmes.

INTO THE NANDA DEVI SANCTUARY

Fortunately, it was during this period that Shipton and Tilman rediscovered, as had been shown by Longstaff and Kellas, that cheap and small expeditions could accomplish a great deal, and they helped pay for them with some very good books. The penetration of the Nanda Devi Sanctuary by way of the Rishi Ganga gorge in 1934 by Shipton and Tilman is one of the great stories of exploration. After the Sanctuary had officially been closed for 18 years to be allowed to 'recover' from the effects of too many expeditions, I was very privileged to be one of a party to be allowed to enter it in October 2000. At a millennium meet in Delhi, several of us, including Ian McNaught-Davis, president of the International Mountaineering Federation, made a special plea to be allowed to enter, to report on the situation and make recommendations for the future. John, the second son of Eric Shipton, who had become interested in retracing his father's journeys, was our trek leader and had the tremendous thrill of leading us into the Inner Sanctuary by the same tortuous route on his fiftieth birthday. Sadly, despite our recommendations for a limited well-supervised opening of the Sanctuary to trekkers and climbers, there has not yet been a positive response from the authorities. One of our party, Hugh Thomson, has written a light-hearted account of our venture.

below: The team which first penetrated the Nanda Devi Sanctuary in 1934, from left to right, Angtharkey, Shipton, Passang, Tilman and Kusang.

right: A climber around 23,000 ft on the first ascent of Nanda Devi in 1936 – the eastern Basin rim on right.

below: The Rishi Ganga gorge proved to be the key to forcing an entry into the Nanda Devi Sanctuary: it had defeated numerous explorers from 1830 onwards.

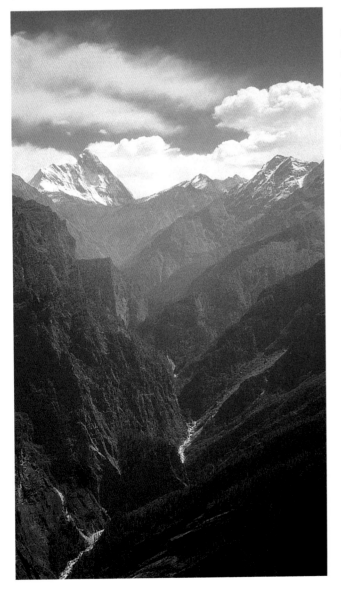

One of my most treasured books is Tilman's own signed copy of Shipton's *Nanda Devi* describing their epic, which was actually dedicated to Tilman. I chanced upon it in Sotheran's Antiquarian Booksellers in 1992. Their exploration in 1934 paved the way for the actual ascent of Nanda Devi in 1936 by a joint American–British party organised by Charles Houston and Graham Brown after meeting on Mount Foraker in Alaska. The party consisted of Houston, Adams Carter, Loomis and Emmons from the USA and Tilman, Graham Brown, Noel Odell and Peter Lloyd from England. On this occasion, Tilman wrote the book and I quote a paragraph describing in his inimitable style the first bivouac at 23,500 feet from which he and Odell set out for the summit, reached on 29 August.

Scenically the position of the bivouac was very fine but residentially it was damnable. It was backed on two sides by rock, but on the others the snow slope fell away steeply, and the platform which had been scraped out in the snow was so narrow that the outer edge of the tent overhung for almost a foot, thus reducing considerably both the living space and any feeling one yet had of security. Necessity makes a man bold, and I concluded that necessity had pressed very hard that night when they lit on this spot for their bivouac. Odell, who had had no sleep the previous night, could have slept on a church spire, and, as I had Houston's sleeping bag and the extra clothing I had fortunately brought up, we both had a fair night. Odell, who was the oldest inhabitant and in the position of host, generously conceded to me the outer berth, overhanging space.

I remember occupying a similar outer berth at our top camp on Kangchenjunga in 1955 after unsuccessfully drawing lots with Joe Brown! When Tilman and Odell reached the summit – the highest point in the British Empire and the highest peak then climbed – Tilman subsequently wrote in his restrained prose: 'I believe we so far forgot ourselves as to shake hands on it.'

TILMAN AND SHIPTON

Tilman was a regular officer in the World War I and was awarded an MC and Bar. He rejoined in the World War II at the age of 41, spending time in the Middle East and being parachuted behind enemy lines to fight with the Albanian and Italian partisans. His great partnership with Eric Shipton began in Kenya in 1930 when they made an adventurous first traverse of the twin peaks of Mount Kenya. I quote from Shipton's account in his autobiography, *That Untravelled World*, in which he concludes that it was probably the hardest climb he had ever done.

THIS PAGE:

above: Shipton in the Beagle Channel, enjoying a new lease of life exploring the mountains and ice caps of Patagonia and Tierra del Fuego 1958–66, including first ascents of Mount Bové and Mount Francis in the Cordillera Darwin.

above right: Camels are the best transport in the Shaksgam, here about to ford the river issuing from the K2 glacier.

OPPOSITE PAGE:

top left: Sunset on Nanda Devi 25,645 ft/7817 m from Patalkhan.

bottom left: Tilman in his 70s enjoyed long-distance cruising in his converted Bristol Channel Pilot cutter *Mischief*.

The rocks on the southern side of Batian were plastered with snow, which delayed us; but conditions improved between the Gate of the Mist and the top of Nelion, which we crossed without a pause and hurried down the gully beyond. There Bill slipped and came on the rope, dropping his ice-axe, which vanished out of sight in a single bound. This near-accident checked our haste. Dusk was falling when we reached the top of the sixty-foot wall above the head of the south ridge, and it was almost dark by the time we had completed the abseil down it.

The clouds had not cleared at dusk in their usual manner, and it looked as though we would have to remain where we were until morning. Later, however, breaks appeared in the mist and the moon came out, providing sufficient light for us to climb slowly down. I felt tired but pleasantly relaxed; the moonlight, the phantom shapes of ridge and pinnacle, interlaced with wisps of silvered mist, the radiant expanse of the Lewis Glacier plunging into the soundless depths below induced a sense of exquisite fantasy. I experienced that strange illusion, not uncommon in such circumstances, that there was an additional member of the party – three of us instead of two.

When Tilman grew too old for strenuous mountaineering, he took up long-distance cruising in a converted Bristol Channel Pilot cutter, built in Cardiff in 1906 and acquired by him in 1954. He named it *Mischief*. His voyages were usually to the Arctic or Antarctic with the objective of visiting some little known mountains or icecaps which he could at least see and explore even when he could not climb them. He got a reputation for austerity and under-provisioning that was legendary but in the main this followed from the quest for mobility and economy. A key food item on land was a bag of chillies, invaluable for making dull food palatable. On his voyages he insisted that every galley should be equipped with Tabasco sauce.

He wrote 15 books: seven on climbing and eight on sailing. He hoped to spend his eightieth birthday in the Antarctic, and sailed in one of *Mischief*'s successors, *En Avant*, from Rio bound for the Falklands on 1 November 1977. The rest is silence. I attended his memorial service several months later in St James's, Piccadilly. I half hoped he would arrive in the middle of it, immaculate in suit with waistcoat, fob watch, carrying bowler hat and umbrella, wondering what all the fuss was about. Emlyn Jones, president of the Alpine Club, spoke in his memory, as did his counterpart representing the sailing fraternity. Most of us mountaineers had little knowledge of the reverence he was accorded by the long-distance sailors for his achievements, and many of them likewise knew precious little about his mountaineering.

Let his biographer, J R C Anderson, have the last word:

His record as traveller and explorer on land and sea is so extraordinary that it can scarcely be overstated. By this time there was little of the earth's surface left to be discovered; had there been he would surely have discovered it. Compared with the acclaim of getting to the Poles, his crossings of Bylot Island and of the Patagonian ice-cap seem small beer, and he himself did nothing to attract publicity save for his ascent of Nanda Devi, which made news in 1936 for the fortuitous reason that it was the highest mountain then to have been climbed. But Nanda Devi was only one incident in his career. The problem in trying to assess his performance is that it was so diverse. The world likes its Einsteins to be mathematicians, its Shackletons to be identified with the Antarctic, its Livingstones with Africa. Tilman travelled and explored wherever he could, from the Congo forest and the fever-ridden marches of Assam to the high slopes of the Himalaya, from China to Chitral, from Baffin Bay to Patagonia. There is a case for regarding him as the greatest individual explorer of the twentieth century.

HOW COULD
BRITISH CLIMBERS COMPETE?

So we approach the end of this period between the wars. It was a time when, in the Alps, the British could not keep up with the leaders of the pack. To keep ahead, in 1919 the French had formed a section of the French Alpine Club restricted to expert climbers called the *Groupe de Haute Montagne* (known as the GHM). They put

above top: The bold British 1937 route up the higher south peak of Ushba, by way of the S E Ridge, the Red Wall and the E Face.

above bottom: The 1937 Caucasus team: Robin Hodgkin, Bob Beaumont, John Jenkins and Michael Taylor. The expedition cost them £72 each.

up all sorts of new routes over the Chamonix Aiguilles. Typically, in August 1924, a strong guideless party, Jacques Lagarde, Jacques de Lépiney and Henri de Ségogne, made an outstanding first ascent of the north face of the Aiguille du Plan, a route which Mummery's party had attempted and which he recorded in the *Alpine Journal* as 'Two days on an Ice Slope'. A number of the GHM members were so committed that they gave up the possibility of professional careers to qualify as mountain guides so they could continue to climb both as guides and for their own fulfilment; men such as Armand Charlet and Gaston Rébuffat were examples. With supreme fitness came greater speed and competence, so that men such as Amstutz and von Schumacher in 1928 could leave the Torino hut at 1 am and be on the top of Mont Blanc by the old Brenva route at 8.30 am. Living close to the Alps, it became a weekend sport. Jacques Lagarde made 16 attempts at the north-east face of Les Droites before he got the right weather and conditions to make the first ascent. How could British climbers compete? Their ambitions mostly extended no further than being able to repeat Geoffrey Young's great routes, some of which he himself repeated one-legged after losing his left limb while serving in Italy with the wartime Friends Ambulance Unit below Monte Sabotino. He vividly remembers: 'On news of the attack for that night, I glissaded down the steep stone flights of stairs from my prophet's chamber under the roof, sliding alternate boot-soles over the edge of each step without check on the tread, after a fashion I had perfected from ice-glissading on glaciers. The headlong glidder kept, I felt, my ice feet in practice; and I have often since that night recalled that last exhilarating occasion of feeling like a free-falling cataract.'

Outside the Alps, the British were doing better, a portent for the future: Reggie Cooke's first ascent of Kabru (24,000 ft/7,315 m) in 1935, John Hunt and James Waller reaching 24,500 feet on Peak 36, now called Saltoro Kangri, also in 1935; Wilfrid Noyce in Sikkim and Kashmir; Robin Hodgkin with John Jenkins, Michael Taylor and Bob Beaumont in the Caucasus in 1937, the first British visit for 23 years. Major achievements here were the first direct ascent of the south peak of Ushba from the south-east and a bold first ascent of the icy north face of Tetnuld (15,918 ft/4,852 m) by a line specifically recommended by the Austrian Caucasian expert Rudolf Schwarzgrüber, and described by Jenkins as 'a slender scimitar-shaped ridge curved upwards to lose itself in a steep ice wall'. Shipton and Tilman, in the same year, were filling in the 'Blank on the Map' in Shaksgam, and Peter Lloyd was writing most significantly about 'Oxygen on Mount Everest, 1938'. As Jack Longland concluded, the seeds of the great renaissance of British climbing after 1945 were already sown.

above top: Hodgkin leading a tricky 'belly traverse' on the E Face of Ushba.

above bottom: The first ascent route up the icy N Face of Tetnuld suggested by Rudolf Schwarzgrüber and achieved by Jenkins and Taylor.

6 POST-WAR – THE ALPS IN THE 1950S AND 1960S

The outstanding feature of immediate post-war climbing in the Alps was the increasing numbers of continental climbers taking part, accompanied by a general rise in their competence. At the top level, the great climbs of the 1930s still set the standard: the north faces of the Matterhorn, Grandes Jorasses and the Eigerwand. Other influential routes were the 1935 ascent of the north face of the Petit Dru by Pierre Allain and R Leininger which set a new standard of rock technique – largely climbed free – and the more sustained use of pitons in the vertical and even overhanging Dolomite climbs such as the north face of the Cima Grande in 1933, which enabled Cassin, Esposito and Tizzoni to have the necessary experience and confidence to succeed on the Walker Spur of the Grandes Jorasses.

Even during the war, some climbing continued; that great Italian climber Giusto Gervasutti, with Paolo Bollini, succeeding on the right-hand Pillar of Frêney in 1940, and the east face of the Grandes Jorasses in 1942 with Gagliardone. But the main immediate post-war activity was in the Chamonix Aiguilles, by climbers from Geneva, members of the GHM and the new young guides of Chamonix, Lionel Terray, Louis Lachenal and Gaston Rébuffat. The publication of new guide books in 1946 and 1947 – the *Guides Vallot* – edited by Lucien Devies, president of the GHM, covering the Mont Blanc massif and the Chamonix Aiguilles were an immense help in giving guideless climbers the confidence to go it alone. So where were the British during these first few years?

Some fine climbers died who might have led a renaissance: Colin Kirkus and Wedderburn were lost in active service; Barford, Kretschmer and Jenkins in a fatal accident in 1947 while descending the Old Brenva. In an era of shortages and rationing and not very much money, the younger climbers grew up in a different atmosphere from the 1930s. They could not afford guides and did not expect to use them anyway, so they tended to stick to the areas covered by the new guide-books in the language they preferred, usually French, rather than German or Italian. An outstanding exception was Emlyn Jones' ascent of the north ridge of the Dent Blanche in 1947 with the guide Remy Theytaz – possibly only the third ascent.

left: The Monarch of the Alps. Mont Blanc from the east, looking across the Brenva face to the Peuterey ridge on the left. The sun highlights the ice-ridge on the old Brenva route to the lower-left middle ground of the picture.

below: The Zinal guide Pierre Bonnard poses on the Rasoir, an awkward gendarme on an ascent of the Zinal Rothorn in 1951.

below right: Ian McNaught-Davis leading the *fissure de la grande-mère* on the Ryan-Lochmatter route on the Aiguille du Plan.

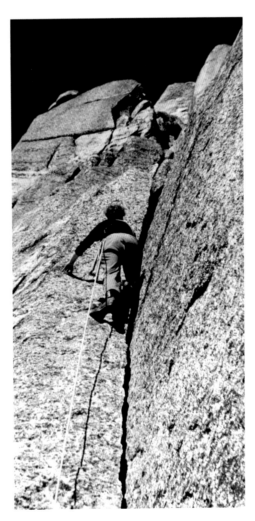

A Controversial Editor

Presiding over the *Alpine Journal* during this post-war period was Professor Graham Brown, known as the 'uncrowned King of Mont Blanc' for his encyclopaedic knowledge of the mountain, and his earlier triptych of great routes on the Italian side described in his meticulously written book *Brenva*, which was not published until 1944. His performance as editor was sadly not as memorable as his climbs. The current editor, Stephen Goodwin, writing as a guest contributor in the sixtieth volume of the *Himalayan Journal*, published in 2004, had this to say:

> Thomas Graham Brown, who took over from Tyndale in 1949, was the last of the AJ's 'awkward squad' of controversialist editors. He had quarrelled beyond all reason with Frank Smythe over their impressive Red Sentinel and Route Major climbs on Mont Blanc and soon brought his capacity for rancour into the business of the AJ. Perhaps as infuriating for those who had to work with him on the Journal was his laxity with correspondence and proofs. The Club was forced to act and Graham Brown was dismissed – the only sacking in AJ history.
>
> The irony was that Graham Brown was in post for a golden period in mountaineering, with the opening of Nepal and the attempts on Everest. His editorial swansong was devoted to the 1953 ascent, with contributions by Hunt, Hillary and other members of the successful team. Graham Brown wrote an introduction in which he waxed eloquent about 'the romance of man's strife against nature', though the word was his journals appeared thanks largely to those who assisted him.

Alpine Club Meets and a First Alpine Season

Responding to this post-war situation, for the first time in 1948 and 1949, the Alpine Club held meets to introduce young climbers to the Alps under the guidance of those with pre-war experience. Although the second was marred by an accident, they served their purpose, in that one of the newcomers was Tom Bourdillon, who, perhaps more than anybody, led the later British renaissance. In a splendid article in the *Alpine Journal* 1990/91, 'The Alps in the 1950s' Bourdillon's frequent climbing partner, Hamish Nicol, describes with the freshness of youth his first Alpine season in 1949.

above: Hamish Nicol relaxes after a strenuous pitch on the west buttress of Coinneach Mhor overlooking Coire Mhic Fhearchair, Torridon.

OPPOSITE PAGE:

above left: Alan Blackshaw leading an artificial pitch on the east ridge of the Dent du Crocodile.

left: George Band making a long stretch on the south ridge of the Aiguille Noire de Peuterey.

When I first saw the Alps in July 1949, I nearly fell off the train with excitement. We were on the little rack railway which goes from St Gervais to Chamonix on the last stage of a two-day journey from London. Suddenly the train turned a corner at Les Houches and the whole North face of Mont Blanc came into view, so close that you could almost touch it. The seracs of the Bossons glacier seemed to tumble and sparkle in the sun. I had never seen anything like it before. I jumped from coach to coach on the rattling train, shouted for joy, tried to climb on the roof to get a better look, and couldn't understand why all the other passengers were not doing the same. I was just 20 years old.

Malcolm Slesser and I had travelled slowly by train to Newhaven, by boat to Dieppe, and then overnight across France, sitting bolt upright all the way, on the hard seats of the SNCF. Dan Steward met us in Chamonix where we spent a frenzied hour buying food and a little equipment, not forgetting that candle lanterns were required on alpine glaciers at night. It does seem incredible that little aluminium candle lanterns were still being sold to gullible alpinists in 1949, long after the invention of the electric torch. The way into the mountains, then as now, was by way of the Montenvers rack railway. This was a coal-fired steam train pushing little carriages, very like the Snowdon mountain railway.

At 4.30 am the next day the three of us set off to climb the Grands Charmoz. We reached the summit at 3 pm in our tricouni-nailed boots and with our hemp ropes, not returning to Montenvers till about 6 pm. I was completely exhausted by my first alpine climb. For the next two weeks we rushed about all over the Chamonix Alps, climbing non-stop but attempting only the easiest routes, such as the Géant by its fixed ropes. There did not seem to be any English people about, but one American spoke to us; he was attached to a guide. Every so often we would descend to Chamonix to buy food and, perhaps, to eat a decent meal. You could eat in Chamonix for 650 francs , which was about 13 shillings [65p]. This was pretty expensive by our standards. As a National Service second lieutenant in the Army, I received 13 shillings a day.

My first season in the alps had been an enormous success for me, though by present-day standards, it was not impressive. We were intensely parochial and had no idea about what, if anything, other British climbers were doing. There were then no monthly climbing glossies full of advertisements. In 1949 there were in fact only two shops in the United Kingdom which specialized in mountaineering equipment: Robert Lawrie in London, and Brighams in Manchester.

Robert Lawrie's was very intimidating. You rang the bell at what appeared to be a smart private house in Seymour Street near Marble Arch. A lady ushered you in to meet Mr Lawrie himself to discuss personally your requirements. Ellis Brigham was more down to earth. A good pair of boots cost a week's wage, he would say, and that's been the case for many years. I used his 'Brigham plates' on my boots instead of tricounis. The teeth were slightly softer, fixed right to the edge of the welt so they could gain purchase on the tiniest edge holds.

INSPIRED BY BERNARD PIERRE

Hamish Nicol was a year ahead of me in the Alps, and he recalls that the continental climbers were years ahead of us. A top French amateur, Bernard Pierre, who spoke English well, came to give several lectures in the UK on his climbs in 1949 with Gaston Rébuffat making second ascents of the extremely difficult Ratti-Vitali route on the west face of the Aiguille Noire de Peuterey, and the north-east face of the Badile. I remember his lecture at Cambridge vividly. Tom Bourdillon would also have heard it at Oxford or at the Alpine Club and took it as a challenge. After an OUMC winter meet in Langdale he invited Hamish to climb with him in the Alps in 1950. They practised some artificial climbing beforehand on a tree in Bourdillon's Buckinghamshire garden where he had driven wrought-iron bars into the trunk on which they could suspend their rudimentary home-made ladders or étriers.

Arriving in Chamonix on 12 July, their first climb was the west face of the Aiguille Purtscheller, by the Rébuffat route, 200 metres, *très difficile*. This was almost certainly the first TD climb done by a British guideless party in the western Alps. There were two artificial pitches but, thanks to their training, they were up in four and a half hours. Their next route was the magnificent 1906 Ryan-Lochmatter route on the Plan. Two fine Oxford climbers, John Hoyland and Paul Wand, had planned to do this in 1934, but were both killed on their way to the Innominata ridge of Mont Blanc – an accident which set back British alpinism for several years.

right: A superb image of the Aiguille du Petit Dru above Chamonix. On the left, the north face. The first ascent of the west face in 1952, facing camera, by crack French climbers, marked a climacteric in Alpine history.

below: Tom Bourdillon in Army uniform in the 1940s.

BOURDILLON AND NICOL ON THE PETIT DRU

Bourdillon and Nicol next planned to try the north face of the Petit Dru, another TD but much longer and more serious than the Purtscheller. On 25 July, they bivouacked at the foot of the huge and frightening cliff. I quote again from Hamish Nicol's article:

It was my first bivouac, and I will never forget the night we spent huddled together on the cold rock. The sky was clear and star-lit, and the town of Chamonix was a blaze of lights at our feet. Our plan was to leave the sleeping bags there and climb over to the Charpoua hut where our friends would be waiting for us. At that time the North face of the Dru had a tremendous reputation. It was first climbed in 1935, and by 1949 there had been something like 30 or 35 ascents. Tom and I left the Bivouac at 5 am the next day, carrying a double nylon rope, a spare rope for hauling up the rucksacks and wearing vibram-soled boots. My ideas had had a good shaking up since 1949. We had some rope slings, some karabiners, a few pitons, a hammer each, one ice axe and one pair of

crampons. Luckily the rock was dry and in perfect condition. We hardly noticed the Fissure Lambert, which is regarded as the first major difficulty. I had certainly led part of it before I realized what it was. When we got to the hard bit, the Fissure Allain, there was no argument: we climbed the Fissure Martinetti which is a lot easier, and a much more sensible way. The last 150 m were steep and covered in verglas, which made them rather serious. The ascent lasted 8½ hours. Our earlier plan to traverse over the Grand Dru came to nothing. There was a thick mist and the weather looked bad. Instead we descended the Petit Dru by a long series of tedious and difficult abseils. Viney and Saxby were waiting for us in the Charpoua hut and gave us a tremendous welcome. I was all for doing another climb, but my companions would have none of it. We must return to Chamonix and have a celebration.

This climb, more than any other, opened the eyes of British rock climbers to what they might achieve in the Alps, based on the skills that they had already acquired on British rock. Bourdillon was keen to improve in the one area of expertise we all lacked – artificial climbing – and his influence helped to overcome the hostility to pitons in the older British tradition. He exuded self-confidence and the courage to challenge accepted limits.

above: Hamish Nicol in action on the Ratti Vitali on the west face of the Aiguille Noire de Peuterey.

CYM AND NANCY SMITH ON THE DIABLE

Another climber with similar talent, Cym Smith, was my predecessor as president of the Cambridge Club, the CUMC. He had been a 'Bevin boy' conscripted by lottery to be a miner instead of doing the customary National Service in the armed forces. He preferred to climb in the Alps with his wife, Nancy, and though she was very good, this probably limited his scope, but even so they made the first British guideless traverse of the Aiguilles du Diable in July 1950, another TD climb. He was most tragically killed on 15 January 1952 in a road accident while motorcycling home from his work in Edinburgh during a snowstorm. Bob Downes, writing about Cym Smith in the jubilee edition of *Cambridge Mountaineering* 1956, reflected:

There were many fine climbers in the Club before him, but somehow his whole approach seems to have been more advanced. Trying and getting up hard routes in bad conditions perhaps was his special contribution, because it influenced his successors so much. Thus a *reputation* for difficulty which a climb might carry was to be discounted until one had met and experienced the actual crack, slab, overhang or whatever else the crux itself was, in whatever conditions. Recklessness, or simply boldness? Who would say; sometimes the margin is finely drawn.

OXBRIDGE RAISES THE STANDARD

Inspired by Bourdillon, Nicol and Smith, in the next two or three years climbers from the Oxford and Cambridge clubs continued to raise the standard, including Westmacott, Rawlinson, Viney and Blackshaw from Oxford, Chorley, Wrangham, Streetly and Sutton from Cambridge. In 1951 Ian McNaught-Davis appeared on the scene from Manchester University ('a tall, loose-limbed North countryman with an infectious grin') with Godfrey Francis, an Oxford geologist who had defected to Cambridge. Nineteen fifty-two was a particularly good season for Cambridge climbers, including two climbs at the upper grade of TD, *très difficile superior*, for the first time: the north ridge of the Peigne (Chorley and Band, with Arthur Dolphin and McNaught-Davis) and the south ridge of the Aiguille Noire de Peuterey (Chorley and Band with Francis and Wrangham). But it was not all Oxbridge; Neil Mather climbed the Peuterey ridge with McNaught-Davis in 1952, and the Ryan route on the Plan in 1953.

But the outstanding ascent that year, even though it was done with a top guide, was unquestionably the Pillars of Frêney on Mont Blanc by Godfrey Francis and Geoff Sutton. This, 'Gervasutti's training climb for the Jorasses' east face' (the right-hand pillar, TD sup), was not in good condition and needed a brilliant lead by Lionel Terray and a great effort on the part of the others. This rope must have been as perfect a guide–client relationship as any in the Golden Age. Altogether it had been a terrific season.

Hamish Nicol, on whose article I have been relying, had a disaster which side-lined him in 1951, breaking his jaw when his partner Dan Stewart tripped on steep ice and they both fell. This, together

with an earlier accident on Ben Nevis, rather queered his pitch for a place in the 1953 Everest team. In his own words, 'I was written off as dangerous, and given a place as a reserve'. In the event, Tom Bourdillon, Michael Westmacott and I were chosen from this active group, with Anthony Rawlinson as another reserve.

THE ALPINE CLIMBING GROUP EMERGES

After the 1952 season, Roger Chorley was invited to speak to the Alpine Club; at the age of 21, the youngest member ever to do so. As a non-member, he kindly invited me along and after the talk the president asked if I would like to comment, as we had done most of our climbs together. I spoke, perhaps not very coherently and as a guest rather out of turn, saying that it was sad that many of our best young alpinists were not members of the Alpine Club, which appeared to be resting too much on its historic reputation, so that they were just not attracted to join, even if they could afford the subscription. There was a long silence. I was eternally grateful when Anthony Rawlinson broke it by standing up and broadly endorsing my statement. It was one of the tiny incidents which illustrated young climbers' dissatisfaction with the Club — reminiscent of the 'Young Shavers' of the 1930s led by Douglas Busk — which resulted in the spontaneous formation in 1952 of the Alpine Climbing Group, a 'ginger group' based on the model of the *Groupe de Haute Montagne*, to link together the new band of young Brits who went for the harder routes, and to encourage more ambitious climbing. Tom Bourdillon was elected the first president. As if to celebrate, early in the 1953 season, Hamish Nicol and Alan Blackshaw climbed the west face of the Pointe Albert, a short 230-metre route but the first *Extrêmement Difficile* (ED) climbed by a British party in the western Alps. It was one of the new post-war ED rock climbs and had first been climbed in 1945 by J and R Leininger.

above left: Climbers reaching the summit of the Matterhorn, with Monte Rosa behind.

left: A snapshot of the west face of the Aiguille du Blaitière where in 1954 Brown and Whillans put up a new route in which the crux became known as the famous 'Fissure Brown'.

THIS PAGE:

above: A break in the clouds around the Drei Zinnen or the Tre Cime di Lavaredo, an atmospheric photo by Basil Goodfellow.

above right: The Biolay Campsite in Chamonix, a favourite location for young British climbers in the 1950s.

'ROCK AND ICE' HIT THE ALPS

One of the early tasks taken on by the ACG, with Ted Wrangham as editor, was to produce guidebooks of selected climbs from the French Vallot guides, but translated into English for the benefit of those with a less than classical education. The Oxbridge domination came to an abrupt end. Members of the Rock and Ice Club from the Manchester area made their first appearance in the Alps. Led by Joe Brown, often partnered by Don Whillans, they had created new standards in rock climbing at home, principally in North Wales and on the gritstone of the Pennines, by their extraordinary ability, honed by constant practice, to jam or lay back their way up fierce cracks. In 1954, these two made the third ascent of the west face of the Dru in two days. Anthony Rawlinson recalls:

> When it was first climbed in 1952, it marked a climacteric in Alpine history. In 1938 the Walker had been the product of Dolomite piton technique in the Western Alps. In later years pitonnage had been yet further developed in the Dolomites, but though inspired by the Dolomites, the technique used by Magnone, Bérardini, Dagory and Lainé to climb, in two stages, the West face of the Petit Dru in 1952 had been practised on the Saussois cliffs near Paris. Their 175 m of continuous pitonnage and multiple bivouacs were something new on a major peak. The number of large rock faces which invite this mode of climbing is limited, so far as major peaks are concerned. It has, however, opened a new series of 'last problems' to the eye of faith. An astonishing later exploit in this genre was Bonatti's solo ascent of the South-west Pillar of the Dru in 1955 … The West face of the Dru is the great single event of post-war Alpine climbing, for it created a new category of expedition.

To add to their success and perhaps even more important, Brown and Whillans made a new route on the west face of the Blaitière. Other British parties had congratulated each other on the first British ascents of routes already described in detail in guidebooks; but here was a British party making a completely new and important route of the highest modern standard of difficulty. It contained two pitches of grade 6, one of which was the famous 'Fissure Brown'. It marked a new stage in the evolution of post-war British Alpine climbing.

BRITISH CLIMBERS ARRIVED!

British climbers had at last arrived in the post-war Alps. Happily they were able to join in the rise in the average level of achievement. Routes reserved for the elite not so long ago, such as the Mer de Glace face of the Grépon, the Ryan-Lochmatter on the Plan, or even the north face of the Dru or the south ridge of the Noire, were becoming standard routes, constantly repeated. This was partly the result of improved equipment, better nylon ropes, warmer duvet bivouac gear, neater and lighter vibram-soled boots. Competence in artificial climbing helped to increase the safety margin on a route, even though no additional pitons or wooden wedges might be necessary. Protection equipment in the form of specially manufactured 'nuts' or wedges which, I think, were largely a British invention, reduced much of the need for pitons, but they did not appear until the mid-1960s. As described in Fyffe and Peter's *Handbook of Climbing*, they evolved from the concept of fitting thin yet strong nylon slings behind smaller flakes and chockstones. It was taken a stage further by wedging pebbles in cracks and then threading slings behind them. The next step was to have ready-threaded chockstones which could be placed, used and removed by the climbing party, and so the first nuts, or chocks, appeared. These were machine nuts with the internal thread removed and put on to a sling.

From this basic yet brilliant idea came, in the mid-1960s, the first nuts specifically produced for climbing. Initially of fairly simple design, hexagonal, rounded or wedged-shaped, these changed into today's more sophisticated and versatile forms and have ousted most other means of protection. The concept of 'clean climbing', where the rock was left unaltered by the passage of climbers, was now a reality and swept the rock-climbing world.

By 1955, there were a lot of British climbers in the Alps. The Oxford and Cambridge contingents had been joined by the Scots and other northerners. In 1955, Tom Patey climbed the north face of the Plan, and Rawlinson and Westmacott the south ridge of the Fou and the Ryan-Lochmatter route on the Plan.

The ascent by Blackshaw and Downes of the north face of the Triolet in the same year was one of the first big ice climbs by a British party. The Couturier couloir of the Verte was climbed by Moseley, Dance, Noyce, Sutton and Brooke; this was before the days of the curved pick, when it was still quite an undertaking. The Cassin route on the Piz Badile fell to Blackshaw, Sutton, Downes and Langmuir in 1956.

THE 'RATTI' ON THE NOIRE

Two of the best routes were again achieved by Tom Bourdillon and Hamish Nicol. The first was the Ratti Vittali on the west face of the Aiguille Noire de Peuterey, first climbed in 1939, being the daunting route Bourdillon had first heard described by Bernard Pierre. Here is Hamish Nicol's account:

It was steep at first, and one has to aim for a little ridge which is a feature of the middle section of the face. The ridge is quite easy, and we could move together carrying coils of rope. The end of this section was marked by a snow-filled gully. Tom pulled the ice-axe out of his rucksack and cut steps across it. On the other side of the gully the climbing suddenly became more serious, the rock blacker, steeper and more greasy. It was very cold. I was looking for the Grade 6 crack which was going to take me up to the Ratti bivouac ledge. The crack was wet, and here and there were patches of ice. Then I was struck clean on the forehead by a drop of water. Another followed. The water came from the lip of the great overhang, and fell a clear distance of 60 m. Somewhere up there, there was a space where the bivouac ledge must be.

I turned my attention to the crack, which was about 6 cm wide, and for 25 m I jammed it, laybacked it, and was sometimes forced to bridge across the corner. I emerged on to the bivouac ledge. Quite a few important climbers had spent the night here, and had left their cigarette packets and sardine tins behind as mementos. It was wide and long enough to lie down full-length, but its chief merit was the huge overhang which acted like a roof; one might have been indoors. From the ledge a crack could be seen running up the overhanging wall, and in it were half a dozen pitons. By 5 pm we were both up, and we could see the summit quite easily, about 300 m away. At 6.45 pm exactly 12 hours from the glacier, we reached the summit of the Aiguille Noire de Peuterey and bivouacked on the East ridge, a few feet below the summit. Next day the washerwomen at Entrèves turned and stared at us walking past. I had a huge tear in my trousers and wondered if anybody would be able to mend them. Ours was the 10th ascent of the Ratti route.

THE EAST FACE OF THE 'CAP'

For five days it rained in Chamonix. Then it cleared enough to allow us to make an attempt on the East face of the Grand Capucin. This climb is so steep that it clears rapidly after bad weather. Our sacks contained food for three days, bivouac equipment, 35 pitons and wooden wedges and 110 m of rope. It was a hard flog up the glacier in soft new snow, sometimes wading thigh-deep. The bivouac platform which is well placed within 15 m of the first Grade 6 pitch was covered with 60 cm of soft now. It was 8.30 pm, and it would soon be dark. After a bit of shovelling with piton hammers an area measuring three metres by one emerged with a gravel base, much better than one might have expected. Tom lit the petrol stove, I cut a few lumps of ice from the cornice behind me, tipped our 20 hard-boiled eggs out of the saucepan in which they had travelled protected, and started to make soup. Our bivouac gear was quite primitive. There were two reasons for this: we were too poor to buy any, and if you carry a lot of stuff you will almost certainly have to use it, because it slows you down. We each had a cagoule and an eiderdown jacket, and nothing else. A bad storm would have caused serious problems. At 3 am two little lights could be seen crossing the glacier. Competitors! So breakfast was a hurried affair, and we started climbing at 6 am. Tom and I pressed on upwards quite slowly, at a rate of about 15 m per hour. Each pitch needed 10 or 15 pitons or wedges, and few were *in situ*. By 4 pm we had reached the 40 m wall which is said to be the crux of the climb. This wall is continuously overhanging and has to be done in two sections, with a stance in the middle, standing most precariously in étriers. It took us four hours to climb the wall, and it was 8 pm by the time we reached the second Bonatti bivouac. This was the largest ledge on the climb so far; it was covered in one metre of snow, but a lot of vigorous stamping and sweeping produced a sort of cave, just big enough for two people to sit down but not to stretch out. I smoked a cigarette and waited for dawn, chin on knee.

Breakfast was eggs, soup and super-milk concentrate, pretty nauseating, and it took two hours. It was still too cold to move off, but by 7 am I was into the 25 m sinuous crack which, in those days, had not a single piton in it. I put in 15, and it took an hour to lead. Just above this Bonatti had spent his third night. He must have been standing on one leg. At 5 pm we reached the summit, abseiled down into the gap behind the Capucin, and rejoined our rucksacks by descending a snowy gully. We reached the Requin hut after midnight. This was the fifth ascent of the East face of the Grand Capucin.

Bourdillon and Nicol seemed to have everything comfortably in hand. What could they achieve in the future? In 1956, Nicol had his final examinations in medicine and had not intended to go to the Alps but Bourdillon persuaded him. Tom Bourdillon and Dick Viney with Roger Chorley and John Tyson walked up to the Baltschiedertal hut and Hamish followed two days later. He arrived at the hut to find Tyson and Chorley alone. Bourdillon and Viney had not returned from their climb. They walked up to the glacier at the foot of the east face of the

above: A rare action painting in grey wash by Edward Theodore Compton, 1849–1921, of climbers surmounting a cornice on the north-east ridge of the Pic Orientale of the Meije, signed and dated 1896.

Jägihorn and found them both there, roped together. They were dead. Their deaths ended the golden age of Oxford mountaineering in the 1950s. Hamish Nicol did not climb again for four years, and never again at the same extreme standard. Tom Bourdillon and Dick Viney were buried in a little cemetery in Visp. The inscription on their grave reads:

They were most rightly reputed valiant, who, though they perfectly apprehend both what is dangerous and what is easy, are never the more thereby diverted from adventuring.

above: 'Between the Lights', sepia washes heightened with white, by Henry George Willink RWS, 1851–1938, painted in 1888. He provided many illustrations for C T Dent's Badminton Library book on mountaineering.

Alpine Centenary

No outward token, but an inward Grace
Binds the six hundred, drawn from every sphere,
Who, when released, their pilgrim's journey trace
Towards some mountain peak 'because it's there'.
Worthy are they, by fortitude and skill,
To join the rope that holds a hundred years
Of high endeavour, which the volumes fill
Of alpine triumphs since the pioneers.
The rugged ramparts of the Alps remain
A challenge to the young to prove their worth:
There, with catly-cautious tread, they train
To reach the highest summits of the earth.
Are all the mighty fallen? Not till time
Robs the last members of the urge to climb!

V Coverley-Price

In 1957, the Club celebrated its centenary, and with an eye on the forthcoming 150th anniversary in 2007, it is perhaps worth recalling how the centenary was celebrated. The *Alpine Journal* of May 1958 is full of it: Geoffrey Winthrop Young creating 'An Alpine Aura', followed by dinners, meets, a certain amount of genuflecting to royalty, and a sonnet.

As usual, I am too flippant. What was more important than all of those was that Club members had played a very large part in making possible the first ascents of Everest in 1953, and Kangchenjunga in 1955, the only two of the 14 8,000-metre peaks which were first climbed by British expeditions. These are achievements which will remain for all time; the best possible way to celebrate a centenary. They are covered in the next chapter and in individual books: John Hunt's *The Ascent of Everest* and numerous others, but for the latter just in Charles Evans' *Kangchenjunga – the Untrodden Peak*.

Back to the centenary celebrations. It was most appropriate that Sir John Hunt (later Lord Hunt), the leader of the successful 1953 Everest team, was the Club's president that year.

CENTENARY DINNERS, RECEPTIONS AND AN AL FRESCO RACLETTE

The special centenary dinner was held at the Dorchester Hotel, London, on 6 November 1957, the date chosen to coincide with that of the historic dinner at The Leasowes, near Birmingham, in 1857, which led to the actual formation of the Club shortly after. Over 400 were present, 55 being official guests representing mountaineering clubs and associations from all over the world. A small band of veterans had attended the Jubilee Dinner in 1907 (C W Nettleton, R L G Irving, R W Lloyd, Tom Longstaff, H J M Pritchard, J O Walker and Geoffrey Winthrop Young) at which Douglas Freshfield had made a remarkable prophecy: 'Will the company which dines here fifty years hence include the conqueror of Mount Everest?' Tenzing Norgay GM was indeed present and amongst the numerous messages and telegrams of congratulation was one from his summit partner, Sir Edmund Hillary, with the Transantarctic Expedition and another from H W Tilman with *Mischief* in Cape Town. A message from HRH Prince Philip, Duke of Edinburgh, Honorary Member of the Alpine Club, was read, as follows:

Throughout its history members of the Club have played a prominent part in the ascent of many of the great peaks and the exploration of the mountain ranges of the world, culminating in the ascent of Mount Everest on 29th May 1953. The Alpine Club has given leadership and inspiration to mountaineers of all ages and countries since its foundation, and I have no doubt that the Club will continue to foster and encourage mountaineering all over the world in the years ahead.

John Hunt concluded his presidential speech with the words:

Finally, Gentlemen, whether we live in the past or in the future, let us all not only look inwards towards each other, but outwards towards other kindred spirits. Because, whatever our differences, here at least on the theme of mountains, we are all on common ground; whether we are Russians or British; whether we are members of this Club or members of the 'Rock and Ice'; whether we climb at all or merely meditate upon the mountain scene. Whatever their scale, their shape or their climate,

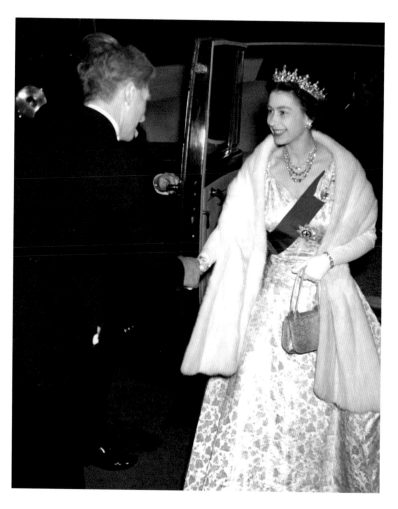

below: John Hunt, Club President 1956–8, welcomes HM The Queen to the Centenary Reception at Lincoln's Inn, 9 December 1957.

above: The Matterhorn is a superb backdrop to the Raclette party hosted by the Seiler family at the Centenary Meet in Zermatt, 20 August 1957.

whether they are the Alps, or the Caucasus, Helvellyn or Himalaya, the mountains are ours to enjoy together now. They beckon to the same spirit which is in all of us; they can be a bond between us. In this, as I see it, lies the true greatness of our sport, and so in this spirit let us go forward together.

Sir Arnold Lunn contributed a final word: 'My only regret is that we cannot welcome here tonight any distinguished lady mountaineers. I recall with shame the deplorable sentiment attributed to a distinguished member of this Club, A D Godley, who said: "I hate those bachelor dinners because I miss the exquisite moment when the ladies leave the table".'

A month after the dinner, in what many regarded as the climax of the celebrations, there was a centenary reception on 9 December, attended by 550 members and guests, in the presence of HM The Queen and HRH Prince Philip. It took place at the Great Hall, Lincoln's Inn, where the Club's jubilee dinner had been held in 1907. It was an historic, happy and serene occasion. While we basked in the rarefied atmosphere of this royal event, it is worth noting that around that time the Club included no less than four members of the Knights of the Garter, an order of chivalry granted by the queen and limited to twenty-four members. They were Prince Philip, Lord Hailsham, Lord Hunt and Sir Edmund Hillary.

London was not the only venue for centenary celebrations. On 19 August, the Swiss hoteliers of Zermatt, and members of the Seiler family had really gone out of their way to make us welcome: Cordon Rouge in the Mont Cervin Hotel, then led by the Zermatt, band to the Monte Rosa Hotel for a first-class dinner with fine wines. A one-metre-high relief model of the Matterhorn, coated with chocolate and sugar, and with the Hörnli hut made of solid chocolate, was brought in and placed before the president and centenary vice-presidents: Herr Alfred Zürcher and Count Aldo Bonacossa.

The following day, two trainloads of members and friends, and a few on foot, made their way up to the Riffelalp where Dr Franz Seiler and his sister, Frau Tschokke, hosted an al fresco Raclette party in bright sunshine with the Matterhorn as a superb backdrop.

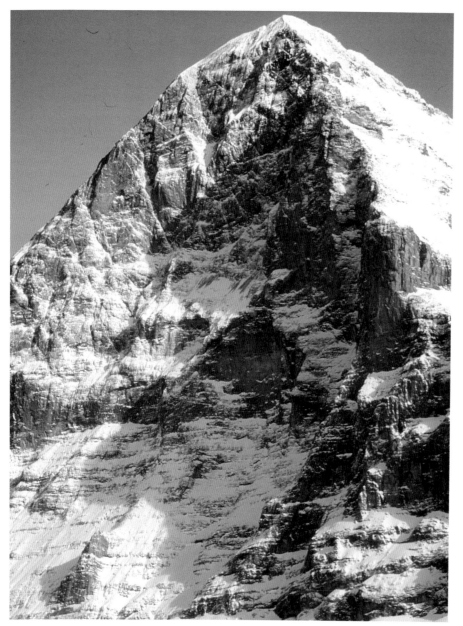

left: The Eigerwand in winter, February 1987, contrasting with the summer image on page 84.

CENTENARY CLIMBS

Christopher Brasher and I were climbing together that summer in the Alps so we booked in for the Zermatt celebration, which as a journalist he planned to write up for *The Observer*. Stormy weather encouraged us to drive farther east and link up with Mike Harris and Peter Nelson for the north ridge of the Badile. We were hit by another storm on the descent and had to seek refuge in a hut on the Italian side instead of returning to our starting point. So we lost a day and missed the Zermatt dinner. The Club organiser was 'white with anger', so we were told. We didn't make the Raclette party either! A tragedy, but we were lucky to get off the Badile safely. The same storm accounted for five climbers on the south face of the Marmolada, and the dramatic rescue of the Italian climber Corti on the Eigerwand, so Chris Brasher had enough copy for his article.

We tried to make amends by following other AC members up to the Monte Rosa hut, where the famous guide Alexander Graven, was now the custodian. We planned to try the north face of the Breithorn by the classic 1906 Young-grat and, as befitted the celebrations, our climbing party was most prestigious: John Hunt with Albert Eggler (both leaders of Everest expeditions), Fritz Luchsinger (first up Lhotse in 1956), Fritz Gansser, John Tyson, John Hobhouse, Chris Brasher and myself. As already described in Chapter 3, it proved a most satisfying climb – just one of the numerous classic routes in the Zermatt area climbed by members during the successful centenary meet, despite rather variable weather.

THE THREE NORTH FACES AND THE BONATTI PILLAR

below: Chris Brasher on the final icy section of the Younggrat, Zermatt Breithorn, 22 August 1957, during the Centenary Meet.

below right: After his companion was killed by stonefall on the Eigerwand at the Flatiron, Brian Nally crosses the Second Ice Field to join Bonington and Whillans on 26 July 1962.

Moving on to the late 1950s, there were now many British climbers with the qualifications and experience to become members of the Alpine Club, if they so wished, and a good number meeting the much more rigorous standards of the Alpine Climbing Group capable of tackling the harder alpine climbs. Routes such as the south face of the Gugliermina, and the north-east face of the Badile were proving popular, but still no British climbers had successfully tackled the Big Three north faces of the Matterhorn, Grandes Jorasses and the Eigerwand. It was just a matter of time and getting the right people together.

One of the legendary figures in Scottish climbing circles was Hamish MacInnes. Quoting Chris Bonington:

> He had started climbing as a lad, hitch-hiked to the Alps just after the war with only £5 in his pocket and had spent his National Service in Austria. There he had earned the nickname 'MacPiton', having acquired a taste for pegging from the Austrians, on the steep limestone walls of the Kaisergebirge. In the early fifties the use of any artificial aids was still frowned on, but Hamish hammered his pegs into Scottish crags with gay abandon, much to the disgust of the staider members of the Scottish Mountaineering Club. This never worried him however, for he had a complete disregard for public opinion and was in every respect an individualist.

In 1958, MacInnes was in a group of six, comprising Chris Bonington, Don Whillans, Paul Ross and two strong Austrians, Walter Phillip and Richard Blach, who completed an adventurous ascent of the south-west Pillar of the Dru. This had been first climbed solo in August 1955 by the Italian mountaineer Walter Bonatti in one of the most audacious ascents in Alpine history which had put all other post-war Alpine climbs into the shade. It would have been a considerable feat for a strong party but as a solo effort, it was incredible.

OPPOSITE PAGE:

right: Hamish MacInnes on his two-man expedition with John Cunningham to Everest in autumn 1953, aborted after learning of John Hunt's team's success in May.

below right: Stephen Venables on a September 1986 ascent of the Eigerwand with Luke Hughes.

THIS PAGE:

below: The north face of the Grandes Jorasses, with the Walker Spur leading to the left peak.

By 1958, four other parties had done the climb, the fastest taking three days over it. After a day of verticality they were delighted to find a bivouac ledge on the very prow of the Pillar the size of a night club dance floor. As they were settling down for the night, there was a thunderous roar and several tons of rock poured down the bed of the gully they had climbed that morning. Then suddenly there was a whistling and a sickening hollow thud as Hamish MacInnes's skull was broken by a single falling stone.

Chris Bonington produced an army field dressing for MacInnes's profusely bleeding head. Astonishingly, he was able to carry on next day. With retreat down the couloir unthinkable, the only way was up. The rope teams were rearranged; the fast Austrians going first, then Whillans nursing MacInnes, and Ross and Bonington bringing up the rear, taking out the pegs. Two more bivouacs and then the difficult descent to the Charpoua glacier. It was the strength of Walter Philip and Don Whillans that got everyone up and down safely.

The very day I was writing this piece, I received a climbing magazine which reported that on 30 June 2005, the Petit Dru suffered another massive rockfall. It seems almost certain that the whole of the Bonatti Pillar has gone!

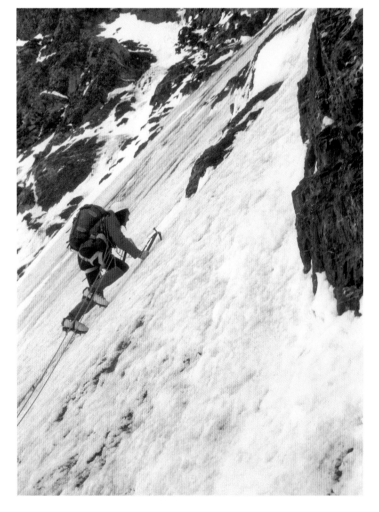

THE WALKER SPUR

Hamish MacInnes recovered well from the fractured skull and arranged to meet up with Don Whillans in Chamonix next year, with a view to trying the Walker Spur of the Grandes Jorasses. Just before leaving, Whillans had a chance meeting with my friend John Streetly. John, in England on a brief visit from his home in Trinidad, had not climbed with Whillans since 1955 when they had a marvellous week together in North Wales romping up the hardest climbs. Despite having no climbing gear with him, his enthusiasm was fired and he arranged to join them in Chamonix. They recruited a young Stockport climber, Les Brown, to make up a four. Jim Perrin takes up the story from his brilliant biography of Whillans:

The ad hoc nature of the party was mirrored by the state of its equipment. John had scrambled together what he could, having arrived in Chamonix without anything. Les, through no fault of his own, had lost his rucksack, all his gear in it, on his last climb, and was forced to climb in the suit he had arrived in, carrying a pair of pyjamas to wear on bivouacs.

They shared out what equipment they had, topped Les's outfit with a discarded trilby found in the rafters of Chalet Austria, and on 22nd July embarked on what they hoped would be the first British ascent of the Walker Spur. In the course of the climb Hamish was affected by the recurrence of symptoms from his head injury, and he and John fell behind whilst Don and Les were delayed by a slow Czechoslovakian party in front. Les Brown tells of how the Czech party pegged and 'frigged' every move, and how, in one Grade Six groove, Don – in boots with a sack on his back – bridged past them and on to the stance. The wide-eyed Czech leader said to Don, 'Sir, you are tremendous, the most fantastic climber in the world.' 'No, mate,' responded Don, 'I'm not the best climber in the world – you're the bloody worst.' They were forced into a bivouac on a climb which, without these problems they might have completed in a day, so fit was Don at this stage in his career. As it was, it gave him particular satisfaction and he thought it the most enjoyable climb he had ever done, but when they descended the Italian side and arrived in Courmayeur, his pleasure was shaded by a degree of disappointment. On the way up the climb, the observant Hamish had noticed

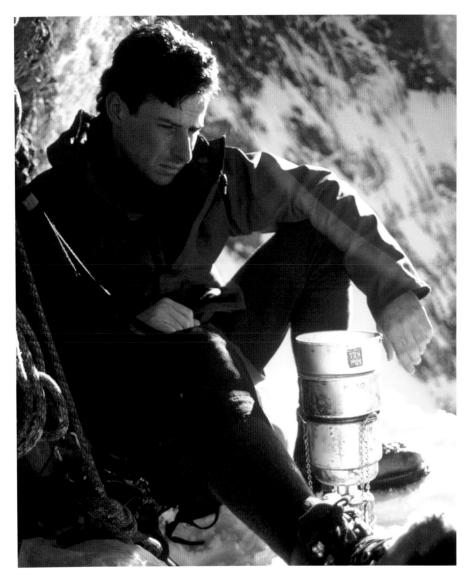

left: Luke Hughes brews up at the Death Bivouac on the Eigerwand, September 1986.

right: Don Whillans, before he lost his cap, on the Central Pillar of Freney, 26 July 1961.

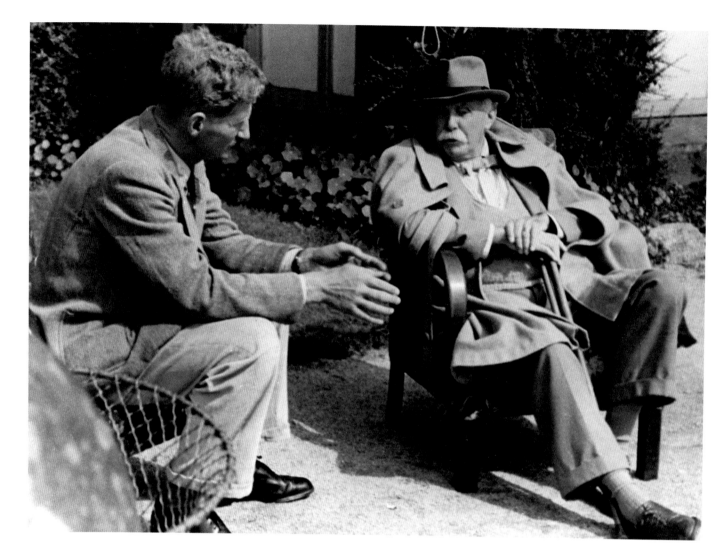

some oddities; discarded Smarties packets, an abandoned jammed knot sling. Had there been a British party on the route before them? He wondered. Back on the main street of Courmayeur two ragamuffin figures called out a greeting — Robin Smith and Gunn Clarke had finished the route the day before. Don had been beaten to the most prestigious first British ascent yet accomplished in the Alps by a couple of Edinburgh University students and a day.

above: John Hunt in conversation with Geoffrey Winthrop Young in the 1950s, when young British climbers were re-establishing the Club's reputation in the Alps.

The ascents of the two teams represented a huge psychological breakthrough for British alpinists, such was the status of the route at that time. Robin Smith was an enigmatic and brilliant climber on both rock and ice — a member of the Scottish Mountaineering Club and Edinburgh University MC rather than the Alpine Club (although he was later persuaded by Dennis Gray to join the ACG) — who left a legacy of wonderful routes on the Scottish mountains. He was a member of the British expedition to the Pamirs in 1962 led by John Hunt and Malcolm Slesser. After a successful ascent of Pik Garmo, he was descending roped up with Wilfrid Noyce when they both fell 4,000 feet to an ice shelf and were killed. Noyce, in his late forties, intended this to be his last expedition. Robin Smith was only 23.

THE MATTERHORN

The first British ascent of the Matterhorn north face was in marked contrast to that on the Walker Spur. It receives one line in the Expeditions section of the *Alpine Journal* for November 1961: 'August 30–31 1961, Tom Carruthers, B.M. Nally.'

Tom Carruthers was a Glasgow climber and Brian Nally a house painter from London. Neither were members of the Alpine Club. That does not imply that they were not good mountaineers, but I had difficulty in obtaining any report of their climb. Eventually, my friend and bibliophile the encyclopaedic Ken Wilson came to my rescue. He located a six-page article in the autumn 1961 number of *Mountain Craft*, written and illustrated by Tom Carruthers, from which this generous summary is taken in order to compensate for its absence from the *Alpine Journal*.

It was Carruthers' first year in the Alps. After climbing in the Polish Tatra mountains in June, and having bad weather in Chamonix for six weeks, he arrived in Zermatt for the first time at the beginning of a settled period of weather, with no climbing partner. Consulting Bernard Biner — a good friend to British climbers — at the Bahnhof Hotel he joined the crowds on the Hörnli ridge for a solo ascent of the Matterhorn — four hours to the top and still feeling fresh. He followed this with a solo ascent of a route on the Breithorn north face. On return, over a pot of tea, Brian Nally introduced himself in a cheery Cockney accent. He had just returned from a solo ascent of the north face of the Lyskanm — a dedicated north face man — already with two abortive attempts on the

below: The Matterhorn. The Hörnli ridge faces the camera, with the hut visible on the left. The north face, on the right remains in shade for most of the day, but is shown better in full sun on p.28. The Furggen ridge is on the left and the Zmutt ridge on the right skyline.

Matterhorn. He invited Tom Carruthers to join him in a third. They sensibly decided to check each other out by climbing the Zmutt ridge first. It went in five hours from the hut. They had got on well together, so decided to go for the north face, and went up to the Belvedere Hotel the next day. They thought of the many excellent British climbers who had never even attempted this notorious face. Could they, two unknown climbers, expect to succeed where others, more experienced, had failed?

The great triangular face of rock, ice and snow measures 3,600 feet from base to apex. Much of it can be hard ice, and the rock is very friable so that pitons do not hold well. The climber seeks security rather than being troubled by overwhelming steepness.

We started at 1.45 am, 29th August, after checking our gear: 5 carabiners each, four ice screws, four rock pitons, cramponning spike, rope, duvet jackets; long pants, extra gloves, food. Crampons on and away. After an hour, we crossed the huge bergschund by a delicate snow bridge and climbed the vertical upper lip. We had a very foreshortened view of the mountain; our three

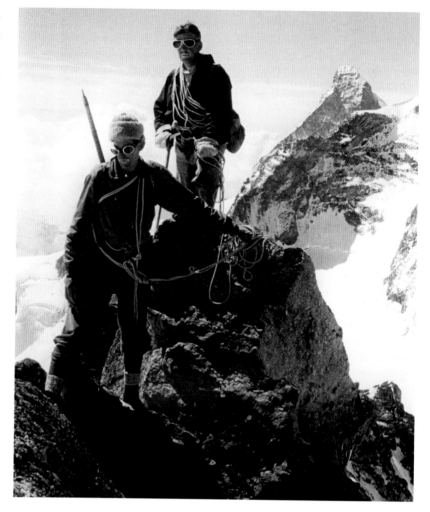

above: Allan Pullinger (Vice-President 1988–9) and Peter Lloyd (President 1977–9) carrying coils on the Rothorngrat in 1962, with the tip of the Matterhorn visible behind.

photographs now seemed suddenly inadequate. We were too far left, and should have reconnoitred the route over the bergschund the previous day. So we now had a time consuming traverse over ribbons of ice – iron hard – and broken rock until we reached the great snow ramp rising into the middle of the cliff. It proved to be 60 degree ice which succumbed to spike and crampon technique without having to cut steps. At the top, we traversed right towards the couloir which is the key to the middle section of the North Face. The unrelenting steepness and even gradient gave a great sense of exposure; no overhangs and intervening bumps as on a rock face. Changing belays, I fumbled and dropped the ice peg I had been using as a hand spike. Then a rock avalanche crashed down the couloir we were about to go up. Somehow we felt safe with our climbing helmets. I had bought mine second-hand from Dieter Marchant; it had already been up the Face twice! By 5 pm we were at the foot of the couloir. The last guided parties had descended the Hörnli Ridge. Now we were alone. We started looking for a bivouac site but there were no ledges. Slightly below the level of the Solvay Hut, we found a spot: two knobs of rock sticking out of the ice. We hammered in four pitons for protection, put on our duvets and pulled our long underpants over our breeches. We prepared tea but in lifting the steaming mug, Nally burnt his fingers and dropped it, spilling the contents over his feet. No oath, no word. We ate our dry supper in silence. It was a long cold night.

We could not move until the sun came up – the face only enjoys it for one hour in the morning – but it thawed us out. Breakfast was steaming porridge and concentrated fudge. We set off at 7 am, leading through endlessly. There were no definite pitches, everything was the same, we just chose the best line using psychological piton belays. We exchanged yells with the tourists on the Hörnli. Then – near disaster. At one awkward point, I asked Brian to place a sound piton runner. Twenty feet on he slipped, and I was whipped off my stance, and the two of us hung suspended from the piton. Unbelievably, I managed to regain my crumbling ledge and Brian to cut a stance in the ice. Then, three rope lengths later, I took off my crampons to negotiate a difficult rock pitch and managed to drop one. Down it went clanging and bouncing in a huge arc. Hell! I had to manage as best I could. At the end of the great coulour, we found we had gone too far left – a second mistake – requiring another time-consuming traverse. The effort was unrelenting, if nowhere extreme; no respite; cracked and crumbling, broken, blasted rock, glued with ice and glazed with verglas. At last Nally shouted, 'I can see the cross on the summit'. The two ridges closed in on us; we were there at 5.45 pm. Brian was an ideal companion, always cheerful, always in his element in this environment of high mountains. In the gathering dusk, we found a generous bivouac platform on the Hörnli ridge, where the first guided parties woke and welcomed us in the morning. Back at the Bahnhof, Herr Biner congratulated us with a Union Jack hung over the door.

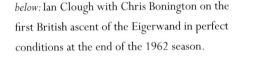

below: Ian Clough with Chris Bonington on the first British ascent of the Eigerwand in perfect conditions at the end of the 1962 season.

THE EIGERWAND

Brian Nally turned up again next year trying the Eigerwand on 26 July 1962, when his climbing partner Barry Brewster, a 22-year-old Bangor University student, was hit by stones, took a long fall, and lost consciousness. Nally held him and did all he possibly could in the circumstances, cutting a ledge in the hard ice, giving him spare clothes and his crash hat and settling him down for the night. Brewster died early in the morning, but then another stonefall swept him from his perch. By chance, Don Whillans and Chris Bonington were lower down on the face, having already decided to turn back with bad weather on the way. They were able to climb up and assist Nally down, with stones still falling round them, until they reached the sanctuary of the Stollenloch Window of the Eiger railway, where the press were waiting for them.

Coincidentally, Tom Carruthers also turned up on the Eiger later that summer, just behind Chris Bonington, this time with Ian Clough. Carruthers was with an

Austrian, Anton Moderegger. Both their intended partners had let them down, so the two decided to team up, having only met for the first time that day and barely speaking each other's language! In Clough's words, 'It seemed foolhardy in the extreme!' Nevertheless, Bonington suggested that if they were climbing at the same speed, then they might join forces, but, if not, the faster party should press on. This was agreed, but, in fact, after leaving their adjacent bivouacs near the foot of the climb next morning, Bonington and Clough were soon well ahead.

What had happened to Don Whillans? Sickened by the publicity and commercialism surrounding the death and rescue of Brewster and Nally, he and Bonington drove east to the Piz Badile and climbed the north-east face in six hours. Both were at the peak of their form and the weather was steadily improving, but Whillans had run out of money and had a lecture date so he headed home. Chris Bonington stayed on in Chamonix, meeting up with Ian Clough, with whom he had been on the Frêney Pillar the previous year. They joined up for a fast ascent of the Walker Spur, reaching the top at 3 pm, and realised that, with the good weather, the Eiger should now be in perfect condition. So they shot off to Alpiglen, and leaving at 4.30 pm settled down in a good bivouac at the foot of the Difficult Crack on the Eigerwand. Conditions were indeed perfect. It was freezing hard, which would keep the stones from coming down next morning. The Crack was dry and clear of ice and the Hinterstoisser Traverse went easily.

above: Chris Bonington uses an ice piton as a spoon during their initial bivouac below the Difficult Crack on the Eigerwand.

left: Luke Hughes on the Traverse of the Gods on the Eiger, September 1986.

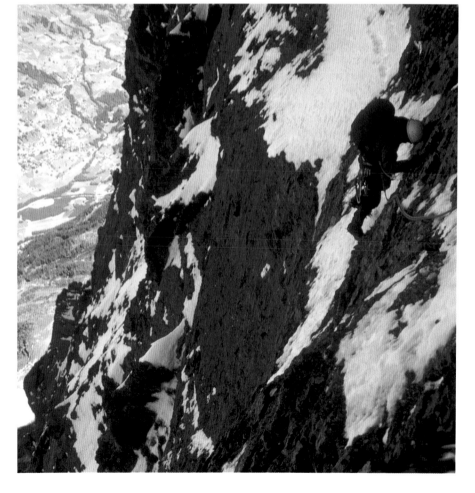

It was quicker going straight up the Second Icefield on front points, leading through and only cutting the odd step. They used the gap at the top between the ice and rock as a handrail to traverse left with barely a pause.

The vast scale of the face caught them out; they turned up too early and had to abseil back down to the Icefield to get to the start of the Flat Iron. A grotesquely twisted piton marked the point where Nally had held Brewster's fall. They were on the correct route, but the Flat Iron is the most dangerous place, a death trap after midday from falling stones. All the way up the Eiger there are grim tokens of other people's misfortune – a tattered piece of material, a broken axe, a piece of old rope: and this all combines to give the face an atmosphere of brooding menace, even when it is in perfect condition and no stones are coming down.

They looked back and could just see the other pair moving very slowly but diagonally across the Icefield. They continued up the Third Icefield and into the shelter of the Ramp up to the famous waterfall pitch. It was mercifully dry, but plastered with verglas. Clough led over a bulge of overhanging ice above. They were now in clouds and to their surprise encountered a pair of Swiss climbers preparing to bivouac. They pressed on across the Traverse of the Gods and round a corner into the White Spider, to be greeted by a falling stone. The afternoon bombardment had begun. They stepped back to a safe, dry bivouac site, just after 5 pm, rather than risk further stonefall.

Next morning, the Spider took five rope-lengths – an oppressive place – to reach the Exit Cracks. There were easy slabs at first, too easy it seemed, when there was supposed to be a grade V steep black nose. Bonington was tempted to try a much harder near-vertical line on the right which proved desperate and took him an hour. Clough followed on a tight rope. The Swiss had now caught up so they were given a top rope. By now they realised they were definitely off route so all four had to abseil down. One Swiss had no idea how to abseil.

below: Tom Patey gives Chris Bonington's new climbing helmet a good test.

He had only been climbing one year! It seemed incredible that anyone would try the Eiger with such scant experience. The correct route was much easier, being free of ice. In bad conditions the easy gullies would become icy chutes. Soon they were on the Summit Icefield and the Mitellegi ridge. It was all over. They had climbed the Eigerwand – and in perfect conditions. They were very lucky. Any unexpected change in the weather could turn the face into a raging maelstrom.

In the early afternoon, they scrambled unroped down the easy west ridge and reached Kleine Scheidegg. There the hotel proprietor asked them for the names of the pair behind them. 'Carruthers and Moderegger; why do you ask?' said Bonington. 'I am afraid they are dead.' 'They were going very slowly. When the cloud lifted they were nowhere to be seen, but then with my telescope I picked out their bodies at the foot of the Face.' Even in those perfect conditions, the Eiger had claimed its victims.

Both the British accidents had occurred in much the same place and in a similar pattern. They had been too slow crossing the Second Icefield and were on the Flat Iron as the afternoon bombardment began. Carruthers' watch had stopped at 5.15 pm. Ian Clough concluded: 'Each year more and more young men of every nationality, blinded by publicity, make their premature attempts on the wall. Some get up, but the roll of honour is long.'

THE CENTRAL PILLAR OF FRÊNEY

In the previous summer one final climb helped to seal the reputation of British climbers in the Alps during this period – the unclimbed Central Pillar of Frêney. This rock buttress high on the south face of Mont Blanc would give the most remote grade VI climb in western Europe. On 9 June 1961, Walter Bonatti and two fellow Italians encountered four Frenchmen bound for the same objective. They agreed to join forces. Leaving their refuge bivouac at the Col de la Fourche at midnight for the long approach route, they managed to climb about two-fifths of the way up the Pillar, which early in the season was still heavily iced. The upper part is a smooth 400-feet rock obelisk. They reached the foot of it when a

storm broke. Confident that they could last it out, they settled down for the night, but it continued unabated. On their fifth day out, they decided to retreat while they still had the strength to do so. Bonatti, emerging as the natural leader, supported by Pierre Mazeaud, a French Deputy, guided them to the Col de Peuterey where, after another bivouac, they continued through the crevasses of the Frêney Glacier to the Gamba hut, with members of the party collapsing on the way. In the end, only three survived: Bonnati, Mazeaud and Gallieni.

This disaster was insufficient to deter Europe's best climbers, provided there was a spell of fine weather. Towards the end of July, Pierre Julien, of the École Nationale in Chamonix, and an Italian, Piussi, helicoptered to the summit of Mont Blanc, to save time, and descended by the Peuterey ridge to the foot of the Pillar. After two bivouacs, Piussi dropped most of their pitons and carabiners and they were obliged to retreat.

Now for the third attempt. Fed up waiting for good weather for the Eiger, Don Whillans and Chris Bonington had met up with Jan Djuglosz, a fine Polish climber, and they returned to Chamonix, recruiting Ian Clough to make up a four. He had already had an outstanding season. On 26 July at the Aiguille du Midi téléphérique they were surprised to meet Desmaison, Pollet Villard and Julien clearly bound for the same climb, but going via the Torino to link up with their fourth man, Piussi. This gave the Brits a head start; from the Col de la Fourche refuge, by 3 pm they were in sight of the now famous Bonatti bivouac, where the great difficulties began. Whillans used the rest of the daylight to prospect the way ahead. To the right of the Pillar, out of sight, was a dièdre, roofed by a huge overhang, but with a chimney through it. Perhaps there was a crack in the dièdre. Next morning Whillans was at his best, using tension traverses and a small ace-of-heart's peg to reach the dièdre. There was a crack, but at one point, working his way through the overhang, his pitons were too narrow and his wooden wedges too big. He decided to climb this part free, first bringing Bonington closer for better protection. It was a truly remarkable lead by Whillans. Then he was suddenly off, ending up 50 feet lower, hanging level with Bonington's shoulders, having lost his cloth cap and piton hammer during the fall. Worse still, his fags and all the party's money were in the cap!

It was now the turn of Bonington, but where Whillans had failed, he did not expect to succeed. He would have to engineer his way up somehow. The French had meanwhile arrived below. Bonington asked for more slings. 'I'll try chockstoning the crack – show the Frogs some Welsh technique.' He jammed some small stones in the crack, threading slings behind them, and clipped in étriers. Tentatively he trusted his weight to them. It proved the key to working through the overhang, with nothing but space beneath, dropping away to the Frêney glacier. He reached a ledge – they were over the main difficulties. It was nearly dark. The 200 feet had taken all day. The other two prussiked up, and took a rope for the French so they could do the same next morning. The Pillar ended in a slender tower; a short abseil, a snow slope and another hour's plod and they were on top of Mont Blanc. A French reporter, dropped there by helicopter, produced a flagon of red wine and fruit juice. Slightly tipsy, they staggered to the Vallot hut and on down to Chamonix.

top left: Don Whillans caught in pensive mood by Ken Wilson.

bottom left: The Pillars of Frêney high up on the southern flank of Mont Blanc, photographed from the summit of the Aiguille Noire de Peuterey. The Brouillard face is beyond the Col Eccles on the left.

7 THE EIGHT-THOUSANDERS

Serious attempts to climb the world's highest peaks really began in the 1920s and 1930s, between the wars. Just three exceeded 28,000 feet in height: Everest (29,035 ft/8,850 m), K2 (28,250 ft/8,611 m) and Kangchenjunga (28,169 ft/8,586 m), given with their latest calculated heights. With the increasing use of metric measurements, 8,000 metres (26,246 feet) has become the touchstone and there are just 14 mountains defined as exceeding this altitude. Eight of these lie all or partly in Nepal, which until 1950 remained virtually closed to foreigners. So the scope for mountaineering expeditions to these peaks was much reduced, and it was really only the top three, plus Nanga Parbat (26,660 ft/8,125 m) in northern Pakistan, which seemed to attract expeditions during that time.

I will, therefore, consider the history of the climbing of these four great peaks before covering the stories of the climbing of the other ten 8,000 metre peaks, which mostly began only in the 1950s. At the same time, may I politely remind the reader that this book is primarily a history of the Alpine Club, so that where Club members were not involved, I must apologise for giving only the briefest mention of great feats of mountaineering carried out by others.

EVEREST

left: Shisha Pangma 26,397 feet/8,046 m the highest mountain wholly in Tibet, was the last of the 8,000-m peaks to be climbed, in 1964 by a team of six Chinese and four Tibetans.

below: Maps showing all 14 of the 8,000-m peaks.

Everest, being the highest in the world, was the greatest attraction. The southern side in Nepal was closed. Only the northern side, which lay in Tibet, could be approached, but it was difficult enough to get permission to enter. The only practical way lay through India, by way of Sikkim, and since the British then ruled India, it was only British mountaineers who had privileged access to the mountain. They made a total of seven attempts between the wars, in 1921, 1922,

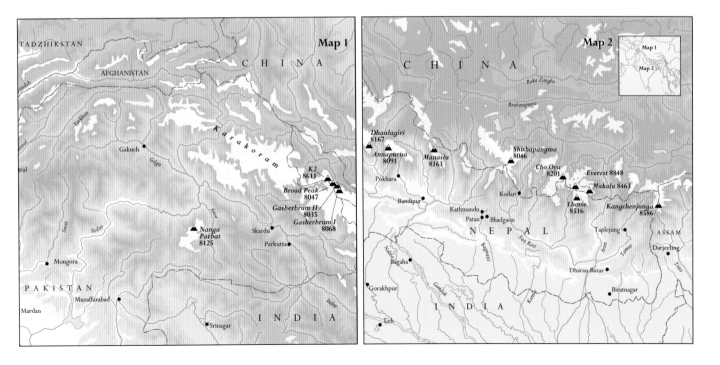

1924, 1933, 1935, 1936 and 1938. All these expeditions were organised by an Everest Committee created jointly by the Alpine Club and the Royal Geographical Society, so virtually all the climbers were members of the Club. As early as 1924, Edward Norton and Howard Somervell reached a record height of 28,126 feet (8,573 metres) on the north-east ridge, with less than 1,000 feet to go. To achieve success, it was felt to be only a matter of time before coinciding a fit and well-supported team with a favourable break in the weather. But this proved elusive, and the outbreak of World War II prevented further attempts.

As mentioned earlier, I included the history of these early Everest climbs in my book *Everest: 50 Years on Top of the World*, published in May 2003 to mark the fiftieth anniversary of the first ascent on 29 May 1953, so I do not propose to repeat the story here.

K2 – SETTING AN ITALIAN AND AMERICAN TRADITION

At the other end of the Greater Himalaya chain lies the second highest peak, K2, in the heart of the Karakoram range in northern Pakistan. As with Everest, the peak lies on a frontier, the north side being in China. The Duke of Abruzzi's expedition in 1909 was the first to reconnoitre the mountain and its ridges from the climbing viewpoint. His diarist Filippo de Filippi describes his first over-whelming sight of the mountain:

> Suddenly and without warning, as if a veil had been lifted from our eyes, the wide Godwin-Austin valley lay before us in its own whole length. Down at the end, alone, detached from all the other mountains soared up K2, the indis-putable sovereign of the region, gigantic and solitary, hidden from human sight in innumerable ranges, jealously defended by a vast throng of vassal peaks, pro-tected from invasion by miles and miles of glaciers. Even to get within sight of it demands so much contrivance, so much marching, such a sum of labour.

They eventually selected the south-east spur as being the only one at all feasible. It is actually a subsidiary ridge which merges with the shoulder of K2 at about 24,600 feet (7,500 metres). It proved too steep for laden porters and the attempt petered out at around 20,500 feet (6,250 metres), but nevertheless they had picked the line by which it was first climbed, now known as the Abruzzi spur or ridge. The duke's reputation and stature – his team included seven guides

from Courmayeur — were enough to deter other expeditions from attempting the mountain for almost 30 years.

The next team to try were Americans in 1938. A German émigré from Dresden called Fritz Wiessner had become an American citizen and joined the American Alpine Club in 1932. Applying through the Club he received permission to attempt K2 in 1938 and, if unsuccessful, again in 1939. Because of business commitments, he withdrew in 1938 while making it clear he wished to lead the 1939 expedition. He was an excellent rock climber; had climbed in both the Alps and North America and in 1932 had been to Nanga Parbat with a German–Austrian expedition. Wiessner recommended that Charles Houston be given the leadership — he had been with Odell and Tilman on the first ascent of Nanda Devi in 1936 — and so began Houston's long association with K2 and the Alpine Club.

Although still a medical student and only aged 25, as with Nanda Devi, he brought together a small cohesive group of friends who formed a great team: Bob Bates, who had traversed Mount Lucania in Alaska with Bradford Washburn; Bill House, who had climbed Devil's Tower, Wyoming, and Mount Waddington with Wiessner; Paul Petzoldt, a Teton guide; Dick Burdsall, who had climbed Minya Konka in China, and a Scot, Captain Norman Streatfeild, based in India, as transport officer. Their team of six Sherpas was led by Sirdar Pasang Kikuli, who had been Houston's personal Sherpa on Nanda Devi and had also been to

THIS PAGE:

above: An avalanche off Wedge Peak, an outlier of Kangchenjunga, named at the far right of the panorama on the opposite page.

OPPOSITE PAGE:

above right: The incredible north ridge of K2 in China. The mountain was not climbed from this side until 1982, by a strong Japanese team, 28 years after the first ascent by an Italian expedition in 1954.

below right: A composite panorama of the Kangchenjunga massif from the north, put together by Frank Smythe when he was a member of Dyhrenfurth's huge international expedition in 1930.

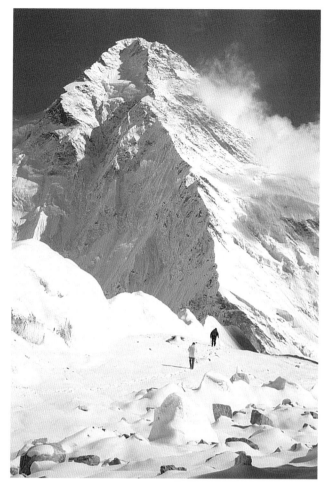

Kangchenjunga, Nanga Parbat and Everest, amassing rather more Himalayan experience than all the team members put together!

After a careful reconnaissance, they again selected the Abruzzi spur, despite its steepness and paucity of campsites. Camps 2 and 3 were located and a camp 4 at the base of a 50-metre vertical rock band at around 22,000 feet (6,700 metres). This was climbed in four hours by an awkward ice-filled chimney by Bill House, their best rock climber, in a superb lead — one of the hardest pitches in the Himalaya at that time — now called House's Chimney. Camp 5 was placed above. It still required two more camps 6 and 7, the latter at 7,700 metres, just 200 metres below the great snowy Shoulder — one of the few easy-angled areas on the mountain. Four climbers, plus Pasang Kikuli (the other Sherpas never climbed above camp 3), established camp 7, where Petzoldt and Houston spent the night. On 21 July, those two ploughed through waist-deep snow above the Shoulder, making slow progress. At just under 8,000 metres, Houston had had enough; Petzoldt carried on another 50 metres, seeing where one might force a route through another rock band. He was about 600 metres from the summit.

Meanwhile, Houston sat looking out towards the junction of the glaciers below at Concordia. 'I felt that all my previous life had reached a climax in these last hours of intense struggle against nature and yet nature had been very indulgent …' Petzoldt rejoined him; they decided to turn back and descending to camp 7 in twilight, used their last match to brew tea.

The weather had been kind to them so far, but Houston realised the risk of being trapped so high on the mountain. Could they get down in a storm? He had been brought up in a tradition of safety and caution, not of fame and glory. They had already done exceptionally well. The expedition book, *Five Miles High*, full of tolerance, good humour and harmonious decisions, records a standard that so many subsequent expeditions to K2 failed to achieve.

Kangchenjunga   Wedge   Peak

THE 1939 TRAGEDY

The 1939 expedition was in stark contrast. None of the 1938 team could afford or wanted to return so soon. Wiessner was known as a difficult person to work with, single-minded and authoritarian, he had difficulty in raising a strong team. He led from the front, with Tony Cromwell as his deputy. Chappel Cranmer and George Sheldon were both 20 and students at Dartmouth College. An odd choice was Dudley Wolfe, a sort of Great Gatsby character well able to pay his own way, but an ungainly climber desperate to prove himself. The last member was a 27-year-old pre-medical student and Teton guide, Jack Durrance, substituting for a last-minute dropout, when Wiessner was already in Europe buying equipment. On arrival at base camp, Cranmer developed what would now be called pulmonary oedema. Although he recovered, he was a non-starter for K2. This time the weather was more normal, strong winds and intermittent storms. Wiessner, out in front with Dudley Wolfe, was keen to press on, but the others below were demoralised. On 30 June, Wiessner climbed House's Chimney with Pasang Kikuli, and hauled up Dudley Wolfe next day to join them in camp 5.

Durrance, acting as doctor, was concerned that Wolfe was spending too much time too high, and he himself on the way to camp 7 began to show symptoms of oedema: violent headache, faintness and breathing difficulties. For his own health, he wisely descended to camp 2, but this left Wiessner and Wolfe out on a limb, with minimal support from below. By 17 July, Wiessner, Dudley Wolfe and Pasang Dawa Lama, the strongest Sherpa, established camp 8 just below the Shoulder and set out towards the summit. The soft snow was too much for Wolfe and he returned to camp 8, where he was destined to spend the next five days on his own. Wiessner and Pasang Dawa Lama eventually pitched a camp 9 around 8,000 metres, at the limit Petzoldt had seen. Above there were two choices: on the right a snow gully below a sérac barrier, which is now the normal route known as the Bottleneck; on the left up broken rocks, preferred by Wiessner the rock expert; both leading to the easier summit snow slopes. The rocks were verglassed and harder than they looked and took all day. By 6 pm they were at about 27,500 feet (8,300 metres), over the worst and a mere 750 feet (250 metres) from the summit. Wiessner was minded to continue climbing through the night, but Pasang was not and refused to go on. Wiessner gave in.

On their way up, Wiessner had noted that the alternative was safer and quicker than he had thought, so they descended that way but, unfortunately, Pasang dropped their crampons. They rested at camp 9. Wiessner thought they could still climb to the summit, but he was deluding himself. They descended to camp 8, where Wolfe was subsisting, but nobody had come up in support with more supplies. Everything started to go wrong. Wiessner and Pasang descended to base, finding on their way that the lower camps had been stripped of stoves and sleeping bags owing to a misunderstanding with the Sherpas. Wolfe had been left on his own. Three Sherpas went up to camp 7 twice to try to rescue him but they were never seen again and Wolfe was left to die. K2 had claimed its first four victims. There were recriminations between the team members, and the American Alpine Club was torn by the controversy.

right: One of Doug Scott's great images of the South Face of K2 seen from high on Broad Peak. The Abruzzi route, by which it was eventually first climbed, forms the right sky-line and the west ridge is the left skyline, beyond the SSW ridge (also known as the Magic Line), which rises from a col at the left edge of the photograph.

of all five came on Pete Schoening and his ice-axe driven into snow behind a rock. He held them all. Houston was concussed. In total confusion they managed to get across to camp 7. When Bates and Streather returned to where Gilkey had been securely belayed in a gully he had gone – carried away by an avalanche. Gilkey's death had saved them.

Now fighting for their own survival, they continued the descent and were reunited with their Hunza porters at camp 2 and managed to reach base camp and a heartfelt welcome by their liaison officer, Colonel Atta Ullah. Charlie Houston concluded, 'We entered the mountain as strangers, but we left as brothers.' Today the survivors of the team are still united in friendship.

Houston turned to the study of high-altitude medicine and became one of the greatest authorities on the subject. When planning to celebrate their centenary recently, the Climbers' Club wondered whether he could be persuaded to come to North Wales as their chief guest. 'Is he still alive?' queried someone. A telephone number was dialled, and the reply came, 'Charlie Houston speaking'. 'Thanks very much,' said the caller. 'You have answered our first question!' Charlie came and received a standing ovation.

Houston, Bates and Streather were all Alpine Club members and are still with us, Houston being made an Honorary Member in 1974, and Streather elected president 1990–2.

below: After crossing the Larkya La 5,200 m westwards, and a long descent to Bimtang, trekkers are rewarded with this great view of the west side of Manaslu 26,781 ft/8,163 m, before they join the popular Annapurna circuit. Manaslu, initially a Japanese preserve, was eventually climbed by Y. Maki's team on 9 May 1956, from the north-east, which is now the normal route (see p.149).

ITALIAN SUCCESS

K2 could not last out much longer. A large Italian expedition had booked the mountain for 1954. It was a combined scientific and mountaineering venture led by the distinguished geologist Professor Ardito Desio. He had been on the Duke of Spoleto's expedition of 1929 which had explored the Baltoro area.

The strong climbing team of eleven were mostly guides, including Achille Compagnoni, Lino Lacedelli and Walter Bonatti, at 24 the youngest member. In contrast to Wiessner, Desio led from behind, exhorting the climbers by a series of messages from base camp, of which number 10 concluded: 'The honour of Italian mountaineering is at stake.'

The 40-year-old Compagnoni was put in charge of the summit attempt. They placed camp 8 at 25,394 feet (7,740 metres) and a camp 9 at over 8,000 metres, from which he and Lacedelli, using oxygen, eventually reached the summit just before 6 pm after their oxygen had run out. At 11 pm they returned to camp 8, falling into the arms of Bonatti, Gallotti and Abram. That is the bare story of this epic, neglecting the reason for Bonatti and the Hunzukut Mahdi having to spend a night out in the open at 8,000 metres owing to confusion over the oxygen sets and a misunderstanding which continues after at least four court actions to this day, even after K2's golden jubilee year in 2004. K2, like Kangchenjunga, was not

above: An Indian Air Force photograph of Kangchenjunga's SW Face showing the route and camps of the first ascent, in 1955.

climbed again for over 20 years. Desio was made an honorary member of the Alpine Club in 1980 and died in 2003, aged 104. He was said to have modelled his K2 organisation on John Hunt's 1953 Everest Expedition, but I think we were a much happier and better-led team.

Bonatti returned to the Alps for his incredible solo climb of the south-west Pillar of the Petit Dru, described earlier. Then in 1957 he was back to the Karakoram, under the leadership of the great Ricardo Cassin, to make, with Carlo Mauri, the first ascent of the soaring granite peak of Gasherbrum IV, at 26,000 feet (7,925 metres) just short of the magic 8,000 metres.

In the Matterhorn centenary year Bonatti crowned his career as the most outstanding alpinist of the post-war era by making a solo ascent of a new route up its notorious north face.

NANGA PARBAT, THE KILLER MOUNTAIN

Whereas K2 came to be regarded as an Italian or American mountain, Nanga Parbat (26,660 ft/8,125 m) in the 1930s was very much 'Unser Berg' to the Germans. Rather ahead of his time, Mummery was the first victim, with his two Gurkhas in 1895, probably swept away by an avalanche when trying to cross into the Rakhiot valley.

The Germans came first in 1932 and then again in July 1934, a strong group led by Willy Merkl, a Bavarian, including Willo Welzenbach, one of their best climbers. They reached the Silver Saddle at 25,000 feet (7,620 m) before a terrible storm broke. Welzenbach, Wieland, Merkl, and six Sherpas died during the desperate retreat. One of the Sherpas, Gayley, stayed with Merkl who was at the end of his tether, and died with him. Another, Ang Tsering, was awarded the medal of the German Red Cross – pinned on by Hitler, so he told me – for his gallantry.

An unusual book, *Tigers in the Snow* by Jonathan Neal, published in 2002, tells the story from the viewpoint of the Sherpas. They had to carry Ang Tsering from base camp to the hospital in Srinagar where all his toes were amputated. A few weeks later the local secretary of the Himalayan Club gave him enough money for the train home to Darjeeling. There he went straight into Victoria Hospital, where the staff found 24 large, white maggots in the holes left by his amputations. He said the flies in Kashmir must have been different from the flies in Darjeeling. The maggots didn't hurt, but they unnerved him. Despite his injuries, Ang Tsering lived until he was 98, an astonishing age for a Sherpa, and I was privileged to meet him in Darjeeling in April 2002, just three weeks before he died of a stroke.

A new assault was launched on Nanga Parbat in 1937, led by Karl Wien, including Müllritter, who had survived from 1934. This had an even more horrific outcome when seven of the climbers and nine Sherpas were overwhelmed by an avalanche in their tents as they slept. Paul Bauer led another expedition in 1938 which was defeated by bad weather, and in 1939 P Aufschnaiter led a reconnaissance to the Diamir, face reaching around 6,000 metres. In 1950, two Englishmen, Thornley and Crace, disappeared on the Rakhiot glacier, bringing the total death roll up to 32.

OPPOSITE PAGE:

right: Jackson (leading) and Band in the Lower Icefall of Kangchenjunga on the 1955 expedition.

THIS PAGE:

below: Nanga Parbat, scene of several German expeditions before it was finally climbed in 1953 – the same year as Everest – in an incredible solo effort by Hermann Buhl.

A SOLO BID BY HERMANN BUHL

Finally, in 1953, the mountain was climbed, just five weeks after the British success on Everest. This was the first major German expedition since the war, called the Willy Merkl Memorial Expedition, being led by Merkl's step-brother, Dr Karl Herrligkoffer, a Munich physician. Herrligkoffer was not a climber himself so, like Desio on K2, he led from below and enlisted Peter Aschenbrenner, another survivor from 1934, as climbing leader. So often this is a recipe for friction developing between lead climbers and the organisation. The ones in front think they are the only ones working, and complain of the delay in stocking higher camps. Herrligkoffer's instructions to come down were ignored and Aschenbrenner went home. Out of this emerged an incredible individual performance by Hermann Buhl. Shortly after midnight on 3 July, he left camp 5 at 6,900 metres for the summit, up 1,220 metres, five miles over the Silver Saddle, up and down the Fore Peak to the Bazhin Gap. There were some awkward pinnacles before the shoulder, but he eventually crawled on all fours to the summit at 7 pm that evening. Overtaken by night on the descent, he had no bivouac gear nor a decent ledge and had to remain on a stance with a rocky back rest. It was astonishing that he survived and got back to his tent at 7 pm, 41 hours after leaving it, where Hans Ertl came out to meet him.

I remember Buhl, and I think it was Ertl, a great climber and film-maker, coming to tell their story at the Alpine Club. Ertl said they had virtually given up hope for Buhl and were busy fixing up a memorial plaque for Willy Merkl on the rocks beside their top camp. As they did so, he couldn't help wondering if Buhl's name should not also be on the plaque. Then he spotted him descending and went out to meet him.

Hermann Buhl, born in Innsbruck, was a phenomenon of the same calibre as Joe Brown and Don Whillans. I love the story of his cycling a 100 miles to Promontogno, walking up to the Sciora hut and then soloing the north-east face of the Piz Badile in four and a half hours. Cycling back immediately, he fell asleep, flipping over the handlebars into the icy torrent of the river Inn. This woke him up, so he carried on down the road shouldering his damaged bicycle! Sadly, he met his end in June 1957 walking unroped over a cornice on Chogolisa in the Karakoram, a very easy thing to do in cloudy or white-out conditions.

KANGCHENJUNGA, THE UNTRODDEN PEAK

More than any other of the world's great mountains, Kangchenjunga is open to public view. Anyone who has seen it from the popular Indian hill station of Darjeeling will agree that it is an unforgettable sight. Rosy at dawn, brilliant and remote in sunshine, cold and repellent in shadow, it seems to float above the haze and darkness of the valleys between, its great mass filling the north-western horizon.

Until about 1850, it was thought to be the highest mountain in the world. I have already mentioned Freshfield's classic circuit of the mountain in 1899, and the ill-fated attempt in 1905 by the Yalung glacier.

Within a year of the founding of the Himalayan Club on 17 February 1928, it received a request from the veteran Heligolander Rickmer Rickmers to help a young Bavarian, Paul Bauer, who planned to bring a party of climbers to the Himalaya: 'They want to test themselves against something difficult,' wrote Rickmers, 'some mountain that will call out everything they've got in them of courage, perseverance, and endurance.'

The two expeditions led by Paul Bauer to the north-east Spur above the Zemu glacier in 1929 and 1931 were classics of their kind. In 1929, they reached a height of 24,272 ft (7,400 m). Their struggle up the Spur for weeks on end, and of their equally laborious struggle down it in bad weather, greatly stirred the climbing world. Colonel Strutt, writing in the *Alpine Journal,* gave it one of his rare accolades: 'A feat without parallel, perhaps, in all the annals of mountaineering.' On their second expedition, after surmounting all the difficulties of the Spur they turned back from 25,263 feet (7,700 metres) rather than embark on a snow slope which they saw to be dangerous. Their effort was a classic example of skill, courage, energy and good judgement.

THIS PAGE:

below left: Charles Evans, the first to climb Everest's south summit, with Tom Bourdillon, in 1953 and leader of the first expedition to climb Kangchenjunga in 1955.

below: Tashi Sherpa, who carried to the top camp on 'Kangch' in 1955 and later, with Dennis Davis, made the first ascent of Nuptse in 1961.

OPPOSITE PAGE:

below right: Celebrating Success! Band and Jackson enjoying 'chang' at Tonglu, June 1955.

Dyhrenfurth's huge expedition of 1930, to the north-west face of the mountain, was described by F S Smythe, who was a member of the expedition, in his book *The Kangchenjunga Adventure*. So far, every visit to the mountain had been either at the end of the monsoon, or during it: Crowley had met with disaster on 1 September; Bauer's first expedition had done most of its climbing during September, and his second expedition during July and August. Dyhrenfurth arrived at the foot of the mountain in the last week of April, and so was the first to be in the right place at what we now regard as the right time, the month of May.

Unfortunately, he went to a face of the mountain more menaced than any other by ice cliffs, and the expedition turned away from Kangchenjunga after the loss of the Sherpa Chettan in an avalanche and the failure of the party to find an alternative route. The highest point reached was about 21,000 feet (6,400 metres).

In those years, while the Yalung or south-west face was neglected, the reputation of Kangchenjunga for bad weather and dangerous ice-avalanche grew: the mountain came to be regarded as more subject to ice-avalanche than any other, and more exposed to heavy snowfall. Smythe, in his widely read book, condemned the Yalung face on the ground that, being south-facing, it would be unusually subject to the danger of avalanche, a view no longer so strongly supported by experience; he thought that the Great Shelf seen from Darjeeling would itself be menaced by avalanche.

Fortunately, not everybody was so daunted, a reconnaissance party led by John Kempe in 1954 recommended a closer look at the Yalung face. So in 1955, the Alpine Club launched a 'reconnaissance in force' to be led by Charles Evans and supported by the Royal Geographical Society and paid for by the newly created Mount Everest Foundation, mentioned in Chapter 8. Before the team left, John Hunt predicted: 'There is no doubt that those who first climb Kangchenjunga will achieve the greatest feat in mountaineering, for it is a mountain which combines in its defences not only the severe handicaps of wind, weather and very high altitude, but technical climbing problems and objective dangers of an order even higher than those we encountered on Everest.'

We were not over-optimistic about our chances. Our task was to examine the upper part of the mountain, with the limited objective of reaching the Great Shelf – a conspicuous ice terrace stretching across the Yalung face at about 24,000 feet (7,315 metres). So far, no party had been much above 20,000 feet on this face. At the same time, just in case things proved easier than expected, Charles Evans was planning to take oxygen and sufficient equipment to launch an attack on the summit.

I was fortunate to be included in Evans' team of eight climbers and a doctor: Norman Hardie, deputy leader, Joe Brown, John Jackson, Tom MacKinnon, Neil Mather, Tony Streather and Dr John Clegg. Our Sherpa sirdar was Dawa Tenzing who had carried twice to the South Col on Everest in 1953. All but one were or became Alpine Club members.

below: Looking west from 28,000 ft/8,535 m on Kangchenjunga, 25th May 1955. On left Yalung Kang. Above the sea of clouds on the horizon are the Makalu and Everest massifs.

Kangchenjunga lies on the border between Nepal and Sikkim. The 1955 expedition would be climbing only on the Nepal side but, not wishing to offend the people of Sikkim, who regard the mountain as sacred, Evans reached a special agreement with their rulers that the climbers would not go beyond that point from which there was an easy route to the top, so would not tread on the summit itself.

The expedition left Darjeeling on 14 March and approached the south-west face by the Yalung glacier. Base camp was set up on 12 April below the Lower Icefall, but after some very technical ice climbing the route was abandoned as being too unstable and dangerous for porters. An alternative approach from Pache's Grave was pioneered successfully to reach a safe site for camp 2 between the Lower and Upper Icefalls, and camp 13II duly placed and stocked part way up the latter.

On Friday 13 May, Evans and Hardie used oxygen for a lightning recce and reached the Great Shelf, continuing up to a potential site for camp 5 at 25,300 feet (7,710 metres), higher than man had ever been on Kangchenjunga. This opened the way for a summit bid in an assault plan involving the whole team. Band and Brown would be the first pair and Hardie and Streather the second. After weathering a 60-hour storm on the Great Shelf, the first pair were placed in the top camp, 6, at 26,900 feet (8,200 metres) halfway up the Gangway on a narrow ledge cut in the ice. On 25 May, after an exciting climb Brown and Band reached the summit at 2.45 pm – a simple cone of snow 20 feet away and 5 feet higher than the ground on which they stood. Hardie and Streather repeated the climb next day. Both parties kept their promise to leave the summit untrodden.

Writing in *The Times* of 3 August 1955, Charles Evans concluded: 'Because it is safe and intricate, and placed in surroundings of fantastic beauty and grandeur, it is not too absurd to hope that this route may be repeated at not too long intervals. As the French climbers' guidebooks are fond of saying, "*Il faut devenir classique*".' It was not climbed again for 22 years, until in 1977 an Indian Army expedition, led by Club member Colonel Kumar, made the second ascent by finally overcoming the Bavarians' north-east Spur.

By the end of 2004, there had been 195 individual ascents, compared to over 2,251 on Everest.

While surfing the Internet in early 2005 on Explorers Web.com looking for ascent statistics, I came across a comparison between K2 and Kangchenjunga just prior to their respective fiftieth anniversary years of 2004 and 2005. By the end of 2003, K2 had also only had some 198 individual ascents, but then a record number of 48 in the anniversary year itself. The writer speculated whether the same thing would happen to Kangchenjunga in 2005, but on the whole thought not and came up with an article entitled: 'Ten Top Reasons for Not Climbing Kangchenjunga' – basically it was 'Too long, too high, too cold, too hard!' He was rather perceptive. The only additional ascent in 2005 was on 30 May by our Alpine Club member Alan Hinkes, who became the first Brit to complete the ascents of all 14 8,000-metre peaks, and the thirteenth person ever to do so.

ANNAPURNA – THE FIRST 8,000-METRE PEAK

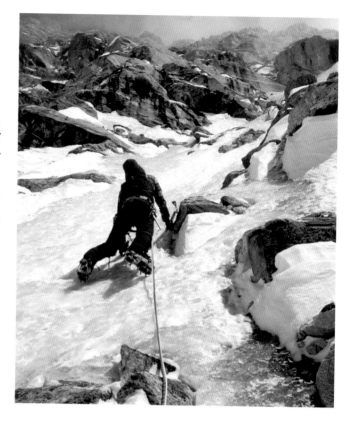

After World War II, the French were the quickest off the mark in returning to the highest Himalayan peaks. Thanks to the drive of Lucien Devies they were able to take advantage of the opening of Nepal in 1949, and obtain permission to try Dhaulagiri (26,795 ft/8,167 m) or Annapurna (26,545 ft/8,091 m) in 1950. Their top climbers, such as Lionel Terray, Gaston Rébuffat and Louis Lachenal, had been able to keep active climbing during and after the war and were obvious candidates. Maurice Herzog, a good organiser rather than a top climber, was appointed leader and the team was completed by Jean Couzy and Marcel Schatz from Paris, with Marcel Ichac as climbing cameraman.

Although they had the rudimentary quarter-inch maps from the Survey of India, it seems incredible now that there were no available photographs. If there had been, they would probably not have made Dhaulagiri their first choice: 'The south face, shining blue through the morning mist, was unbelievably lofty, not of this world. We were speechless in face of this tremendous mountain.' They soon turned their attention to Annapurna on the other side of the impressive Kali Gandaki gorge. It took them a month to find a way in to establish a base camp below the north side, which appeared to offer a possible route to the top. It was now 23 May, leaving only a couple of weeks before the monsoon might be upon them. They worked out a route and carried loads below the potentially dangerous Sickle ice cliff barrier and up a steep gully that led to the upper slopes. Herzog was performing well and teamed up with Lachenal for a summit bid while Terray – perhaps the strongest – carried on stocking camp 4. Supported by two Sherpas, they set up their final tent at 23,950 feet (7,300 metres).

The tent half collapsed during the night and they had trouble with the stove, so set off at 6 am without food or drink. It was brilliantly fine but cold and windy. The slope did not look difficult so they climbed unroped, panting heavily with each step. At 2 pm, 3 June, they reached the summit – the first persons to climb a peak of over 8,000 metres. But that was only part of the story. Storm clouds were gathering from the south. On the descent, Herzog lost his gloves. They staggered separately down to the top camp. Lachenal fell through a crevasse. Terray and Rébuffat helped to rescue them but both were badly frostbitten. Lachenal lost his toes, and Herzog all his fingers, but it was a price he seemed willing to pay. In his expedition book, which is said to be the most successful mountaineering book ever, he concluded: 'Annapurna to which we had gone empty handed, was a treasure on which we should live the rest of our days. With this realisation we turn a new page: a new life begins. There are other Annapurnas in the lives of men.'

above: Georges Bettembourg leading an ice pitch on the face below the North Col of Kangchenjunga in 1979.

above: Peter Boardman and Joe Tasker, climbing with Doug Scott up the north side of 'Kangch', pause at the Pinnacles on the west ridge before making the third ascent in 1979, and the first without supplementary oxygen. They were at the same point where Joe Brown and George Band had reached the ridge in 1955 by way of the south-west face.

CHO OYU –
BY THE GRACE OF THE GODS

When we met over lunch in Vienna in January 1956, Herbert Tichy kindly gave me a copy of the original German edition of his book *Cho Oyu: Gnade der Götter* – by the Grace of the Gods. He was an Austrian anthropologist, more of a mountain traveller than a climber and, like Alexander Kellas, he enjoyed the company of Sherpas, often travelling with them alone. His sirdar was Pasang Dawa Lama, who had climbed so high on K2 with Fritz Wiessner in 1938. For his expedition to Cho Oyu (26,906 ft/8,201 m) in 1954 he added only Sepp Jöchler and Helmut Heuberger to his team of seven Sherpas. It could not have been a greaer contrast to Professor Desio's cavalcade with 500 porters to K2 in the same year. Unlike Shipton, in the abortive British attempt of 1952, Tichy had no qualms about trespassing across the Nangpa La into Chinese territory to set up base camp on what was likely to be the easier north-west side of Cho Oyu in Tibet. In their first attempt they were caught in a storm and Tichy was badly frostbitten trying to save his tent. On their second try, climbing in agony but determined not to be beaten by a rival Swiss party, he was nursed by Jöchler and Pasang to the summit, which was reached at 3 pm on 19 October. Reflecting on the climb 30 years later, Tichy wrote: 'Life there becomes a thrilling and happy experience. True, thoughts become confused, but vision – and I don't just mean what you see, I mean inner vision, too – becomes more acute. It allows you to forget everyday worries. That may sound contrary, but most people who have been above 8,000 metres – and there are now many of them – will vouch for this experience.'

Makalu – Ten on Top

In 1955, the French redeemed their harrowing experiences on Annapurna in 1950. The expedition was a model of organisation under the leadership of Jean Franco, and reached the summit on 15 May, just ten days before the British climbed Kangchenjunga. During a reconnaissance the previous autumn, they had also made the first ascent of Makalu II, or Chomo Lonzo (25,640 ft/7,815 m). On Makalu (27,766 ft/8,463 m), over three successive days, all nine European climbers reached the top, as well as their sirdar Gyalzen, an unprecedented event. Lionel Terray and Jean Couzy, neither of whom had the chance of reaching the top of Annapurna in 1950, were the first summit pair. But Franco's expedition book was not nearly as successful as Herzog's on Annapurna. As Mick Conefrey remarks in his recent book, *A Teacup in a Storm*: 'Suffering sells. There is nothing like a good frost-bite story or near-death experience to shift an exploration book.' Painography pays!

1956 A Bumper Year, Lhotse, Manaslu and Gasherbrum II

Lhotse, at 27,940 feet (8,516 metres) forming part of the Everest horseshoe, was now the world's highest unclimbed peak. The Swiss, with the support of their Foundation for Alpine Research, decided to make a second ascent of Everest and tackle Lhotse as well. Under the leadership of Albert Eggler, they were successful

below: A telephoto of Makalu, Lhotse and Everest not long after dawn, from the North Col of Kangchenjunga.

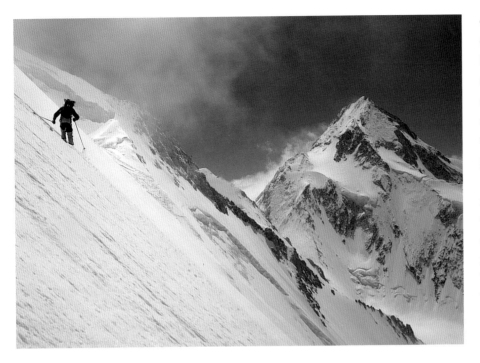

above: Iain Peter, until recently head of the National Mountaineering Centre at Plas-y-Brenin, skis down from the summit of Gasherbrum II on 9 July 1987. Beyond is the south-western flank of Gasherbrum I.

on both counts. On 18 May, using oxygen, Ernst Reiss and Fritz Luchsinger climbed Lhotse up a couloir from the South Col, in five and a half hours after leaving their tent, despite a cold and stormy day. It was the first ascent of an 8,000-metre peak by the Swiss.

The 8000-metre peaks were falling fast. Tilman's small party in 1950 were the first European mountaineers to approach Manaslu (26,781 ft/8,163 m) in Nepal, close to the Tibetan border. They decided to leave it to better men. When much later I crossed the 5,200-metre Larkya La to the north of the mountain with a trekking party after a snowstorm in 1999, I also agreed it looked very impressive. It had become a Japanese preserve; four expeditions, one after the other, explored climbing possibilities from the north side as well as via the east ridge. Eventually, under the leadership of Y Maki, it was climbed from the north-east side, by what later become the normal route, on 9 May by T Imanishi and Gyalzen Norbu and on 11 May 1956 by K Kato and M Higeta.

Gasherbrum II (26,360 ft/8,035 m) is generally considered the easiest of the eight-thousanders. The Gasherbrum group was first explored in 1909 on the Duke of Abruzzi's expedition, and in 1934 an international expedition led by G O Dyhenfurth reached about 6,250 metres on the south side. An Austrian expedition under Fritz Moravec made the first ascent by the south-west ridge, then crossing near the top to the east ridge. Larch, Willenpart and Moravec topped out on 7 July. In 1984, a Frenchman and a Swiss skied down from the summit!

BROAD PEAK

Martin Conway bestowed the name on this mountain in 1892. It has three summits, the highest 26,400 feet (8,047 metres). Vittorio Sella brought back photographs in 1909. The first attempt to climb it was by a German–Austrian expedition led by Herrligkoffer in 1954 but they chose a poor route and gave up around 6,900 metres.

Then in 1957, an Austrian team of four came out: Marcus Schmuck, Fritz Wintersteller, Hermann Buhl, and a young alpinist, Kurt Diemberger. It was a modern alpine-style expedition with three high camps, but moving continuously up the mountain: no high-altitude porters; no fixed ropes. Climbing in pairs, Schmuck and Wintersteller summitted first. On the final day, Buhl was going more slowly, perhaps he had not recovered fully from the ordeal of Nanga Parbat. Diemberger went back to accompany him to the summit in the failing light, so Buhl became the first man to be on the first ascent of two 8,000-metre peaks but he did not have long to enjoy the achievement.

They split up, the first pair to make the first ascent of Skilbrum (23,345 ft/7,420 m) and the second pair to try Chogolisa (25,110 ft/7,654 m). Turning back when the weather deteriorated, they descended unroped on a corniced ridge in white-out conditions. Diemberger drew ahead. When Buhl didn't appear, he climbed back up and found a jagged bite in the cornice with tracks leading into it. It is an easy thing to do. I was on a similar corniced ridge on Rakaposhi in 1954, in clear weather, climbing second in a roped party of four. The leader was following tracks from two days previously – obviously too close to the potential fracture line – when the whole lot suddenly collapsed and the two men behind me were precipitated over the edge together with tons of snow. Instantaneously, I had to plunge down the opposite slope to counterbalance them; the rope bit deeply into the crest and fortunately held. Without a rope my two companions would certainly have died.

GASHERBRUM I, THE HIDDEN PEAK

Martin Conway coined the name Hidden Peak (26,470 ft/8,068 m) to distinguish it from its neighbour, Gasherbrum II. Dyhrenfurth's 1934 international expedition got to about 6,300 metres and a French one led by Henri de Ségogne in 1936 to some 6,900 metres on the South Spur. But it needed a post-war American team in 1958 to pull it off. It was led by a lawyer, Nick Clinch, who was to become their most successful expedition leader, and also a close personal friend. Peter Schoening, who had held the incredible multiple fall on K2 in 1953, went to the summit with Andy Kauffman. The following year Nick Clinch was elected to the Alpine Club and made an honorary member in 1999.

His parents lived in Dallas and I was most grateful to him in 1959 when I was posted by Shell to the desert oil town of Midland in West Texas not knowing anybody. He sought me out and invited my wife and me to spend New Year with them in Dallas. By local tradition, we ate black-eye peas on New Year's Eve and on New Year's Day had tickets for the University football game at the Cotton Bowl with Texas playing Syracuse. As a new patriot, when the teams entered the stadium, I joined in the stirring tones of 'The eyes of Texas are upon you …' with my right palm clasped firmly over my heart.

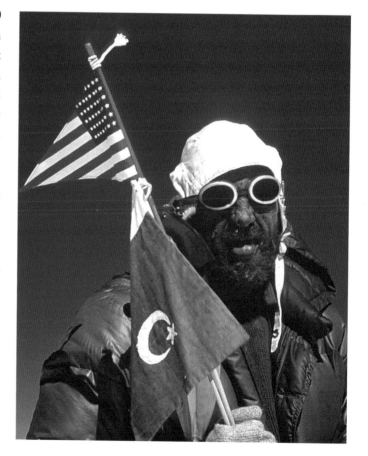

below: Andy Kauffman on the summit of Gasherbrum I (named Hidden Peak by Conway in 1892) which he reached with Peter Schoening on 5 July 1958. This is the only 8,000-m peak first climbed by an American team, led by Nick Clinch.

DHAULAGIRI

Dhaulagiri (26,795 ft/8,167 m), the sixth highest, proved a tougher nut to crack than most of the other eight-thousanders. The first aerial photographs were taken in 1949, and over the next decade there were four successive expeditions by French, Swiss, Argentinian and Austrian groups. These were on the north side and generally failed around 8,000 metres. One of the problems was the lack of suitable ledges for tents high up. There was even talk of taking up some explosives to help create them. Then in 1960 the Swiss, Max Eiselin, led a group following the north-east ridge which gained the summit on 13 and 23 May: Forrer, Schelbert, Vaucher, Weber from Switzerland, Diener from Germany, and Diembeger from Austria, with the Sherpas Nima Dorje and Nawang Dorje, all without using oxygen. An unusual feature was that a Pilatus Porter light aircraft was used to fly equipment in to the base camp.

So Kurt Diemberger became the second person, after Hermann Buhl, to be on the first ascent of two 8,000-metre peaks, but he still lives to tell the tale. He very kindly gave me in April 2000 a signed copy of an amazing 360-degree panoramic photograph from the summit of Everest which he took on 15 October 1978. He is another honorary member of the Alpine Club and did much of his high-altitude filming and climbing with Julie Tullis, from Britain, another member who died after reaching the top of K2 in 1986. It was a very sad year in which a total of 13 people died on that 'Savage Mountain' in a series of accidents, when they were caught up in a prolonged storm. Here Kurt reflects on his climbing philosophy:

When Hermann Buhl fell to his death in 1957 and I was left to find my own way back down through the mist to the valley, across the snowfields and icefalls of Chogolisa, it certainly cost me one of my seven lives. In the summer of 1986, when I was making a summit attempt on K2 with Julie Tullis, and not only my companion but four others in our group of seven lost their lives, those long days of storm and the never-ending descent just as certainly robbed me of another. How do you explain survival? Left on your own, where does the 'Never give up!' come from? It is something that has often puzzled me.

I believe what is important for survival is that the people who climb high must not just aim for the top single-mindedly, but also be very critical of the way they carry out their undertaking. Reinhold Messner has described me as the 'only mountaineer to have survived throughout the whole history of 8000 m climbing and remained active'. I have to say, I have seen a lot of changes.

below: A 'rope' bridge on the way to Gasherbrum, made mostly of twisted twigs rather than rope.

SHISHA PANGMA, THE LAST EIGHT-THOUSANDER

All the other 13 eight-thousanders were climbed in the decade from 1950 to 1960. But Shisha Pangma (26,397 ft/8,046 m), formerly better known by its Indian name of Gosainthan, lay totally in Tibet and this was out of bounds to all but Chinese and Tibetan climbers. And it was they who made the first ascent in 1964, after a reconnaissance the previous year. They had a large team, and on 2 May six Chinese and four Tibetans reached the summit by the north-west face and north ridge.

While doing the background reading for this book, I came across an interesting Shisha Pangma story in Michael Ward's autobiography, *In This Short Span*. In 1962, there was a China–Nepal Boundary Commission. The Nepalese co-chairman mentioned to Colonel Charles Wylie, who was then the British military attaché in Kathmandu, that the Nepalese might give permission for a British party to attempt Shisha Pangma. Although it might be on the Tibetan side of the watershed, it could be approached through Nepal and one need not descend below 19,000 feet into Tibet where the nearest habitation was over 20 miles away. Michael Ward was not one to pass up such a golden opportunity for the last unclimbed 8,000-metre peak, so he quickly sought support from the Alpine Club, wrote to the Mount Everest Foundation asking for funding, and put together a potentially very strong team. They waited for the formal permission to come from the Nepalese Government and then, in Michael Ward's words:

'It was not until May 1964 that we saw in the newspapers that the Chinese had climbed the mountain from its Tibetan side, taking a party of 195 mountaineers. Ten of them had reached the summit, and a bust of Mao Tse-tung had been placed there together with the Chinese National flag. That was the end of British interest in Gosainthan, and all that remains of our aspirations are two large and bursting files'.

THE REASONS FOR SUCCESS?

So how can one explain this sudden success on all the 8,000-metre peaks after a century of striving? In a nutshell: politics, science, planning and leadership. Between the 1930s and the 1950s, including the war years, there had clearly been time for considerable improvement in clothing and equipment, development of climbing boots and new textiles and materials; lighter and stronger nylon ropes, and particularly improved oxygen apparatus considered to be necessary for at least the top three peaks. Of great importance was the better knowledge of high-altitude physiology, the process of acclimatisation and the effects of dehydration at high altitude; thanks largely to the studies of scientists such as Dr Griffith Pugh from the Medical Research Council who was specially attached to the British Cho Oyu Expedition in 1952 and to the successful Everest Expedition the following year. Then there was the breaking of a psychological barrier, similar to that of the four-minute mile. Once one or two had been climbed, then all the rest were possible! The opening of Nepal to mountaineers in 1950 brought six new 8,000-metre peaks totally into the arena, plus the Nepalese sides of Everest and Kangchenjunga which had previously been out of bounds.

Finally, one sees the benefit of setting clear objectives, thorough planning and organisation, together with inspired leadership. John Hunt's Basis for Planning drawn up in London before the expedition's departure, and included as Appendix III in his book *The Ascent of Everest*, provided a template on which all later siege-style expeditions could be modelled, as acknowledged by leaders such as Professor Desio, Charles Evans and Christian Bonington.

THE FIRST BRITONS ON 8,000-METRE PEAKS

To conclude this chapter I have researched when British mountaineers succeeded in climbing all the 8,000-metre peaks. The last to be climbed was Makalu on 9 October 1995, more than 42 years after the first ascent of Everest by a British team led by John Hunt in 1953 when Edmund Hillary, from New Zealand, and Sherpa Tenzing Norgay reached the summit on 29 May. So no Brit actually stood on Everest's summit until Doug Scott and Dougal Haston succeeded by the south-west face route on 24 September 1975.

Here is the complete British list, as far as I have been able to ascertain, thanks largely to the data given in Richard Sale and John Cleare's *On Top of the World* (2000), published by HarperCollins. Nearly all the climbers were members of the Alpine Club. All climbs are by the first ascent route except where indicated. A cross after the name denotes 'died on the descent'.

Peak	Location	Metres	Feet	Date	Names
Everest	Nepal/Tibet	8,850	29,035	24.9.75	Dougal Haston, Doug Scott
				26.9.75	Peter Boardman (Nos 50, 51, 52)
					Mick Burke † (all SW face)
K2	Pakistan/China	8,611	28,250	4.8.86	Julie Tullis † , Alan Rouse †
				2.9.93	Jonathan Pratt, Dan Mazur (US)
					(W ridge/SW face)
Kangchenjunga	India/Nepal	8,586	28,169	25.5.55	Joe Brown, George Band
				26.5.55	Norman Hardie (NZ), Tony Streather
Lhotse	Nepal/Tibet	8,516	27,940	10.5.95	Keith Kerr
Makalu	Nepal/Tibet	8,463	27,766	9.10.95	Andy Collins, Jonathan Pratt (SE ridge)
Dhaulagiri	Nepal	8,167	26,795	18.5.80	Alex MacIntyre (E Face to NE ridge)
Manaslu	Nepal	8,163	26,781	12.5.89	Alan Hinkes (S face)
Cho Oyu	Nepal/Tibet	8,201	26,906	30.4.88	Dave Walsh
Nanga Parbat	Pakistan	8,125	26,660	21.7.91	Dave Walsh, Roger Mear
Annapurna	Nepal	8,091	26,545	20.5.70	Henry Day, G F Owens
				27.5.70	Don Whillans, Dougal Haston (S face)
Gasherbrum I (Hidden Peak)	Pakistan/China	8,068	26,470	4.8.94	Jonathan Pratt (Japanese couloir)
				12.8.94	Andy Collins (Japanese couloir)
Broad Peak	Pakistan/China	8,047	26,400	25.6.83	Roger Baxter-Jones, Andy Parkin, Alan Rouse,
				28.6.83	Doug Scott
Shisha Pangma	Tibet	8,046	26,397	28.5.82	Roger Baxter-Jones, Alex MacIntyre,
					Doug Scott (Central couloir SW face)
Gasherbrum II	Pakistan/China	8,035	26,360	28.6.87	Richard Thorns
				9.7.87	Iain Peter, Donald Stewart

The country whose mountaineers were the first to climb all 14 eight-thousanders was West Germany, followed by Japan and Switzerland.

8 Exposed Ridges, Steep Faces, to the 1970s

THANKS TO THE MOUNT EVEREST FOUNDATION

In some ways it was a relief to get the first ascents of all the 8,000-metre peaks out of the way. 'Now we can get back to some real climbing' was the verdict of the keenest mountaineers. There were literally hundreds of unclimbed 6,000-metre and 7,000-metre peaks presenting exciting challenges which did not require such elaborate planning, organisation and fund-raising, the use of expensive oxygen apparatus, or a lengthy period of acclimatisation to extreme altitude. Himalayan mountaineering could become an enjoyable holiday activity again!

In this respect, British climbers have been greatly helped by the creation of the Mount Everest Foundation (MEF), which also took over the role and assets of the Joint Himalayan Committee. This was an imaginative and far-sighted initiative set up after the first ascent of Everest in 1953, being financed from the proceeds of some £100,000 raised from John Hunt's expedition book, Tom Stobart's film, and the lectures which the team members gave throughout Britain during the following year. I myself spoke six times in the Royal Festival Hall. The MEF's principal aim is to encourage exploration and science in the world's mountain regions, and it is a registered charity. It is managed jointly by the Alpine Club and the Royal Geographical Society, with a screening committee to interview potential expedition leaders to ensure that their team has the competence to undertake their chosen objective, which has to be a new peak, or route, or high quality exploration or research – not just repeating a known climb. Armed with the MEF's 'seal of approval', the embryo expedition can more easily seek additional funds and donations to cover the balance above the members' own contributions.

Originally, we thought that the fund would be dissipated within 10 to 15 years, but the management committee invested the capital prudently and mostly only distributed the annual dividends to provide priming support for expeditions. An exception was Charles Evans' successful 1955 expedition to Kangchenjunga, costing £13,652, which was totally funded by the Foundation. Each year now the Foundation pays out in total some £20,000 to £30,000 to about 30 to 50 expeditions and at this rate could continue indefinitely. Since its inception, it has dispensed £780,000 to 1,400 expeditions to greater mountain ranges in all parts of the world: China/Tibet, USA, Antarctica, Greenland and Kyrgyzstan currently being the most popular destinations. These are mostly smaller lightweight expeditions, often carried out in Alpine-style continuous movement in contrast to the siege tactics frequently used on the Himalayan giants. This support

left: Evening light on the south face of Annapurna. The British route of 1970 is broadly up the left-hand spur.

below: Bill Ruthven, the dedicated Hon. Secretary to the Mount Everest Foundation, at the Alpine Club Annual Dinner on 3 December 2005. The website is **www.mef.org.uk**

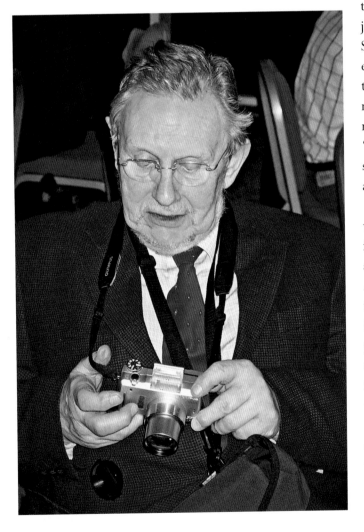

by the MEF is the envy of climbers in other countries. Over the years, it has also had a snowball effect in training and giving experience to future leaders. A participant on his or her first successful expedition will soon want to apply for a grant to launch or lead their own group.

I will now highlight some of the successes from the 1950s and 1960s involving British climbers who were also mostly members of the Alpine Club.

THE MUZTAGH TOWER
(23,860 FT/7,273 M)

The Muztagh Tower was discovered and so named by Martin Conway in August 1892 during the first expedition to the upper Baltoro glacier in the Karakoram. It was Vittorio Sella's famous telephotograph, taken from the south-east, on the Duke of Abruzzi's expedition in 1909, that created the legend of the unclimbable mountain. 'It appears, and perhaps is, a true monolith, a rocky mass of single formation – without traces of breaks or divisional planes – no other of any comparable size is known to exist on the globe.' But Conway recognised that its extremely precipitous appearance from the upper reaches of the Baltoro glacier is deceptive. It is a relatively thin but elongated peak, whose south-east arête appears quite accessible. 'It is the peak we ought to have climbed, for its position is superb.'

From the age of 14 when he first read about the mountain in R L G Irving's *Romance of Mountaineering*, John Hartog dreamed of climbing the Muztagh Tower. In May 1956, Ian McNaught-Davis, then in East Africa, agreed by letter to join him and share the leadership and financial responsibility. The other two members of the party, Joe Brown and Tom Patey, only joined up in March, less than three weeks before their ship sailed. Nobody had ever previously dared to attempt the mountain. It had two possible ridges, the north-west and south-east, each leading to a summit, with the two summits being about 400 yards apart, separated by a col less than 100 feet lower. After reconnaissance, they decided on the north-west ridge from the Chagaran glacier, aiming to summit early in July.

McNaught-Davis and Patey were the first to reach the col at the foot of the ridge and were impressed by what they saw. It was going to be hard and exposed. They knew that a strong French expedition was also in the Karakoram that year: Guido Magnone, Robert Paragot, Keller, and Contamine. To his con-

below: The diagram shows the opposing ridges taken by the British and French teams on the first ascent in 1956.

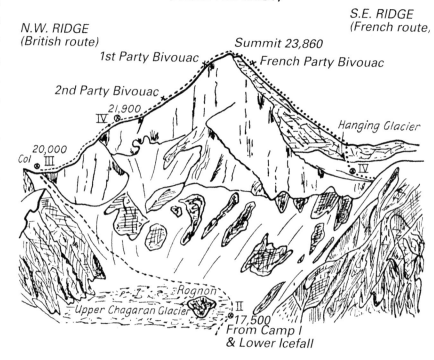

MUZTAGH TOWER (FROM THE WEST)

N.W. RIDGE
(British route)

S.E. RIDGE
(French route,

1st Party Bivouac

Summit 23,860

French Party Bivouac

2nd Party Bivouac

21,900
IV

Hanging Glacier

20,000
Col   III

IV

Rognon

Upper Chagaran Glacier

II

17,500
From Camp I
& Lower Icefall

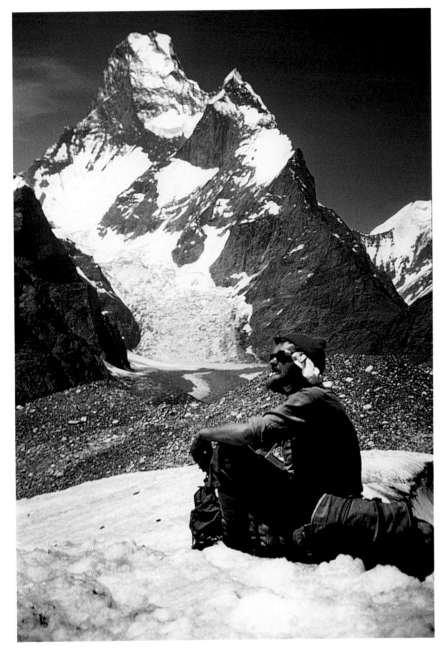

above: Ian McNaught-Davis contemplates the challenge of the Muztagh Tower, looking utterly impregnable from the south-east.

sternation, on 18 June at base camp, Hartog was handed a letter from Magnone saying that they too were planning to climb the Tower, but would now switch to the south-east ridge from the Younghusband glacier. It would be an international race for the summit!

A thousand feet of rope was fixed up to camp 3 on the col at 20,000 feet and a final camp 4 at 21,900 feet. Brown and McNaught-Davis made the first attempt on 6 July, both describing it as the hardest day's work they had ever done in their lives. They reached the west summit at 6.30 pm, visited the col between the summits, then returned 300 feet down the ridge to bivouac for the night. Patey and Hartog followed the next day: Hartog describes how 'the individual moves, on rock ledges, across icy couloirs, unstable snow slopes, a rock chimney, an *à cheval* across a chockstone wedged across the top of an ice-gully, were far more frightening to me the first time up than a second time, either up or down'. Thanks to the steps cut or consolidated by the first pair, they reached the west summit four hours sooner and had the energy to continue to the east summit, including a tricky little grade V slab, and according to John's aneroid, it was the true summit, just three metres higher. They too bivouacked on the descent, Tom Patey concerned about frostbite but John Hartog could wiggle his toes so felt happy. Next morning Joe Brown and Ian McNaught-Davis came up some way to meet them. Hartog wrote: 'How exciting that meeting was; they were so glad to see us, with we to see them. I'd picked up a glove Joe had dropped higher up and gave it to him. He was touched. Mac said I was so excited that I was talking as if I was drunk. But I was, intoxicated with happiness; alcohol isn't necessary to achieve that state'. In the event it was John Hartog who fell sick, exhausted and got frostbitten toes, and had to be carried out with the generous help of the French expedition, who also climbed the mountain by their route on 12/13 July. Hartog thought the mountain was technically the hardest climbed in the Himalaya to that date and said: 'The kindness of the French remains for me one of the noblest deeds in the history of international mountaineering – the conversion of rivalry to great friendship and affection.'

RAKAPOSHI
(25,550 FT/7,788 M)

This is a most beautiful mountain domi-nating the fabled Hunza valley in northern Pakistan. Unlike the Muztagh Tower, Rakaposhi required several seri-ous attempts before it succumbed, by way of the south-west spur and south-west rdge, to a British/Pakistani Forces Expedition in 1958. The base camp was at only 14,500 feet, so some 11,000 feet and a considerable distance of climbing was involved, offering problems of organisation and logistics comparable to those of the higher 8,000-metre peaks. Our Cambridge party in 1954 (which was privileged to receive the Mount Everest Foundation's first ever grant of £1,000) managed to climb a prominent feature on the ridge known as the Monk's Head, to about 21,000 feet (6,400 metres). We felt we had opened the door to the summit, but a British–American four-man team in 1956 established that three more camps were still necessary above the Monk's Head and they failed only 1,500 feet

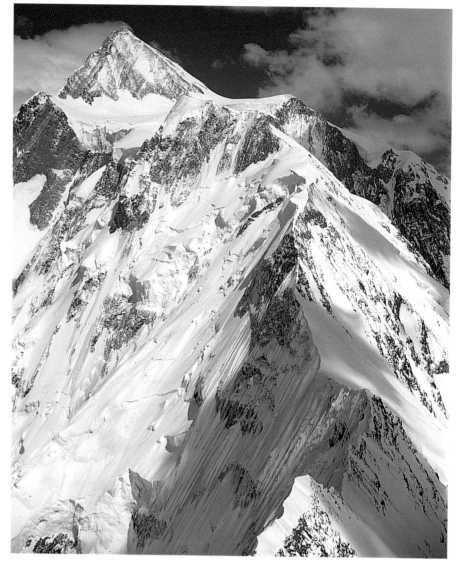

above: A view of Rakaposhi in 1954, looking along the north-west ridge from the top of the 19,350-ft Secord Peak.

from the top. All three expeditions had hair-raising experiences of one kind or another; collapsing cornices, spectacular falls, electric storms and a giant windslab avalanche.

'Commando Climber' Captain Mike Banks of the Royal Marines organised and led the 1956 and 1958 expeditions, keeping an eye open for Tom Patey, fresh from the Muztagh Tower, who was due to undergo National Service and now appeared, not entirely by coincidence, in the Royal Navy as Surgeon-Lieutenant Patey, serv-ing in the Commando School where Banks himself was stationed, and from which he joined the 1958 expedition. Tom Patey describes a little incident climbing with Richard Brooke up the 1,200-feet face from the Kunti glacier to the crest of the south-west spur:

> I was only 200 ft from the crest. The snow was excellent for kicking steps with a firm surface crust. Suddenly a shout broke the stillness. 'I say, I'm certain I felt the slope move just now.' I made a mental note for the physiological diary: 'Brooke, hallucinations, not yet fully acclimatised.'

above: Two shepherd boys visit the Rakaposhi base camp.

right: A diagram of Rakaposhi from the south-west, showing the route and camps up the south-west spur and ridge of the first complete ascent in 1958.

His next shout, seconds later, was drowned in a dull roar as the whole slope avalanched. An area about the size of a football field broke away above and below us. At the instant we felt ourselves moving we drove our axes firmly into the stable underlying névé and hung on grimly. A tremendous weight of snow piled up against my body, but just as the pressure became unbearable I managed to deflect it past me with a mighty heave. The crisis was all over in ten seconds, but perhaps a minute later we saw the debris spill out on the lower slopes 2,000 ft below.

The silence was broken by Richard, picking his words deliberately with an admirable display of *sang-froid* as befits an Alpine Club member. 'This place is distinctly dangerous. I propose that we turn back.'

The two were stunned by the incident; giant windslab on a scale beyond their experience. The snow that day was the firmest they had met on the mountain. Despite such incidents, on 25 June Mike Banks and Tom Patey were able to battle the last 1,500 feet from their high camp to the summit, reached at 2 pm, fighting for every step in blizzard conditions.

Patey had quite severely frost-bitten fingers and on the descent treated himself with Priscal and an intravenous injection of Heparin to help thin the blood. There was some talk of his losing the top joints of his fingers. 'That would ruin your chances as a surgeon, wouldn't it?' asked Banks. 'I suppose so, but I was worrying about not being able to play my accordion!' he replied. There was little more to add, concluded Patey in his autobiography, save that Hunza apricots are the most luscious fruit known to man, and on our return to the valley we did them full justice.

MEMORIES OF TOM PATEY

Very sadly, Tom Patey was killed on 25 May 1970 when abseiling from a Scottish sea stack. He was just 38 years old. He had settled as a local GP in the fishing port of Ullapool in one of the most beautiful parts of north-west Scotland. He was a master climber, brilliant at moving fast over difficult ground and at his best on mixed routes of rock, ice and snow. I first met him in the bar at Pen-y-Gwryd. He produced a sheaf of large photographs of an astonishing sandstone sea stack, a 450-feet unclimbed admonishing finger of rock, the Old Man of Hoy. 'It's just made for a television spectacular,' he said. Indeed, after several trials by seasickness, and tribulations with gannets, fulmars and loose rock he had made a daring first ascent by the east face with Chris Bonington and the Rhodesian Rusty Baillie in 1966. Thanks to Chris Brasher and Alan Chivers of BBC Outside Broadcasts it all came about, and 15 million people thrilled to the live spectacle of six expert climbers at work on this incredible pinnacle. Years later in 1988, aged 59, I had the thrill of becoming the oldest man to have climbed it – with a very good leader – but this accolade was resoundingly passed to Mike Banks when he climbed it in 1990 and again in 1994 at the age of 77, in aid of 'ME', the Chronic Fatigue Syndrome. Tom Patey was the greatest entertainer in the climbing world – a composer of ballads about the Alpine Club or his friends, Joe Brown and Christian Bonington. His songs are satirical without being vicious and I cannot resist including here and now, the one about Sir Chris, who was then President of the Alpine Climbing Group and who currently is the august Chancellor of Lancaster University. It is sung to St Gertrude, the familiar tune of 'Onward Christian Soldiers':

below: The irrepressible Tom Patey playing his accordion despite badly frost-bitten fingers.

> Onward, Christian Bonington, of the ACG
> Write another page of Alpine history
> He has climbed the Eigerwand, he has climbed the Dru –
> For a mere ten thousand francs, he will climb with you:
> Onward, Christian Bonington of the ACG
> If you name the mountain, he will name the fee.
> Like a mighty army, faithfully we plod,
> Treading in the footsteps Bonington has trod.
> From the Direttissima loud Hosannas ! ring –
> Grave, where is thy victory, O death, where is thy sting?
> Onward, Christian Bonington joyfully we sing,
> Down with McNaught-Davis, Bonington for King.
>
> Live transmission will commence shortly after ten
> From the Kleine Scheidegg and the Alpi-Glen.
> Do not miss this spectacle, you can watch for free:
> Bonington is on the wall, Tune in on B.B.C.

Onward, Christian Bonington of the B.B.C.
Fighting for survival, and a token fee.
When they climbed the Eigerwand, those two gallant men
They received a message (sent) from Number Ten:
Well done chaps, Macmillan said, Victory was your due;
Well done Christian Bonington the Führer's proud of you –
Onward, Christian Bonington, hallowed be thy name,
Digging out a belay in the halls of fame.

CHRIS BONINGTON'S EXPEDITION APPRENTICESHIP

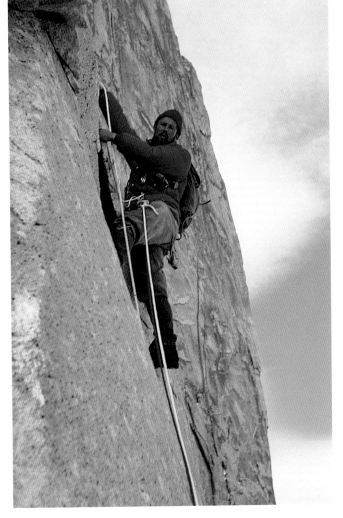

below: Chris Bonington on the steep upper section of the Central Tower of Paine.

Sir Christian John Storey Bonington is tough and competent enough to withstand such leg-pulling. It was in the early 1960s that he began to extend his reputation as a top alpine climber to the Greater Ranges and serve his expedition apprenticeship. In 1960, he climbed Annapurna II, a 26,041-feet (7,937-metre) peak just below the magic 8,000-metre level. This was a traditional Combined Services siege-style expedition led by the very experienced former Gurkha officer, Jimmy Roberts and with a strong team of Sherpa high-altitude porters. On the final push, Dick Grant, Ang Nyima and Chris Bonington reached the top using oxygen.

The summit day was a long hard slog, but the pyramid itself suddenly gave some real climbing, scrambling over broken rock, scrabbling up snow-covered ice. I forgot my fatigue and became immersed in the climbing and then suddenly we were on top, the mountain falling away on every side, my first unclimbed peak and to this day the highest unclimbed peak I have ever attained.

But though that success was all important to me, my richest memory of that expedition was walking out with just Tashi, the oldest of our Sherpas, over the Tilitso pass, first discovered by Maurice Herzog in his 1950 recce, and enjoying three days of quiet companionship with this immensely wise and compassionate Sherpa.

Next year both Bonington and Tashi joined an expedition to Nuptse, at 25,850 feet (7,879 metres) the last unclimbed summit of the Everest horseshoe. Led by Joe Walmsley, this was a less structured venture, seven individualistic climbers and six dedicated Sherpas. They shared the load-carrying and lead climbing up the virgin south face using up all their fixed rope and having to buy more locally. Morale flagged. Two of the

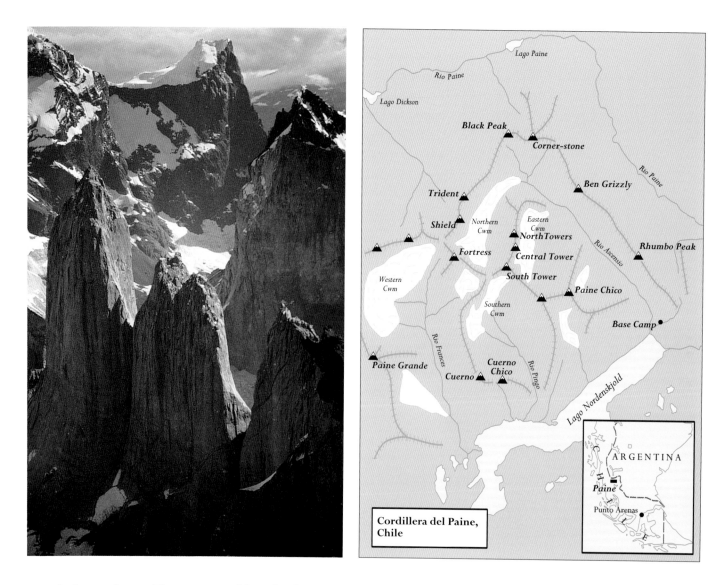

Cordillera del Paine,
Chile

team had to go home. The rest argued but slowly gained height in a drawn out battle of attrition. At last they were working well as a team. Dennis Davis and Tashi moved up to make the first ascent on 16 May and then Jim Swallow, Ang Pemba and Chris Bonington repeated the climb the next day.

Two years later he was in southern Chile joining forces with Barry Page, Derek Walker and Vic Bray who had been there the previous year, 1961, and discovered the enormous potential of the Towers of Paine for superb rock climbs. Don Whillans, John Streetly and Ian Clough completed the strong team, bonded by previous climbing experience together. The sheer-sided Central Tower was the obvious challenge, although only 8,760 feet (2,670 metres) in height. From a col between the North and Central Towers, they made some progress until the ferocious winds struck, ripped their tents to bits, and forced them to retreat back to the valley for Christmas. It was Don's inspiration to replace the torn tents with a rigid prefabricated timber and tarpaulin box erected at the foot of the Tower – the 'Whillans Box'. A sign outside in bold yellow letters proclaimed 'Brittania Hut – Members only'. This became the prototype for the box tents used on the southwest face of Everest in the 1970s, with improved design by Hamish MacInnes.

above: A map of the Cordillera del Paine.

above left: An aerial view of the Towers of Paine, with the Central and North Towers in the foreground and the Fortress beyond on the right.

below: Whillans and Clough admire the first ever 'Whillans Box', proof against the ferocious winds that had ripped their tents to bits.

At the end of December, an Italian team arrived, also bound for the Central Tower. As with the Muztagh Tower, a certain rivalry developed! Eventually, during two fine days, Whillans and Bonington made a bid for the summit. They reached it at dusk and bivouacked just below the top. Descending next morning, they passed the Italians on their way up. They had been using sisal ropes as fixed ropes which were easily frayed by the wind and twice when they suddenly parted there were near fatal accidents. Badly shaken, Chris left the expedition to explore southern Chile with his newly wed wife, Wendy. After these three contrasting expeditions, Chris spent some seven years building up a career as a photo-journalist before he returned to expeditioning. Nevertheless, as he wrote many years later, they provided a foundation on which to build, not just the techniques of leading and organisation, but finding a deeper and more profound enjoyment of the mountain environment and the people with whom he climbed.

ANNAPURNA SOUTH FACE

In the late 1960s, the Himalayan countries were closed to foreign climbers because of political tensions Kampa Tibetan rebels were fighting the Chinese from bases in Nepal and India and there were continuing problems in Kashmir between Pakistan and India following Partition. When the Himalayas re-opened in 1969, there was a flood of expeditions. Since all the 8,000-metre peaks had been climbed by their easier routes and many of the 7,000-metre peaks as well, attention was turning to the big unclimbed walls such as the south-west face of Everest, the Rupal face of Nanga Parbat and the west buttress of Makalu.

Chris was itching to get back on a climbing expedition, and a photograph of the south face of Annapurna fired his imagination. He decided to go for it. The Mount Everest Foundation agreed to underwrite the cost; Don Whillans designed the box tents, and also his waist harness from which many other designs have evolved; Mike Thompson planned the food. Chris co-ordinated it all, learning on the job. 'In many ways,' he wrote, 'the South Face of Annapurna was the greatest challenge that I have ever faced and the most satisfying climb, since it was such a step into the unknown, into the realms of expedition leadership on a mountain face that was bigger and steeper than anything that had previously been attempted'. He was learning that 'the best position for the leader of a large expedition is at the camp immediately below that of the lead climbers. Here he can keep in touch with what is going on at the front and have a good feel for how the supplies are flowing up the mountain. This was the position adopted by John Hunt at the crucial stages of the 1953 Everest expedition and it still seems a sound one on more technical climbs.'

Base camp was at 14,000 feet, giving a full view of the daunting 10,000-feet wall of steep ice and rock they had come to climb. An ice ridge led up to the mid-height snow slopes; above was a prominent rock band expected to be the crux. He estimated three days for the Ice Ridge but it took 18, with climbers taking turns to tackle the tortuous ice bosses and cornices. Mick Burke and Tom Frost climbed the Rock Band in several days of sustained effort, thereby opening the route to the summit. Don Whillans and Dougal Haston then moved up to the top camp, 6, at 24,000 feet, sitting out a week of bad weather. Then as it improved, they made a one-day dash for the summit, climbing unroped for most of the way. A blurred 16 mm movie frame shows Don at the summit. There was a sad price to pay for the achievement. As they were clearing the mountain, Ian Clough, with whom Chris had climbed both the Walker Spur and the Eigerwand, was swept to his death when an ice wall collapsed below camp 2.

EVEREST THE HARD WAY

On all four of his siege climbs on 8,000-metre peaks, and again in 1982, members of Chris Bonington's team had lost their lives: Tony Tighe in the Khumbu Icefall in 1972; Nick Estcourt in a huge windslab avalanche low on K2 in 1978; Mick Burke alone near Everest's summit in 1975; Peter Boardman and Joe Tasker on the unclimbed pinnacle section of the north-east ridge of Everest in 1982. However careful one tries to be, it just goes to show that climbing the highest peaks is a statistically dangerous activity. This is a risk that the whole team accepts in its desire to achieve success on a mountain, whether by a large siege-style expedition or a lightweight alpine-style push. Friends and relations of the bereaved may regard it as a selfish unjustified activity, but if the climbers wanted to eliminate risk, they would never leave base camp and would have to suppress those very qualities of enterprise, initiative and boldness that their friends and relatives admire.

above top: Don Whillans' victory pose on the summit of the Central Tower of Paine.

above: Whillans at Base Camp waiting for a fine spell.

left: Ian Clough traversing the fixed ropes on the steepest part of the Ice Ridge on the Annapurna South Face expedition, 1970.

Bonington went on to establish his public reputation on Everest, particularly in leading the first ascent of the south-west face in 1975, *Everest the Hard Way*, which I have described in my previous book. Through his continuing high-standard climbs, his books and his lectures, and his presidency of both the Alpine Club and the British Mountaineering Council, he has become a public spokesman on mountaineering and an ambassador for the sport. He was knighted in 1996. Reinhold Messner, the first person to climb all 14 8,000-metre peaks, generously says of Chris Bonington: 'When we go back to the 70s, Bonington was really the motor. And British climbers should understand that without him they would not have been leading in this period.

He was not the best climber, but he looked for the best ones. He organised the expedition; he found the money. And he had the idea for the Annapurna South Face. All over Europe – not only climbers but also normal people who were interested in mountaineering – we understood that this was something new, something great.'

AMA DABLAM

From the rigours of 8,000-metre peak expeditions, it is a relief to backtrack a little to what else was happening to British climbers in the late 1950s and 1960s. Anybody following the trail to Everest cannot fail to be captivated by the sheer-sided peak of Ama Dablam (22,493 ft / 6,856 m), dominating the skyline beyond Thyangboche monastery. The name means 'Mother's Locket', the mountain's long ridges resembling the enfolding arms of a Sherpani, and the upper hanging glacier being her Dablam or pendant locket. The mountain is photogenic from every direction. In 1953, I remember George Lowe, with all his New Zealand ice-climbing experience, saying, 'That peak will never be climbed.' A rash statement! You just have to spend longer looking at it first.

In 1960–1, the members of the Silver Hut Expedition, more properly known as the Himalayan Scientific and Mountaineering Expedition, led by Sir Edmund Hillary, spent all winter looking at it. They were primarily investigating the long-term effects of high altitude on man, based on the comparative comfort of a laboratory at 19,000 feet close to the Mingbo La, a pass just a mile and a half from Ama Dablam. There were four mountaineers in the research team, Barry Bishop, from the National Geographical Society, Michael Gill and Wally Romanes from New Zealand, and Alpine Club member Michael Ward. It was impossible to ignore the peak, even if it had not been so beautiful and looked so inaccessible. They confirmed with the scientific director, Griffith Pugh, that they had permission to climb mountains in the Mingbo valley. So during a slack period at the end of February, they determined to have a look at it. Michael Ward gives a detailed account in the *Climbers' Club Journal* 1962. Previously, Cunningham had reached about 20,000 feet on the south-west ridge but had been stopped by an overhang. They decided to investigate further where the ridge became a series of ragged and jagged turrets.

above: Members of the Annapurna South Face team, 1970, after the climb. Originally eleven climbers and six Sherpas, augmented by some 'London Sherpas' and a television team.

right: Kate Phillips at the top of the Ramp on Ama Dablam, climbed on 4 April 1990. She was only the second Briton up (after Mike Ward on the first ascent on 13 March 1961) and her companion, Brendan Murphy, was the first Irishman.

Luckily the more difficult pitches were on the sun-warmed east side of the ridge. Key features were a Yellow Tower, a Red Tower and a First and Second Step. They needed numerous pitons, a couple of wire ladders and 1,500 feet of fixed rope. Their two good Sherpas, Pemba Tensing and Gumen Dorje, were very apprehensive, saying it was a 'Sahib's path' and not a 'Sherpa path'. The team spent a week preparing the lower rock section above the Second Step. Their camp 4 was an ice cave on a sloping snowfield, still 1,500 feet from the summit. The last part was a series of snow and ice flutings, very impressive as they swept in parallel silver lines towards the blue sky and the summit ridge. The climbers followed a convenient diagonal fluting, in places very icy and steep at a general angle between 40° and 50°. Instead of the narrow ridge they had expected, the top was a snowcap, seamed by a crevasse, of about 100 yards by 30 yards.

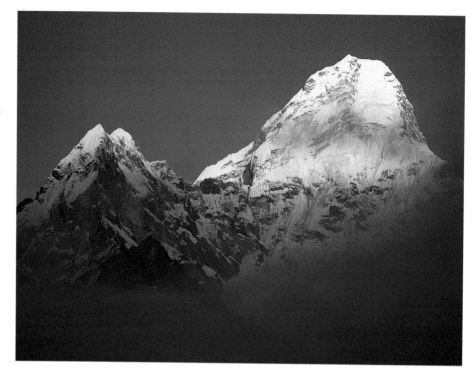

It was 13 March 1961, but the climb was not yet over. While helping to clear the lower part of the mountain, carrying very heavy loads, a rock gave way under Gumen Dorje and he broke his leg. He had to be carried down over very tricky ground and evacuated to Kathmandu. Michael Ward concluded: 'in length, character and variety I would compare the climb with the routes on the Italian side of Mont Blanc. The solitary situation of Ama Dablam, the great beauty and character of the mountain, the tenuous line of the route and the Alpine standard of difficulty made this a most memorable climb on an outstandingly lovely peak.'

It actually qualified as a winter ascent and the Kathmandu authorities considered it had been done without sufficient prior permission, so Ed Hillary had to fly back specially to Kathmandu to make amends! Ama Dablam has since deservedly become one of the most popular serious climbs in the Everest region.

above top: Sunset on Ama Dablam, chosen as the Club's Christmas card in about 1980.

above: The summit of Ama Dablam. The rope of three climbers making the first ascent on 13 March 1961 is just visible near the top of the snow and ice flutings.

INVITATION TO PERU

In the *Alpine Journal* volume 60 of May 1955, there appeared an article by one of our American members, John C Oberlin, entitled 'Invitation to the Andes'. It printed an enticing picture of mountaineering in Peru, illustrated by magnificent photographs of unclimbed peaks: Chacraraju, Pyramid, Huagaruncho, and Taulliraju. It ended: 'if you accept the invitation of the Andes of Peru you may glimpse the white spire of Salcantay from the rock-cut ruin of Machu Picchu far above the Urubamba gorge, you may lean against a palm tree in the plaza of Yungay to look upward at the peaks of Huascarán and the Huandoys, and there is no end to the trail leading into those enticing mountains'.

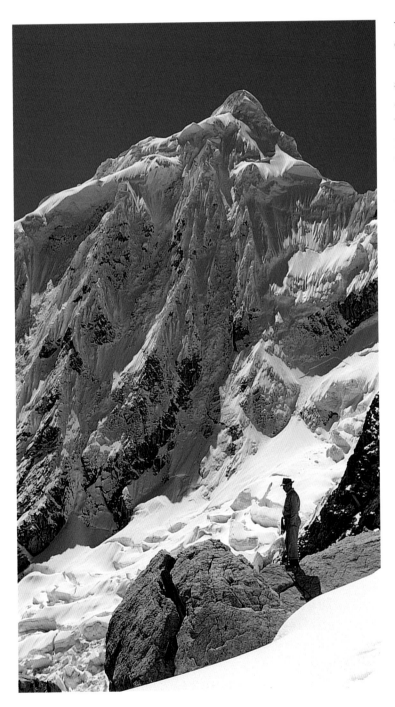

below: The sheer south face of Huagaruncho, near Huachon. We were told the Incas had placed a cross of gold on the summit!

To my knowledge, British mountaineers had not previously climbed in Peru. They had been to Ecuador (Whymper 1879–80). Aconcagua (FitzGerald and Vines 1897), Boliva (Conway 1898), Chile (Temperley 1912) and to Venezuela (Gunther and Chenery 1939–40). Six of us needed no second invitation: John Kempe, Jack Tucker, Donald Matthews (the nucleus from the Kangchenjunga 1954 reconnaissance), Michael Westmacott, John Streetly and myself, so we formed our own private party, our departure westward prompted by the red tape and expense associated with travel in the Indian and Nepal Himalaya. On arrival in Lima, one could just catch a bus or hire a truck to the Cordillera Blanca or adjacent ranges and climb wherever one wished without let or hindrance; no permits required or royalties to pay. Referring to the lesser ranges, Oberlin wrote: 'Undoubtedly Huagaruncho (18,797 ft/5,729 m) has achieved the greatest notoriety. Several attempts have been made on it without discovering a certain way to the top. Although below the 6,000 m mark it will be a great prize.'

When we arrived at the nearest village of Huachon, we were told that the Incas had climbed the mountain 400 years ago and left a cross of gold upon the summit. So they could understand our desire to retrieve it!

It proved an exciting climb. Trying the west ridge, we were forced by double cornices on to the steep south face, where we were astonished that soft deep powder snow could remain in place at such an angle; in the Alps it would have avalanched. Fortunately, where it had been disturbed it would freeze during the night and the next day prove rather more stable. Eventually, after days of hard work, on 17 August 1956 Westmacott and Streetly made it to the top in a white-out, but there was no cross of gold!

THE PUMA'S CLAW

During an earlier phase of the expedition, four of us had visited the Cordillera Vilcabamba beyond Cuzco and Machu Picchu in order to establish the precise location of another virgin peak, Pumasillo, at 20,490 feet (6,245 metres) claiming some notoriety as probably the highest virgin peak outside Asia. We did not have time to get really close, but it looked challenging so I recommended it to an enthusiastic Cambridge Mountaineering Club group as an objective for 1957. John Hunt agreed to be their patron and 'greatly helped us in our problem of getting an expedition with an average age of 22 taken seriously'. This also proved an exciting snow and ice route involving artificial climbing, and all seven climbers reached the summit in three separate groups, the first being on 23 July.

Young John Longland on the second rope describes the trail of devastation left by the first pair. 'Blades of snow had been felled like trees to leave narrow, airy walks, cornices sculpted, and towers of snow and ice had had their tops lopped off. Never have I seen such cornices as we steeple-chased along!' And finally the top: 'Ten feet of a pointed cone of snow and I was on the finest and most gratifying summit that I have ever been lucky enough to reach.' The terse cable to their patron summed up the whole exploit: 'All up, all down, all well, Pumasillo.' Joint leader Simon Clark, with Mike Gravina the first on top, wrote the delightful expedition book, *The Puma's Claw*, which concluded after their final dinner:

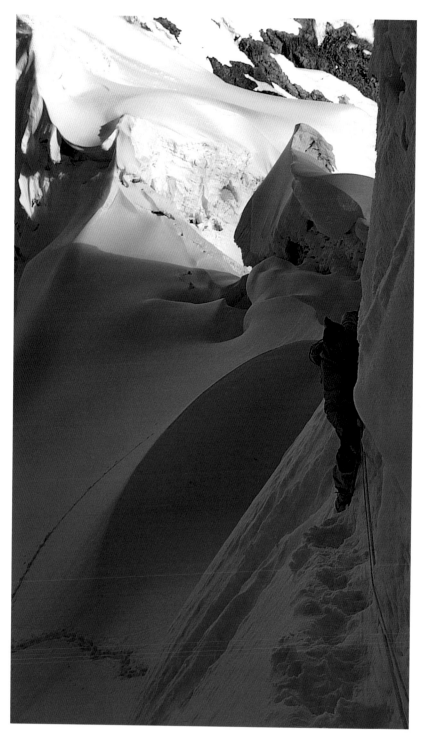

We took our rum to the bonfire which Harry had made close by: As it grew later someone produced the packets of fireworks we had bought in Chaullay before deserting the road on our way to the Vilcabamba. We splashed paraffin on the burning branches, and as the flames roared up I could feel the scorching heat on my chest, and at the same time the cold of the Andean night through the back of my duvet. So the evening grew to a close, with rum, a blazing fire, squibs bursting and spitting, and friends grouped around telling stories and singing, face now lost in shadow, now lit by a sudden flame.

above: John Kempe rounding an icy corner on the south face of Huagaruncho.

right: Simon Clark, moving up to summit Pumasillo on 23 July 1957, the 'Puma's Claw'.

RETURN TO THE FROSTY CAUCASUS

I think it was in 1953 that Dave Thomas, a member of the Climbers' Club, wrote a letter to Bulganin (who together with Nikita Khrushchev was then all powerful in the USSR) asking whether a group of British climbers might be allowed to climb in the Caucasus, continuing the tradition begun in 1886 by Dent, Donkin, Freshfield and others. Astonishingly during this Cold War period he received a reply that the time was not yet ripe, but low-key discussions were continued through other sporting and cultural links by Chris Brasher, Christopher Mayhew MP and the Soviet ambassador in London, Mr Malik. Meanwhile, John Hunt had visited Moscow in 1954 to tell Soviet mountaineers about the ascent of Everest, and two Russians, Eugene Beletski and Eugene Gippenreiter, had come to London to lecture to the Alpine Club in 1955. Finally, early in 1958, permission was received to climb that summer in the area of Ushba and the Bezingi glacier. It was a real coup; since the Russian Revolution in 1917 only one British expedition had climbed in the area, in 1937. We were an informal group of friends,

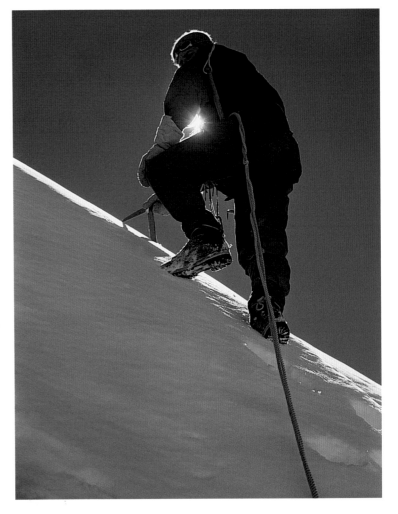

above: Mike Harris completing the new route up the south rib to the east peak of Dych-tau, July 1958. One of my best climbs.

being given added status by John Hunt, who asked to join the party. I was lucky to be included as the ninth and positively last member when I had a fortuitous six weeks leave from my new employer, Shell. We were worried about our level of fitness; the Russians would clearly expect us to be the 'A' team. Dave Thomas weighed nearly 17 stone but reduced this by a rigorous regime, eating only three oranges a day, to 14 stone before we left. Others trained by doing the Welsh Three-Thousanders. Mike Harris, by far the fittest, did the round in 9 hours and 20 minutes and also led Cenotaph Corner, one of the fiercest Welsh rock climbs at that time. Chris Brasher and I tried some weight-lifting at the Imperial College gymnasium but for some exercises I could only manage the bar alone at first!

In the event, we were stormbound on Ushba, living in an ice cave until we cut our losses and moved to the Bezingi in a tented camp beside a group from the Russian Academy of Sciences. Dych-tau, Koshtan-tau and the peaks on the Bezingi Wall were all over 5,000 metres. There were no huts, you carried everything yourself, perhaps for several days. It was like the Alps in the 1920s but up to 1,000 metres higher. Four of us climbed the north ridge of Shkhara, Mike Harris, Derek Bull, Anatoli Kustovski, a Russian Master of Sport, and myself, descending by the original Cockin route, and having four nights out on the mountain. From our vantage point we looked across at the south face of Dych-tau, on the other side of the Bezingi glacier, and we could see the line of the route pioneered by Mummery and Zurfluh in 1888. Just beside it was another clean rock rib leading directly to the east peak of Dych-tau. We were told it was unclimbed, so Mike Harris and I decided to have a go at it while another party, of Hunt, Brasher, Alan Blackshaw and Eugene Gippenreiter, would repeat the Mummery route and show us the best way down the north side from the top. Sadly, Brasher became unwell and they decided to turn back. They had already had an adventurous climb on Jangi-tau on the Bezingi Wall, having to turn back after overcoming the technical difficulties just 500 feet short of the summit in dangerous snow conditions.

Our route proved superb, just at the limit of my capability and I was happy to let Mike Harris lead one or two artificial pitches. Against all Russian ethics, we were doing without a tent to save weight. For our three bivouacs, I took a bright red nylon tent-sack I had been given by Sporthaus Schuster after lecturing in Munich. Not knowing the route of descent, we wasted time and exceeded our self-imposed 'control time' which the Russians required us to stipulate in advance. So our friends were obliged to come out to rescue us, but we were safely off the mountain when we met them on the glacial moraine. I think it was the best climb I ever did.

right: Master of Sport Anatoli Kustovski and Derek Bull, right, erect the Russian four-man tent (held up by ice-axes).

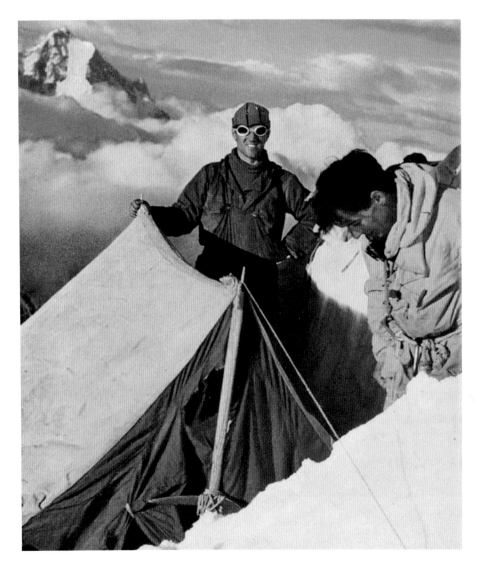

We met unrivalled hospitality and made many good and true friends, yet
there was always an undercurrent of competition. After we climbed Shkhara the
Russians sent a party of four to repeat it. Two were killed. Nevertheless, they
sent a second party who managed to complete the climb. After Dych-tau the
Russians tried to repeat our route also. We had left before they returned, but
later learned they had spent nine days on the mountain, partly in storm, and
came off the rib probably at the crux and finished up the ice gully between the
east and west peaks. 'We froze toes a little,' said their letter. They were tough!
We hoped that the expedition book, *The Red Snows*, authored jointly by Hunt and
Brasher, would be read without prejudice on both sides of the Iron Curtain.

RED PEAK IN THE PAMIRS

After entertaining a Russian team in North Wales and Scotland in 1960, the
opportunity arose for a joint expedition with Russians to the Pamirs in the
summer of 1961. Both the Alpine Club and the Scottish Mountaineering Club
submitted separate proposals, initiated by John Hunt and Malcolm Slesser
respectively, but were unexpectedly asked to combine in a single group of

below: Summit talks on Peak Communism in
the Pamirs, a high-speed ascent led by Anatoli
Ovchinikov, during the British-Soviet
Expedition, 1961.

twelve to be joined by six Soviet mountaineers headed by Anatoli Ovchinikov. John Hunt was invited to be the overall leader. The plan was to climb in two areas: first the Vavilova glacier, hoping to climb Peak Garmo (21,637 ft/6,595 m), and then, when well acclimatised, ascend Peak Communism (24,470 ft/7,459 m). They split into three groups: four Brits and two Russians in each, Wilfrid Noyce leading the Garmo group.

After successfully climbing Garmo, Noyce and Robin Smith were descending roped together wearing crampons when a fatal slip occurred. They were on soft wet slush overlying ice, one pulling off the other, and both fell 4,000 feet to their deaths. Wilfrid Noyce, first to the South Col on Everest in 1953, and now in his late forties, intending this to be his last expedition; Robin Smith, a brilliant Scottish rock and ice climber, only 23 years old. It was a sad and difficult situation. Had the Brits been climbing independently they would probably all have returned home immediately, but the Russians clearly expected the expedition to continue. In the end, six Brits agreed to stay, John Hunt returning with the others.

Ian McNaught-Davis now takes up the story:

The plan of action was resolved from one single axiom – to get up Peak of Communism as quickly as possible. Anatoli Ovchinikov produced a scheme which would, in theory, get us to the top of Peak Communism, thirty miles away and 16,000 ft above our Base Camp, in ten days, with five days to get down again. There would be no rest days, no fixed camps, no room for weakness, accident or illness. We had, after a month of astute evasion, at last been caught in the web of a Russian 'sports plan'. Malcolm Slesser and his Scottish colleagues, used to having to adopt similar measures to reach their native crags, were almost enthusiastic. The English trio were resigned and somewhat glum.

The first day into new pastures started badly. The Russians rose early and ate their food in silence; Slesser, in a flurry of camp activity, lectured Joe and myself on our sloth. Then, his Scottish temperament strained to the limit, he shouldered his pack and marched towards the rising sun. I thought of his martyred expression and felt guilty, Joe slept on. This was a routine that seemed destined to repeat itself day after day and, in the spirit of Anglo-Scots relations, I vowed to be an early starter the following day. Food poisoning and dysentery hit the British contingent. Two more days to the summit and three days down to our last food dump. I counted them like a prisoner counting his sentence. I realised that whatever happened we were going to cover the 5,000 ft that remained to the top in the next thirty-six hours. It was just a long hard slog. We had always thought that the final section to the summit would be a monotonous slope of ice. To our delight we now found in front of us a crenellated knife-edge running up to the base of the summit pyramid. On each side beautiful fluted slopes of ice fell 6,000 ft to the glacier. It was the most enthralling section of climbing we had found in the whole visit, as if enjoyment of the Pamirs was proportional to the agony suffered to find it.

Throughout the whole ascent, we relied heavily on our Russian comrades, the leadership of Anatoli Ovchinikov, and the confidence they had in their 'sports plan'. Although the climb was rarely pleasurable it was nevertheless unforgettable.

9 BIG WALLS AND
ALPINE-STYLE,
1970s ONWARDS

In October 2004, Club member, and director of the annual Kendal Mountain Film Festival, John Porter, put together an illustrated lecture entitled 'Wild, Stylish and Innovative 1975–86', which he introduced as follows:

The ascent of Everest's South-west Face in 1975 was a watershed in British mountaineering, marking the last of the big siege expeditions. In the same year, Dick Renshaw and Joe Tasker made an audacious Alpine Style ascent of the South-east Ridge of Dunagiri in the Garhwal Himalaya; it set the scene for a decade of unprecedented lightweight ascents by British climbers on major Himalayan and Andean peaks. Key personalities of this period were Alex MacIntyre, Peter Boardman, Joe Tasker, Doug Scott and many others of a generation that nearly climbed itself into extinction. The death of Alan Rouse on K2 in 1986 marked the end of that era.

Although I would not agree entirely with John's summary – for example our British Services expeditions continue to mount siege-style climbs on Everest, and successfully on Kangchenjunga in 2000, in order to give experience to greater numbers of their personnel – he rightly draws attention to the increasing number of audacious alpine-style or so-called 'capsule-style' expeditions overcoming great technical difficulties and carried out by very small teams of climbers – often just a pair – relying totally on their own abilities to extricate themselves if they get into difficulties because of bad weather, an impossible route, or accident.

Such has been the proliferation of activity in the last 30 years that there is no way in this short summary that I can give due credit to all the daring British ascents of this period. I can only select a few of those which seem to me to mark the highlights and the new trends made possible by advances in clothing, equipment, techniques and the sheer adversity and misery that top modern climbers are prepared to suffer in order to complete a new climb or a first ascent.

left: South face of Changabang, 1978. Two étriers hang from the first overhang on the headwall. Peering over the bulge, Kurtyka, climbing in seventies-style double boots, was delighted to discover a single curving crack piercing the smooth shield above.

below: After completing a new route with Allen Fyffe up the south-east buttress of Kalanka, Bob Barton took this photograph of Dunagiri, first climbed in 1947 by André Roch's Swiss team up the S W Ridge (left sky-line). In 1975, Dick Renshaw and Joe Tasker climbed the S E buttress, one of the hardest routes to be climbed 'alpine-style' at that time.

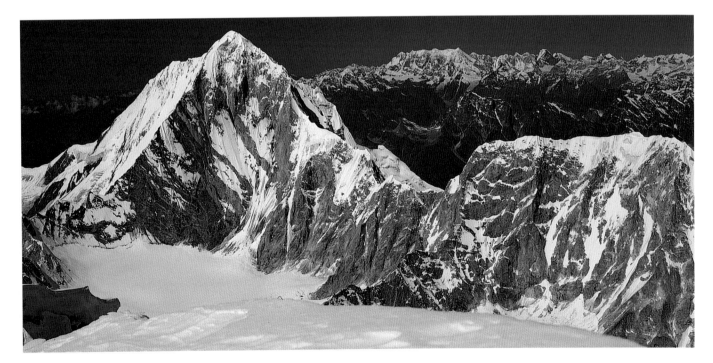

FROM THE EIGERWAND TO DUNAGIRI

Joe Tasker spent seven years in a seminary training to be a Catholic priest. He and his climbing partner, Dick Renshaw, tested themselves on the Eigerwand – a traditional summer ascent in 1973. Three years later, they came back to try it in winter.

> 'Having climbed it once, we were coming back because it was the longest and most complex route we could think of and, if we dared admit it to ourselves, the most difficult. We wanted something substantial, something we could get our teeth into. We did not want to overcome a mountain with ease, we needed to struggle, needed to be at the edge of what was possible for us, needed an outcome that was uncertain. Sometimes I wondered if climbing had become an addiction, if the pleasure of this drug had gone and only the compulsion to take it in ever stronger doses remained.'

This time the Eiger took them six days after leaving the station at the foot of the mountain – the first British winter ascent. In mid-afternoon they got down to the small hotel on the railway line. 'I left Dick at the table to go and buy the train tickets for our descent to the valley. As I walked away I heard an incredulous Englishman asking: "You mean you only bought one way tickets?"'

Tasker and Renshaw went on to climb in alpine-style, the south-east ridge of Dunagiri in the Garhwal Himalaya. 'It was a bold ascent by any standards,' said Chris Bonington, 'outstandingly so for a first Himalayan expedition. Dick was badly frost-bitten and this led to Joe inviting Peter Boardman to join him on Changabang and the start of their climbing partnership.'

There is an article in the *Alpine Journal* 1976 in which Joe goes into unusual detail in discussing the techniques, equipment and clothing for tackling winter ice. Before trying the Eigerwand in winter, they tested their gear in a five-day climb on the north face of the Lauterbrunnen Breithorn: Damart underwear; one-piece polar suit with Velcro flaps for relief; a Tenson salopette that would not trap moisture; on top a Ventile jacket. They each had a woollen shirt and two wool jerseys.

> In spite of the discomfort from our hands and the uncertainty inherent in such an undertaking, in some ways the week on the Eiger was a pleasure. I had looked ahead beforehand with trepidation at the thought of the long cold nights and the interminable ordeal they might be. But it turned out that once having carved out a ledge, cramped as it might be, we were able to have a long rest instead of the hastily snatched moments of half-wakefulness before the pre-dawn start of a summer climb. Even though it some-

right: Dick Renshaw climbing on Dunagiri.

below: A diagram of Dick Renshaw and Joe Tasker's route up Dunagiri's S E buttress. On the last 1,000 ft of descent, totally exhausted, they chose different routes but met up safely at base camp.

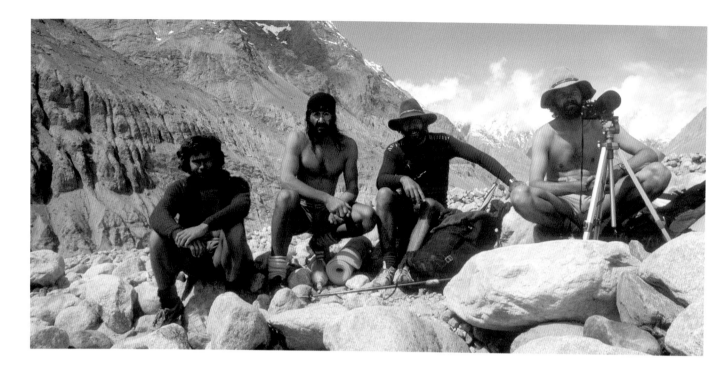

above: Dick Renshaw, Doug Scott, Peter Boardman and Joe Tasker en route to K2 in 1980.

times took two hours, well into the night, to prepare a space, and another hour to cook we were still left with eight or nine hours rest before needing to move again. Consequently we were well rested for most of the climb and though relieved eventually to be off the mountain were not too fatigued. The bivouacs were even more enjoyable as a result of our eating well. Looking back on the ascent it seems to have gone without a hitch, but I only need to cast my mind back a week further and think of the wretched nights spent in the snow-storms on our first attempt, of sitting shivering, damp and cold under a bulging rock sheltering from avalanches, waiting till dawn for the furtive nerve-wracking descent on unsound pegs and wading through waist-deep snow at the bottom, tired but relieved to be down. I have only to think back to this to realise that the Eiger is not finished; on the successful ascent we just had very good luck.

So they were already attuned to hardship when the two of them decided to drive out to India in a battered grossly overloaded Ford Escort van. In his first book, *Savage Arena*, Joe Tasker's account of their expedition to climb Dunagiri (23,180 ft/7,066 m) by the south-east ridge takes up 50 pages but conveys brilliantly all the freshness – and frustrations – of a first Himalayan experience. Dick went for an interview by the Mount Everest Foundation in the Council Room of the Royal Geographical Society to seek approval and a grant. A huge polished table runs the length of the room and on one side are ranged the mostly grey or white-haired dignitaries who conduct the interview with the applicant, who sits alone across the table.

'Why are there only two of you?'
'What if one sprains an ankle?'
'Who have you consulted about your plans?'
'What mountain do you intend to climb?'

A frail-looking, white-haired gentleman at the far end of the table, who seemed to have been asleep, opened his eyes and asked: 'Why don't you try Kalanka?'

'It looks too easy,' replied Dick without hesitation or embarrassment. Later he discovered that the white-haired gentleman was Eric Shipton, who had explored and climbed in the area since long before either of them had been born, and still knew it better than anyone.

From a photograph they chose Dunagiri, climbed only once before, by its south-west ridge, in 1939, by a Swiss expedition led by André Roch. On their way, they called in to see Ken Wilson, then editor of *Mountain Magazine*: 'I like it, I really like it. You guys just going off, chucking your gear into the back of a van and going to the Himalayas. It's got to be the shape of things to come. Great. Go for it!'

'The vertical interval of the route we had chosen was the same as the North face of the Eiger. It did not look as difficult so we estimated we would take four days to reach the summit and allowed ourselves two days to descend. Our food and fuel was calculated accordingly. Six days' rations and a litre of fuel, the same as for the Eiger in winter.'

It took them six bivouacs to reach the summit. The south-west ridge looked too complex to descend, so they would retrace their steps, abseiling down the upper barrier of rock. At the most, it would take two days, they thought, with no more fuel and only a few scraps of food. Becoming progressively weaker, without water, it took them four days, their throats too parched to swallow the remaining morsels. Encountering bare hard ice, their blunted crampon spikes would not hold.

'Wearily and inevitably, but with surprise, I fell, banging down the ice to be stopped 20 ft below the ice peg, dangling from the end of the rope. Dick's fingers became horribly frost bitten. Pulling the ropes down after an abseil was exhausting. Somehow I had lapsed into letting Dick do all the thinking and leaned more and more heavily upon him psychologically; I did the physical tasks and he did the brain work. I was the hands to his mind. I felt as if all my climbing life had been a preparation for this; a constant rehearsal so that when the need arose every movement came automatically.'

With 1,000 feet to go, there was a choice of routes: a gully one side, or an easy shorter slope on the other involving a longer walk round down the glacier. In their exhaustion, Dick preferred one, Joe the other. They parted. Joe could see the wise grey heads of the MEF Committee wagging their disapproval: 'We told you so; it was too much for the two of you!' 'The decision to come this way, to separate from Dick, had been the decision of a mind deranged from thirst, hunger, cold and physical deprivation.'

Fortunately, they met up safely at base camp. Dick flew back to get his frost bite treated. The van was not going to make it. Joe traded it, in Afghanistan, for a seat on a bus back to England. They were short of funds. He sold a pint of blood for £5. 'The easiest money I had ever made.' Things were beginning to go right at last.

CHANGABANG

While they had been climbing on Dunagiri, every morning the sun had risen behind the monstrous fang of Changabang. Joe began to have visions of climbing the incredible, ice-smattered precipice of its west wall. He could not propose it to Dick, who was still under treatment. Instead, he mentioned it to Peter Boardman, the national officer of the British Mountaineering Council in Manchester, who had reached the top of Everest while Joe had been to Dunagiri. Peter seemed to be of the same inclination and share the same spirit as himself. A new partnership was born.

Changabang was first climbed in 1974 by an Indian/British team led by Chris Bonington and Balwant Sandhu by the East Ridge, the easiest route on the mountain. 'Yet,' wrote Doug Scott, 'we had climbed for 18 roped pitches up and along a beautiful knife-edged snow arête, overwhelmed with the setting as much as by the fine climbing and the good company we shared'.

The attempt by Joe Tasker and Peter Boardman on the 5,000-feet virgin west face was to push the standards of technical rock climbing at altitude to new heights. It involved over 25 days of climbing, mostly on rock up to VI/A2 standard. They used big-wall tactics to overcome the difficulties, though in the upper part it relented to mixed climbing and, finally, easier snowfields. Their success was hailed as a landmark in Himalayan climbing and I believe the route still remains unrepeated.

OPPOSITE PAGE:

far right: The south face of Changabang. The 1978 route reaches the crest of the lower buttress from the right, then up the headwall (on page 178) to the Cyclop's Eye, a good bivouac site, and on to the summit icefields.

right: A diagram of Changabang's 5,000-ft virgin west wall, overcome on 15 October 1976 by Joe Tasker and Peter Boardman, and hailed as a landmark in Himalayan climbing.

THIS PAGE:

below: The granite tooth of Changabang is on the perimeter of the Nanda Devi Sanctuary in a restricted area inaccessible to climbers for many years until 1974, when it was climbed by the relative easy East Ridge.

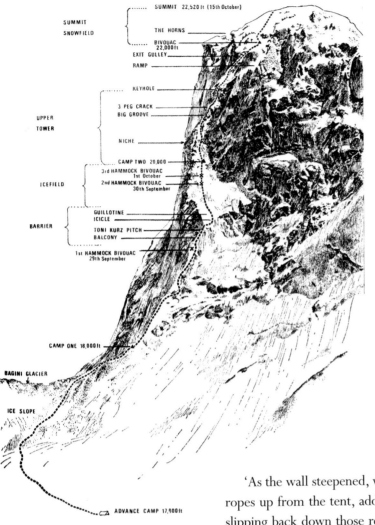

SUMMIT 22,520 ft (15th October)

SUMMIT
SNOWFIELD

THE HORNS

BIVOUAC
22,000 ft

EXIT GULLEY

RAMP

KEYHOLE

UPPER
TOWER

3 PEG CRACK
BIG GROOVE

NICHE

CAMP TWO 20,000

3rd HAMMOCK BIVOUAC
1st October

ICEFIELD

2nd HAMMOCK BIVOUAC
30th September

GUILLOTINE
ICICLE

BARRIER

TONI KURZ PITCH

BALCONY

1st HAMMOCK BIVOUAC
29th September

CAMP ONE 18,000 ft

BAGINI GLACIER

ICE SLOPE

ADVANCE CAMP 17,000 ft

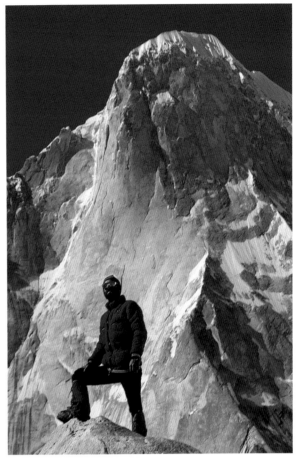

'As the wall steepened, we made slower but still steady progress, fixing a line of ropes up from the tent, adding more rope each day as we pressed on further, and slipping back down those ropes each evening to the haven of the tent.' They were adopting the so-called capsule style, enabling a better rest before a true alpine-style push to the top, which involved two bivouacs in hammocks and two further conventional bivouacs. 'At long last we were clawing our way to the top of the slope awesomely poised 5,000 ft above the precipice of the West Face. A few points of metal on our boots and metal tools in our hands were all that kept us there. The top was simply an end to the struggle upwards!'

'Pete and I were united as one person, if need be one spoke for both; we had emerged from the trial of six weeks of confinement together with a friendship which needed no words.'

They were now set for a whole series of expeditions, to K2 in 1978 unsuccessfully, but with great success on Kangchenjunga (28,169 ft/8,586 m) with Doug Scott in 1979 – only the third ascent, and the first without oxygen – and then on Mount Kongur (25,325 ft/7,719 m) in China in 1981 with Chris Bonington, before Joe Tasker and Pete Boardman sadly disappeared high up on the pinnacles of the north-east ridge of Everest in 1982.

In addition to their climbs, they left a legacy of fine writing in each of their two books, which happily led to their memory being perpetuated in the annual Boardman Tasker Prize for Mountain Literature.

TRIUMPH ON TRANGO TOWER

One of the most spectacular needles in the Karakoram is the clean-cut Trango Tower (20,508 ft/6,251 m), sometimes also called the Nameless Tower. Joe Brown noticed it on return from the Muztagh Tower in 1956 and dreamed of climbing it, but it was not until 1975 that he returned there with a six-man team led by J V (Mo) Antoine.

Once established at the foot of the monolith, they took turns, climbing in pairs, fixing ropes on the lower pitches. The rock was superb; solid and at a high enough angle even for Martin Boysen, who enthused over beautiful jamming and delicate wall climbing.

With only 250 metres to the summit and still five hours of daylight, Boysen was struggling up an awkward overhanging 12-cm-wide off-width crack when near disaster struck. His left knee jammed in the crack! Despite all sorts of contortions it remained so for nearly three hours. When he finally freed it by cutting through his trouser leg with a piton, his knee was swollen and gashed and hands covered in blood. Out of supplies and short of time, they were forced to abandon the climb.

Despite repeated 'never agains' from Brown and Boysen, they returned next year and Boysen was able to settle his score with the crack but there were still numerous hard pitches above. On 8 July, Boysen and Antoine made the summit, fixing ropes, and were followed next day by Joe Brown and Malcolm Howells. In all, there were over 20 grade VI or harder pitches on the route, which was quickly recognised as a major *tour de force*, being climbed at a time before camming devices or Friends had been invented for use in wide or flared cracks as running belays for improved protection. It was not repeated for 14 years and then by two Japanese to rescue another, Takeyasu Minamiura, who had soloed a new route on the east face, jumped from the summit and snagged his paraglider on the cliff face 80 metres from the top!

There are now at least eight different routes on the Tower, now mostly climbed free with just nuts and Friends for protection, with the climbers wearing rock slippers, rather than the cumbersome big boots used by Boysen. It has become a deservedly popular challenge for the world's best rock climbers.

below: A most dramatic image of the Trango Tower, climbed as a major *tour de force* in 1976 and not repeated for 14 years. There are now eight or more routes on the Tower, a real challenge for the world's best rock climbers.

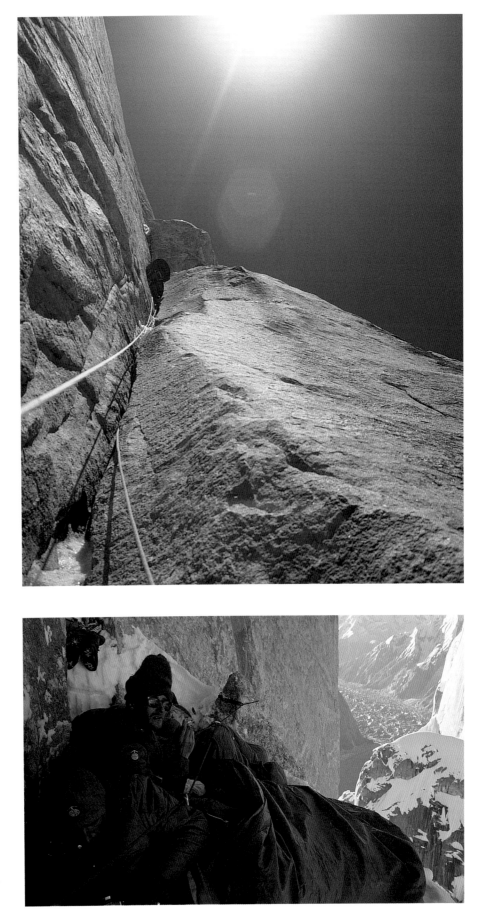

above right: The Fissure Boysen, scene of a horrific event in 1975 for Martin when his knee became firmly jammed in the crack for nearly three hours.

right: A reasonably comfortable bivouac after such a nasty experience!

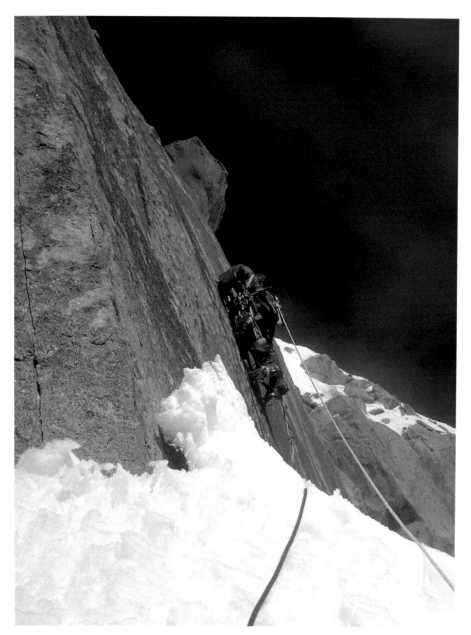

left: Doug Scott climbing using tape étriers on the hardest pitch of the 250-m summit tower of the Ogre in July 1977.

OPPOSITE PAGE:

right: Mo Anthoine, Clive Rowland and Paul Braithwaite enjoy a tea break at Camp I on the Ogre.

ORDEAL ON THE OGRE

This history would not be complete without recalling another epic the following year, 1977, in the central Karakoram. The mountain was Baintha Brakk (23,900 ft/7,285 m), more commonly known as the Ogre, a complex three-headed giant above the Biafo glacier. This was Doug Scott's expedition with six climbers, climbing in three pairs, and initially trying out different routes as the best way was not immediately obvious. Scott and Paul (Tut) Braithwaite started up the impressive rock buttress of the Central Spur but a dislodged rock hit Braithwaite on the thigh and put him out of effective action. Meanwhile, Mo Antoine, Clive Rowland, Chris Bonington and Nick Estcourt spent ten days fixing ropes up steep rock and ice ribs to the left of the Central Spur, ready for an alpine-style push to the top. While Antoine and Rowland dropped back for a rest, Bonington

and Estcourt unexpectedly took off for the main central summit. They made a spirited attempt over four days but, realising they did not have enough gear, settled for the easier west summit at 7,224 metres, some 200 feet lower. Estcourt had acquired a throat infection, so he and Braithwaite opted out and, after a rest, Bonington rejoined the other three in the Shoulder Camp at about 6,700 metres. They traversed the west summit and descended to a snow hole, previously occupied by Estcourt and Bonington, under the final rock tower of the Ogre's main peak.

On 14 July, Scott and Bonington set out, taking most of the climbing gear, with Rowland and Antoine following and filming their progress. With Bonington still recovering and Scott feeling relatively fresh, he took the lead up the sheer granite face. When a crack petered out he asked Bonington to lower him from a peg so that, by galloping backwards and forwards, he could pendulum across to another crack on the right and continue up it to the top of the wall. It was the hardest climbing he had ever done at that altitude, and Bonington was suitably impressed. A final overhang was overcome by combined tactics, Scott standing on Bonington's back. They reached the top at 7 pm, just as the sun disappeared below the horizon.

Without sleeping bags and with only very light clothing, they hustled down at once. While abseiling down, Scott was tensioning across some water-streaked rock which, in the cold night air, had frozen to verglas. His feet skated off and, out of control, he crashed across the rock, slamming his feet on rocks on the other side of the couloir. He lost his glasses and ice-axe and, as he dangled and then manoeuvred himself onto a tiny ledge, he realised he'd broken both legs at the ankles! Bonington abseiled down and took over and they spent a bitterly cold night on a snow patch.

They managed to descend and traverse across to the snow cave, with Antoine and Rowland digging great bucket steps in which Doug Scott could crawl back on his knees. Then followed storm and starvation as a blizzard penned them in for two days. Clive Rowland led them over the west summit to regain the fixed ropes, Scott wearing out the knees of five pairs of over-trousers. At one point he abseiled off the end of the rope but managed to grab a fixed rope. Chris Bonington did the same and broke a couple of ribs in the process, leading to incipient pneumonia. It took them eight days to get off the mountain, with Scott crawling last into base at 10.30 pm. 'No one else but you could have made it back,' said Chris. A team of Balti porters carried Doug to the helicopter pad near Askole, and back in the UK he made a complete recovery.

Unlike so many of their friends, both Chris and Doug have survived their astonishing climbing careers and authored magnificent illustrated coffee-table books published by Diadem in 1989 and 1992 respectively, from which I have been able to draw this and other accounts of their achievements. They have both been honoured for their contributions to mountaineering, and served in succession as presidents of the Alpine Club.

above: A diagram showing the various camp sites and routes being tried on the Ogre (opposite).

right: The Ogre, or Baintha Brakk, a complex three-headed giant above the Biafo glacier in the Karakoram.

ALPINE STYLE FOR ALL

Extending alpine-style ascents to the very highest peaks had been encouraged by the three-day dash in 1975 up the north face of Hidden Peak (26,470 ft/8,068 m) in the Karakoram, by the Austrians Reinhold Messner and Peter Habeler, as a preliminary to their landmark ascent of Everest in 1978 for the first time without supplementary oxygen. It now seemed that no peak on earth was immune to a rapid lightweight ascent, and Doug Scott, Joe Tasker and Peter Boardman's climb on Kangchenjunga the following year just confirmed the fact. Another fine climb in that area was the ascent of Jannu (25,295 ft/7,710 m), one of the most beautiful mountains imaginable, first climbed by a French team in 1962, and repeated in 1978 by young British climbers, Alan Rouse, Brian Hall, Roger Baxter-Jones and Rab Carrington.

Another star on the horizon, dedicated to alpine-style, was Alex MacIntyre who, with Doug Scott and Roger Baxter-Jones, made a rapid lightweight ascent of the unclimbed south-west face of the Tibetan giant Shisha Pangma (26,397 ft/8,046 m) in May 1982. For MacIntyre 'the face was the ambition; the style was the obsession'. It was a reaction to the heavy siege-style expeditions of the past. His book, written with Doug Scott, became the winner of the first Boardman Tasker Prize in 1984. Sadly, soon after the climb MacIntyre was killed by stonefall on Annapurna's south face and Baxter-Jones by an ice-avalanche on the Aiguille du Triolet. At the top of the world the casualty rate is high.

I began this chapter with John Porter's commentary on the period 1975–86, and his statement that the death of Alan Rouse on K2 in 1986 marked the end of that era. At the time, Alan Rouse and I were both vice-presidents of the British

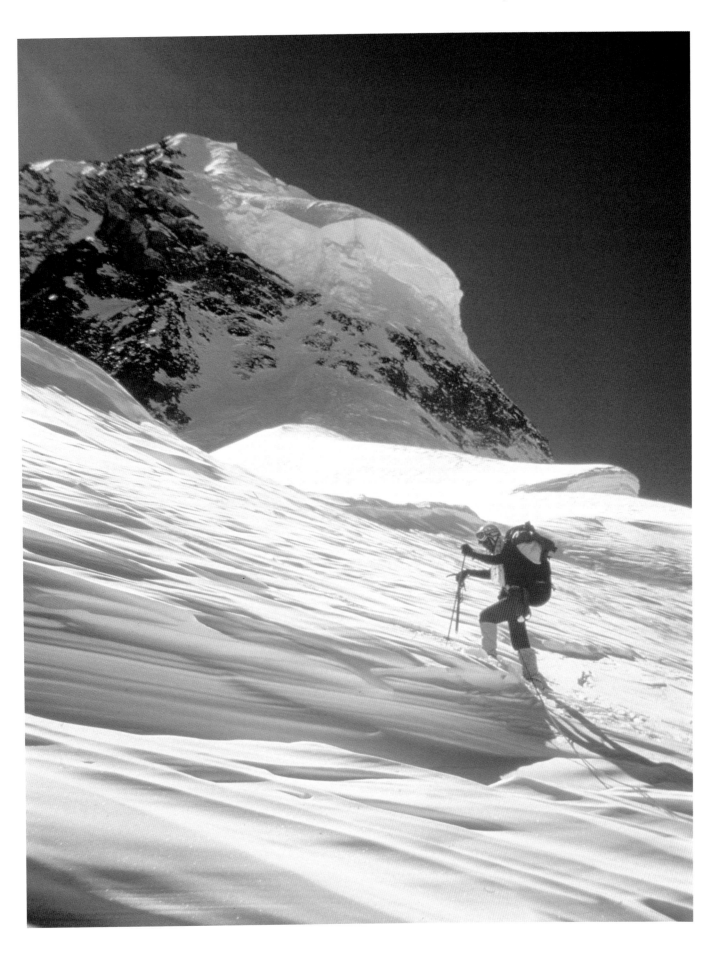

Mountaineering Council. I heard of his death in a mid-night radio report as I drove home from central London. He had been leading an eleven-man British team to the unclimbed north-west ridge of K2. They did not succeed and he was reluctant to return to England without one more attempt on the mountain. To quote Jim Curran: 'It was curious that Al, who was originally so determined to climb a new route on K2, eventually committed himself to the Abruzzi Spur, where the most he could hope for was the dubious satisfaction of a first British ascent, but he would be only the sixty-fourth person to climb K2, which was really no big deal in Al's own highly competitive view of his place in the world of mountaineering.' He linked up with 'Mrufka' Wolf, who was originally with a Polish south-west ridge expedition.

The full story is beyond the scope of this narrative. It was a disaster. There were too many climbers on the Abruzzi ridge and too few tents when a storm hit them on 5 August, and raged until the 10th. The indestructible Kurt Diemberger was also there with his regular British climbing and filming partner, Julie Tullis. On their summit day, Rouse had exhausted himself through breaking the trail most of the way to the summit. Diemberger and Tullis also summitted but Mrukfa Wolf, who was going too slowly, was persuaded to turn back. Alan Rouse and Julie Tullis both died at camp 4 on the Shoulder. Mrukfa Wolf,

above: Kurt Diemberger at K2 Base Camp in 1986 with his regular British climbing and filming partner, Julie Tullis. Julie also died of exhaustion at Camp 4 on the Shoulder while returning from the summit. She was a Black Belt in martial arts.

descending slowly on her own, never arrived. Only Kurt Diemberger and the Austrian Willi Bauer from that disparate group reached base camp alive but both suffering severely from frostbite. So ended the dreadful summer of 1986, when no less than 27 people climbed K2 but 13 died in the process.

In happier times, on 10 March 1984, Alan Rouse had contributed to an Alpine Club symposium on *Lightweight Expeditions to the Great Ranges.* He described 'the best trip ever' in 1976–77.

right: Kishtwar Shivling, climbed by Dick Renshaw and Stephen Venables in 1983. The peaks of relatively modest height in this area are ideal for small teams.

A nine months' climbing expedition covering most of South America, particularly Patagonia and Peru. We left in three climbing pairs, Rab Carrington and myself, Brian Hall and John Whittle, Alan and Adrian Burgess; accompanying us were various wives and girl friends. (Although a rather different set of wives and girl friends was present by the end of the expedition.) For all of us this was a highly successful expedition and we managed seventeen major first ascents between us. Each pair operated entirely separately on the mountain but we offered each other moral assistance at Base Camps as well as the possibility of a rescue if needed. During the course of the trip we occasionally swapped partners.

Sadly, they were not as well organised on K2.

KISHTWAR HIMALAYA AND RIMO GROUP

I continue with short accounts of climbs in two areas of northern India which are less well known to mountaineers but full of potential for challenging alpine-style climbs. Kishtwar, situated north-east of the Chenab river, is one of the most enchanting regions of the Himalaya with peaks in the range of 6,000–6,560 metres. The first major ascent was not until 1974 when Chris Bonington and Nick Estcourt climbed Brammah I by its south-east ridge.

In 1983, Dick Renshaw and Stephen Venables decided to try Kishtwar Shivling (19,816 ft/6,040 m) by the north face, which rises in a single sweep of 2,500 metres from the Bujwas nullah, which is also an improbable trade and pilgrim route over the Umasi La (5,330 metres) to Zanskar. Their base camp was a flowery meadow fringed by stands of Himalayan birch. The real climbing began from their advance base at about 4,500 metres. They needed two bivouacs on the face and a third on the east shoulder. They encountered numerous patches of superb rock and mixed climbing and some steep ice to gain the summit, with another two days and 25 abseils to return to base. They had been gone for twelve days.

The hardest climbs in the Bujwas cirque have been on Cerro Kishtwar (20,340 ft/6,200 m), so named because of its similarity to the monolithic Patagonian peaks. In 1991, Brendan Murphy and Andy Perkins almost reached the summit after a 17-day epic on the east face, and it was left to Mick Fowler and Steve Sustad in one of their hardest climbs to complete the first ascent in 1993 by the precarious mixed terrain of the north face. There is no shortage of good climbs in Kishtwar, ideal for small teams making minimal impact, without the need for fixed ropes or a single bolt.

The second area is the Rimo group in the eastern Karakoram some 150 miles (250 kilometres) to the north-north-east of Kishtwar Shivling, still in India but close to the de facto border with Pakistan and China. The main highway is by the Siachen glacier, whose upper reaches were controlled by Pakistan, and the eastern approach up the Nubra valley, closely guarded by India – all part of the sad Kashmir dispute since Partition in 1947. By 1985, the Indian army controlled the entire Siachen glacier and the government was prepared to allow joint Indian and foreign expeditions to the area. A British team was invited to join a group from the Bombay Mountaineers, led by Harish Kapadia, and this was the first of many happy collaborations with him.

Arriving in early June, the joint eleven-member team was able to cross the Terong river easily and become the first party since the famous Dutch couple, Dr Philip and Jenny Visser in 1929, to reach the Terong glacier system. Here were several peaks, including Rimo I, II and III, all over 7,000 metres and all unclimbed. The major success was Dave Wilkinson and Jim Fotheringham's first ascent of Rimo III (23,727 ft/7,233 m), by its north-east ridge. The highest, Rimo I (24,239 ft/7,385 m), proved more demanding, comparable to the Eigerwand in winter conditions. Victor Saunders and Stephen Venables spent six days on its south-west ridge, retreating from 6,850 metres after Venables had the embarrassment of dropping a rucksack full of bivouac gear. 'I stared with incredulous horror as the sack gathered speed, sliding then somersaulting, bouncing and bursting as it disappeared to plunge 1000 m into the North-west cwm. Sleeping bag, duvet vest, food, tent poles and, most vital of all, the gas stove had gone. One tired, careless mistake had ruined everything.' There was no time for a second attempt.

Success came finally in 1988 to a large well-organised joint Indian/Japanese team. They took a more direct line up the south face to reach the previous high point and, taking no chances, fixed over 3,000 metres of rope and placed two more camps, at 6,750 metres and on the west of the ridge at about 7,000 metres. On 28 July, Joshio Ogata and three companions reached the summit, and over two days six more repeated the climb.

In total, the 1985 expedition made eight first ascents, including Rimo III. They explored three large glaciers and reached five cols, crossing two of them. It was an international success and the start of a continuing friendly association between the Alpine Club and the Bombay Mountaineers.

above: Peaks I (right) and III (left) of the Rimo Group, approached up the Siachen glacier — the objective of a Joint British and Bombay Mountaineers team in 1985 which made eight first ascents including Rimo III.

Stephen Venables recounted both expeditions in his first book, *Painted Mountains,* which won the Boardman Tasker Prize for the best mountaineering book of the year in 1986. As detailed in my Everest book, he went on to become the first Briton to climb Everest without supplementary oxygen, in 1988, by a new route up the Kangshung face from Tibet. He is the current president of the Alpine Club and most appropriately will continue to preside throughout its 150th anniversary year.

I should not close this chapter without some mention of former Alpine Climbing Group and current Alpine Club member Chris Jones. In the 1960s he moved to California and did some very high-quality routes with American climbers, some of which he wrote up for the *Alpine Journal*. In the 1969 *Journal* he describes a first ascent of the Amazon face of Yerupaja, Peru, carried out in fine alpine style in July 1968. Then in December of the same year, only the third ascent of Fitzroy in Patagonia, being the first ascent by the south-west buttress, was made by a group that included Yvon Chouinard, Lito Tejada-Flores and Chris. The 20-hour climb included some 17 technical pitches. They had to stay in the area for eight weeks until the stormy weather at last gave them the opportunity to go for it. The same journal describes the first British ascent of the famous Nose of El Capitan, Yosemite, by Mick Burke (who sadly disappeared close to the summit of Everest in 1975) with Rob Woods, ten years after Warren Harding's pioneering first ascent.

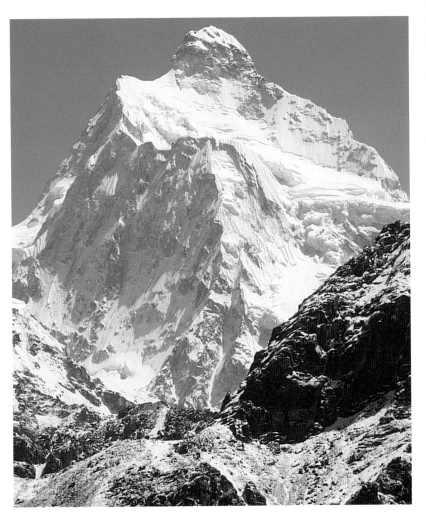

below: Trekkers get this unforgettable view of Jannu when they traverse the Mirgin La from Tseram to Ghunsa in the Kangchenjunga region. See p.192 for the second ascent by a British group in alpine style in 1978.

The 1970 *Journal* tells of Jones' ascent of the Salathé Wall – only the second route made up El Capitan – with Gary Colliver, 19/23 June 1969. 'At that time', relates Jones, 'although it had had six ascents, they had all been by legendary hard men – whereas we were neither legendary nor hard. Perhaps his best route was an ascent with the American George Lowe in the 1970s of the north face of North Twin, known as the 'Eiger of Canada'.

All this experience qualified Jones to write his book *Climbing in North America*, published in 1976, and enthusiastically reviewed by Edward Pyatt in the 1977 *Alpine Journal* as an outstanding contribution to mountaineering literature. 'The author', says Lito Tejada Flores in his foreword, 'is a foreigner, an expatriate English climber. And as such, seems to have the detachment and perspective needed to form a broad, objective view of the American climbing scene'. Ken Wilson, former Editor of the magazine *Mountain,* cites Jones' contribution to the sport as as great as that of Mick Fowler at the present time.

10 THE LAST TWENTY YEARS (1986–2006)

PRAISE FOR THE ALPINE JOURNAL

In preparation for this last chapter on Alpine Club members' achievements throughout the world, I reviewed the last 25 years of *Alpine Journals*. It is an astonishing record of mountaineering adventure and scientific observation with its roots going back to 1863. The most recent editors are to be congratulated on maintaining a consistently high standard: Edward Pyatt, John Fairley, Professor Ernest Sondheimer, Johanna Merz, Ed Douglas and, currently, Stephen Goodwin.

A 1989 report on the future role of the Alpine Club (prepared during my presidency under the guidance of His Honour Judge Michael Baker) invited the editor to commission articles 'grouped round the great issues of the day'. Previously, they had been listed in no particular order, so in her first *Journal* in 1992–3, Johanna Merz introduced a more logical format with a main theme that year being the environment. Her editorial included a Club Policy Statement on climbing ethics. In particular, the Club:

1   supports the use of protection and belaying techniques which cause minimal damage to the rock; pegs, nuts, slings, etc. which use natural rock features are felt to be acceptable. But the use of bolts and the chipping or altering of rock features is to be deprecated;

2   believes that the mountains should be left as they are found; equipment abandoned should be kept to an absolute minimum and no litter should be left on the approach, around huts, at base camp, or on the mountain;

3   encourages small expeditions to the Greater Ranges and minimal impact on the local environment.

Johanna Merz concluded: 'There is something obsessional about climbing which perhaps encourages mountaineers to be rather pre-occupied and inward-looking; many of us take refuge in the belief that threats to the mountain environment are someone else's responsibility. But we cannot insulate ourselves from these problems.' It is important that the Club sets an example and makes a positive contribution towards addressing these issues.

THE MOUNTAINEER'S MOUNTAINEER

In reading the accounts of various expeditions, particularly the smaller British ones, it is gratifying how many of them acknowledge the financial support of the Mount Everest Foundation, often with matching funding from the Sports Council (now Sport England) channelled through the British Mountaineering

left: Look, no hands! One of today's British rock superstars, Leo Houlding, executes a 'double dyno' while leading a free variation 'Passage to Freedom' on an original aid climb 'New Dawn' by Royal Robbins on the Nose of El Capitan, Yosemite, October 1999.

Council. This has greatly helped to give young climbers experience of the Greater Ranges, and the opportunity to organise and lead their own expeditions. This is the common thread linking successive *Journals*. One name appearing regularly is that of Mick Fowler, often, but not always, in the company of the architect, now turned professional mountain guide, Victor Saunders.

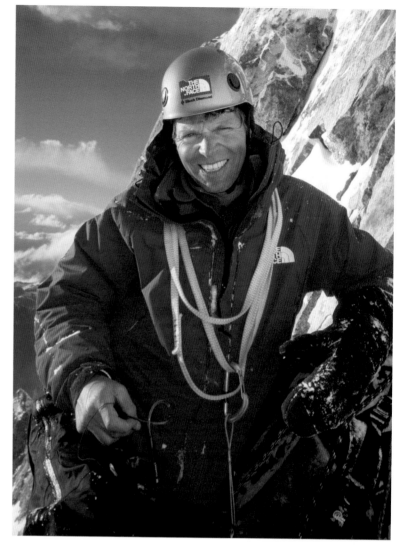

Mick Fowler holds down a responsible job with the Inland Revenue (recently valuing the shares of unlisted companies), so he has had to seize every opportunity outside office hours to indulge his pastime. This has varied from climbing the overhanging shale cliffs of Henna in north Devon to the friable chalk of Beachy Head (pioneered by the infamous Aleister Crowley). Scottish sea stacks or winter ice climbs could be grabbed by a team of four driving in two-hour spells overnight on Fridays from London and back again on Sunday night, fresh for an 8 am start at the office. However, during one particularly cold spell in February 1987 Fowler discovered a challenge almost on his own doorstep. One of the huge drainpipes on the ornate façade of St Pancras Station had sprung a leak high above the pavement.

'The ice had formed in a particularly friendly position. Of three parallel drainpipes two were almost completely encased up to a height of about twenty metres. The third one was unaffected, thus enabling protection slings to be threaded round it just above the support brackets. Wonderful – a vertical ice streak of frighteningly pure (and very brittle) water ice with excellent protection – assuming of course that the Victorian drainpipe supports were up to the task.' With friend Mike Morrison belayed to a convenient parking meter, and feeling slightly silly wearing plastic boots, crampons, helmet and flailing two ice-axes, he set to work. The encased drainpipes were clearly visible and caution was required not to damage them. After eight runners and an exact 19.2 metres, he came to the leak and the end of the ice. Some sculptured gargoyles five metres higher might not have stood the strain so he duly lowered off from a sling stretched behind all three pipes.

As the crowd dissipated, presumably disappointed at the lack of injury or death, and the second man, Chris Watts, was barely five metres up, a blue flashing light appeared. But the police were too late to stop them. The caption to a front-page photo in the *Daily Telegraph* next day read, 'Fireman making safe a sixty-five foot icicle on St Pancras Station last night!'

THE GOLDEN PILLAR OF SPANTIK

An *Observer* feature later acclaimed Mick Fowler as 'The Mountaineer's Mountaineer', his name put forward by the likes of Andy Fanshawe, Victor Saunders and Joe Simpson. The climb that really established his reputation, together with Victor Saunders, was the Golden Pillar of Spantik in 1987. I had actually seen it during our 1954 expedition to Rakaposhi when we paid a courtesy visit on the Mir of Nagir, beyond whose domain the mountain lay. On the north side a large monolithic pillar catches the evening sun and gives the peak its Burushaski name, Ganesh Chish, which means Golden Peak. The Pillar is of metamorphic limestone, converted to a compact marble, and soars 7,220 feet (2,200 metres) from the glacier. The summit at 23,054 feet (7,027 metres) is about 980 feet (300 metres) higher and set back about 3 kilometres from the Pillar.

They had seen it in 1984 when attempting to climb Bojohagar, a mountain directly above the Karakoram Highway, so several of the same team from the North London Mountaineering Club returned to support Fowler and Saunders. The Pillar was divided into four sections. First a 400-metre pinnacle, the First

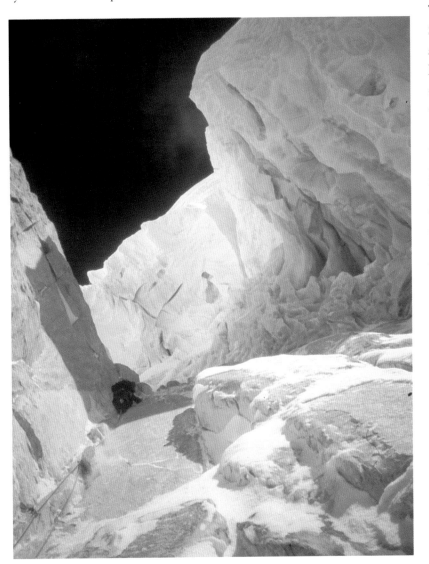

Tower, barred access to the long serpentine Snow Arête. The Snow Arête ended in a small step, which led to the third section, a tiny hanging glacier. The fourth part was the point of the exercise: 3,937 feet (1,200 metres) of wall, like a great spear thrust into the sky.

While Fowler and Saunders reconnoitred the approach to the Pillar, the others prospected an easier descent route. A spell of bad weather left them just ten days for the climb before Fowler was due back at his desk on 23 August. It was their last chance. By 5 pm on the second day, they were doing well. They had reached a possible bivouac site at the Amphitheatre above a 1,000-feet section of slabs. On day 3, it began to snow heavily and they had to bivouac early. Next day was clearer, but still overcast and they began to follow lines on the right wall of the Pillar. They had a miserable bivouac with no ledge. They used the tent as a hanging bag, inside which Mick spent the night dangling in his harness while Victor stood in his rucksack. Next day, looking up they could see the final ramps but they were not easy: blank rock, no runners, so very poor protection, with the impending side wall pushing you off balance. Then came a final vertical book-shaped corner under an ear-shaped sérac. Above, the snow leading to the plateau was thigh deep, but after another commodious bivouac, they ploughed on. At 12.45 pm on 11 August 1987 they were on top.

Within an hour a storm overtook them; winds brought drifting snow and white-out. Their tracks disappeared. Somehow they found their tent, and next day searched for the right line off the plateau to hit their descent ridge. If they missed it, they would be abseiling from snow bollards over large séracs into space. They survived. In fact, Mick calculated he could even get back to the office by Monday 16th. 'Why the great rush?' asked Saunders. 'Then I will have saved a whole week's annual leave,' replied Fowler. He did; by 9.30 sharp, those Civil Service shoes were under that Civil Service desk!

Quoting Fanshawe and Venables' *Himalaya – Alpine Style:* 'few would argue that this original ascent ranks as one of the hardest achievements ever accomplished in the Karakoram. It is distinguished by its sustained, technical nature, at least twenty pitches of mixed climbing at Scottish grade V and above. In 1991 another team attempted to repeat the Golden Pillar by taming it with bolts, but they did not get very far. Let us hope that future parties will respect the clean, bold style in which the Pillar was first climbed and leave their bolt kits at home.' Mick Fowler and Victor Saunders were perfect examples of the Club's stand on climbing ethics.

right: The Golden Pillar of Spantik, climbed by Mick Fowler and Victor Saunders in 1999, which really established their reputations.

below: The Arwa Tower's elegant but blank N E Face was rejected by Mick Fowler and Steve Sustad in favour of a more feasible route up the N W Face of this 6,352-m peak in the Garhwal Himalaya close to the Chinese border.

TOWARDS THE PIOLET D'OR

Mick Fowler continued enterprising first ascents during his limited vacations: in September 1993, with Steven Sustad, a four-day climb up the 1,000-metre north-west face of Cerro Kishtwar (20,340 ft/6,200 m) in the Kishtwar Himalaya; in 1995 a first venture to Nepal, succeeding on the north-west buttress of Taweche (21,463 ft/6,542 m). Climbing with Pat Littlejohn, they took five and a half days to reach the summit on 28 April. The route was 43 pitches long with an overall grade of ED Sup. In April 1999, it was the turn of the Arwa Tower (20,840 ft/6,352 m) in the Garhwal Himalaya, close to the Chinese border. This wild, ice-streaked rocky spire was first photographed by Harish Kapadia, editor of the *Himalayan Journal*, who is a genius at discovering attractive virgin peaks. Fowler was partnered again this time by Steve Sustad, originally from Seattle but living in Britain for many years. Unable to locate any mashed potato powder in Delhi, they lived on an alternating diet of noodles and lurid 'peach'-flavoured baby food.

More recently in 2003, with Paul Ramsden, Fowler responded to the overtures of Tamotsu 'Tom' Nakamura, our Japanese member, who for several years has been exploring the fantastic climbing potential of 'the Alps of Tibet' or 'East of the Himalayas, (from north-west Yunnan to south-east Tibet) and reporting his finds each year since 2000 with enticing photographs in the *Alpine Journal*.

Flying in to Chengdu, they chose a peak called Siguniang with an unclimbed north face, which, from photographs, looked to be very daunting compact granite. However, they found a way up a continous ice *goulotte* hidden from view. Even so the route

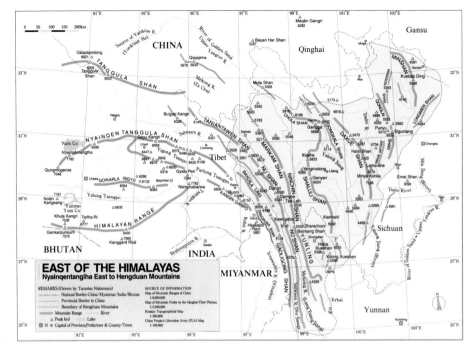

was extremely demanding technically, occupying them for a week with very uncomfortable restricted bivouacs on minimal ledges. The French climbing establishment were so impressed that they awarded them their *Piolet d'Or* for the best route of the year, the first time this has ever been given to a British pair. Chris Bonington has written of Mick Fowler's 'extraordinary collection of new routes whose common denominator is immense seriousness and individuality'.

above: The region of numerous unclimbed 6,000-m peaks, recently researched and photographed by Tom Nakamura, and included as end papers to challenge future mountaineers.

MORE ALPINE STYLE

Another pair of dedicated climbers, although operating normally at a slightly less extreme level, is the husband and wife team of Roger Payne and the New Zealander Julie-Ann Clyma.

Roger Payne was general secretary of the British Mountaineering Council from 1995 to 2002 and then took a part-time post as Sports and Development Director with the International Union of Alpine Associations (UIAA) which gave him a little more time for guiding and expeditions. His bureaucratic experience equipped him admirably for teasing out permits to climb in previously restricted areas close to the frontiers of India, Pakistan, Tibet and the former Soviet Union. Meanwhile, Julie-Ann Clyma, originally trained as a physiologist, had also qualified as an international mountain guide. In summer 1991, with a larger group, including also Iain Peter, Allen Fyffe, Rick Allen, Shaun Smith and Simon Yates, they climbed the world's most northerly 7,000-metre summits, the elegant Khan Tengri (23,000 ft/7,010 m) and Pobeda (or Victory) Peak (24,406 ft/7,439 m) in the Tien Shan range, also known as the Celestial Mountains.

In October 1994, Payne and Clyma cleverly contrived a way of 'entering' the Nanda Devi Sanctuary, which had been closed since 1982 for environmental reasons. They climbed the East Peak (24,390 ft/7,434 m) of Nanda Devi by its south ridge, which rises from the eastern rim of the Sanctuary at Longstaff's Col, so you don't actually have to set foot on the floor of the Sanctuary itself. This proved a quadruple first ascent: British, New Zealand, female, and in fine alpine style!

Most recently they made the fourth ascent of Chomolhari (23,930 ft/7,294 m), which lies on the border between Tibet and Bhutan. It was first climbed in 1937 in a sterling effort by the indefatigable Freddy Spencer Chapman with his single Sherpa Pasang Dawa Lama. I recall that Chapman once wrote that 'a fit man should be able to continue on the level or downhill *indefinitely*'. He later published his wartime Malaysian adventures behind the Japanese lines as a best-seller, *The Jungle is Neutral*. The King of Bhutan has forbidden attempts on Chomolhari from the Bhutanese side, but Payne and Clyma were surprisingly able to get permission from the Tibetan side to make a successful ascent in spring 2004.

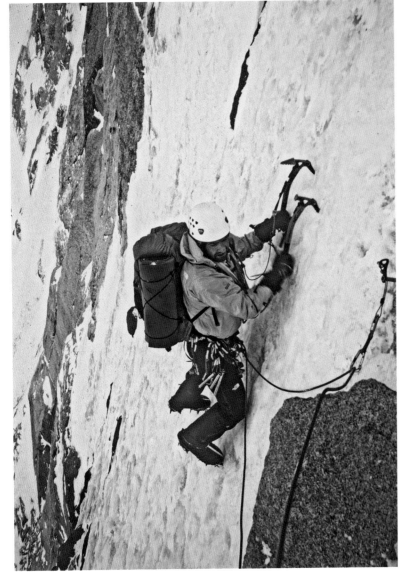

CHANGABANG AGAIN

Payne and Clyma have shown commendable persistence on one particular mountain, Changabang, in 1996 and 1997, in a period when I happened to be Roger Payne's 'boss', as president of the BMC. He was probably only too pleased to be away from the office. Julie-Ann Clyma wrote in the *Alpine Journal*: 'Perhaps the most special mountain is the one that captures your imagination in your early climbing years – the one that is so big, so hard, so impossibly beyond your ability that it could only ever be a dream. For me, Changabang was such a mountain.' Fifteen years after Boardman and Tasker had made their landmark ascent of the west face, she found herself looking at the north face of that 'Shining Mountain'. The dream had become reality, and the impossible even began to seem possible.

With the closure of the Nanda Devi Sanctuary in 1982, one now had to approach Changabang from the north, as it is on the northern rim of the Sanctuary. Nevertheless, the approach is easy: two days drive from Delhi, then just two days walk to base camp. Clyma describes the main part of the north face: 'A stupendous sweep of steep, clean granite, with improbable ice formations stuck randomly to it.' There were several possible starts leading to a central icefield. Then an upper snow spur led to a groove system which would exit high up on the East Ridge, the original line of ascent of the mountain.

With Andy Perkins and Brendan Murphy, they were a team of four and planned a capsule-style ascent, with the two pairs sharing the leading and load-carrying. They chose a route that began on the right side of the obvious buttress. After some four days on the face, with very uncomfortable bivouacs, they were in the area of the central icefield when Andy Perkins was smitten with severe food poisoning. There was also a sudden deterioration in the weather. They prudently abandoned the attempt before they got over-committed. But they soon vowed to return.

Next year, 1997, they returned as a team of six, Brendan Murphy now joined by Andy Cave, with Mick Fowler and Steve Sustad as the third pair. With their increased knowledge of the face, they were determined to try alpine-style climbing as three independent pairs. Payne and Clyma chose a line to the left of the others. After four days of superb sustained mixed climbing they reached the foot of the central icefield – their high point of 1996. Thereafter, climbing on hard green ice or strenuous mixed grooves, the deteriorating weather began to take control. After three more days, in which they reached the ice tongue just above the upper icefield, they withdrew. Getting down safely now became their prime objective. In all, Payne and Clyma spent twelve days on the sheer face.

Andy Cave now takes up the story. He and Brendan Murphy chose a central line, with Steve Sustad and Mick Fowler following two days behind because of the limited bivouac sites. With nine days' food and ten days' gas, their sacks weighed 20 kg. They were hampered by the daily afternoon storm and they wrecked their ice screws trying to drive them into the steely ice. Spindrift swept down the route. By the time they reached a bivouac site at the edge of the snow arête at 11 pm on the fourth day they were exhausted. When they rested next day, Fowler and Sustad caught them up. The steep upper grooves involved some of the most challenging climbing yet. Each pitch had a sting to it. On the eighth day, Andy Cave hacked through the cornice onto the east ridge. They had climbed the face. It was his birthday next day and Brendan Murphy produced six Snicker bars he had secretly carried up.

A day later, on 1 June, Fowler and Sustad reached the summit ridge, but Sustad slipped on balled-up crampons and the pair fell 200 feet. Steve sustained broken ribs and was in pain, so the four climbers teamed up to descend by the normal route on the south side. It was bitterly cold and they were utterly exhausted. Only a few more abseils to go. One was too steep for Sustad in his injured state so Murphy volunteered to set up another anchor to the right. Seconds later a muffled noise came from above. Way up, one avalanche released another and another. Murphy saw it coming, but had no sling to clip into the ice screw. He was just swept away, with no chance of surviving. He would rest in one of the most remote and beautiful mountain valleys on earth.

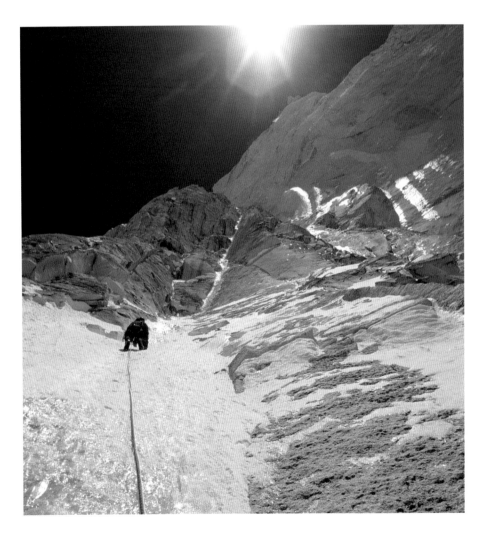

left: Andy Cave on steep thin ice, a crucial section that linked to the upper grooves in 1997.

right: Brendan Murphy leads the ice tongue during day six on Changabang in 1996.

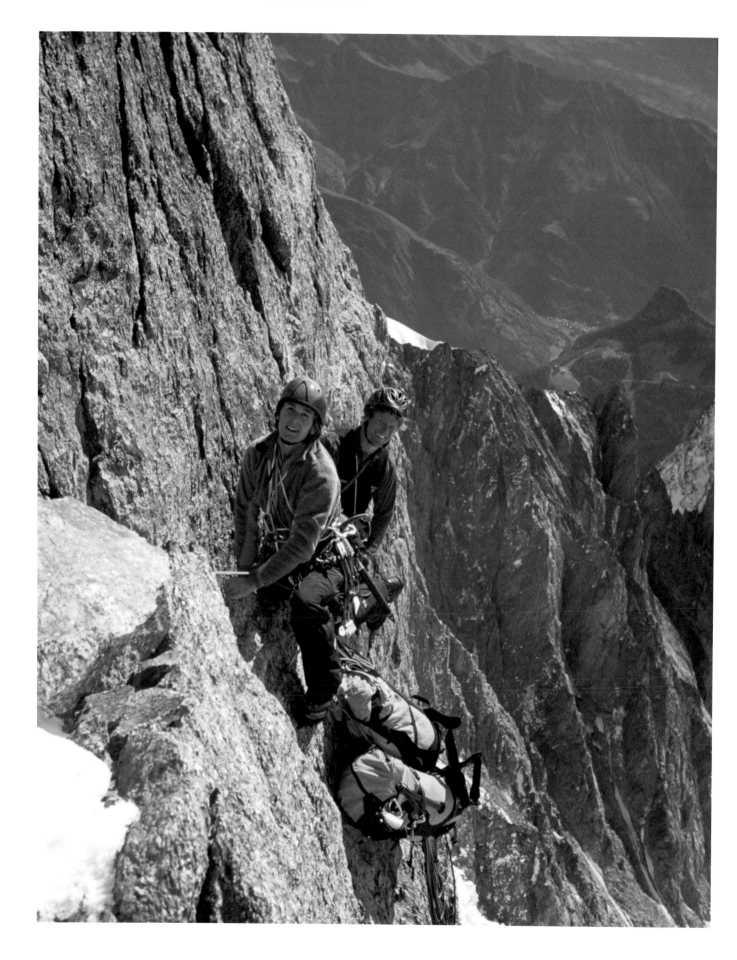

A CHANGE OF PACE –
THE PEAK-BAGGERS

left: 'Are the Alps exhausted?' was the cry in Leslie Stephen's day, but Julie-Ann Clyma and John Harlin III (photographed by Roger Payne) are still exploring new ground *From Dawn to Decadence* on Mont Blanc's Innominata Arête, 17/20 September 2004.

below: Alps 4000: Simon Jenkins and Martin Moran basking in contentment back at the Schreckhorn hut after the 16-hour traverse of the Lauteraargrat.

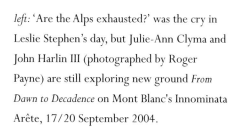

Martin Moran and Simon Jenkins had a busy 52 days in the summer of 1993. Their plan was to make a non-stop traverse of all the 4,000-metre peaks in the Alps of western Europe. As professional guides, they were mostly on familiar ground but the final commitment implied the loss of a third of their annual earnings as guides and personal expenditure of some £10,000 to equip and support the venture.

There is no official list of 4,000-metre peaks, but they accepted a minimum 35-metre height separation to define individual summits, and produced a total of 75. They arranged high-level support teams for the major sections of the Bernese Oberland, Zermatt skyline, and the Mont Blanc massif, with wives providing valley back-up and communications. As a change of exercise, they would bicycle between the main massifs and use skis in the Oberland. Going from east to west they would start with the Piz Bernina and finish with the Barre des Écrins.

The Piz Bernina was climbed on 23 June in a blizzard, and the day's cycling over the Oberalp, Furka and Grimsel passes was as tough as any effort on the mountains. The Schreckhorn–Lauteraarhorn traverse gave some of the finest space-walking in the Alps. Near exhaustion at the Mönchsjoch hut was saved by the arrival of the support team. 'I devoured six fried eggs in as many minutes,' said Martin Moran, 'each with a thick slice of bread, followed by a family-sized tin of peaches; I was still ready for another meal three hours' later.'

They ploughed up the Hasler Rib of the Aletschhorn and skied the Mittelaletsch glacier, using 130-cm Kästle Firn Extrems with Silvretta 404 bindings. Then the weather collapsed. They climbed the Dom in a white-out but further progress was impossible and forced a detour to the valley floor. Snow had fallen thickly down to 7,874 feet (2,400 metres) and the Täschhorn's usually benign south-east ridge proved to be a corniced monster of Andean proportions. Their support team kept them going over Monte Rosa and they were nearly struck by lightning at the start of the Breithorn traverse. Then five days of brilliant weather; the snow-plastered Matterhorn was magnificent and totally deserted; the Dent Blanche a spectacle of ethereal winter beauty. Another storm put fresh snow on the Schalligrat of the Weisshorn which they avoided by uncharted couloirs on the east face and then descended the north ridge. They had closed the Zermatt ring and dared to think of finishing – if Mont Blanc was kind.

They climbed Les Droites and the Aiguille Verte separately rather than the difficult linking ridge. The west ridge of the Jorasses seemed the most nerve-racking so far, with threatening weather and a rescue operation going on below. With thunder rumbling over Mont Blanc, they touched the Madonna on the Dent du Géant and fled to the col where a support camp awaited. They squeezed Mont Blanc's twelve tops into a 36-hour fine-weather window promised by the Chamonix weatherman. The Bionnassay's summit ridge was a razor-edge. After 33 hours on the move, they gained the sanctuary of the Eccles hut. The storm held off just long enough for the Aiguille Blanche de Peuterey, and the descent to the Val Veni into the arms of their wives.

They beat another storm to the top of the Gran Paradiso, followed by a glorious hike into the Vanoise. They followed the wheels of the Tour de France up to the Col du Galibier with a tremendous view of La Meije and the Barre des Écrins from the pass. But the Écrins was an anticlimax; they were too tired and jaded to appreciate the finish after 52 days from 23 June to 13 August. Martin Moran concluded: 'For Simon and myself the journey rekindled the fire of true Alpinism as perhaps it was practised in the days of Winthrop Young, Knubel and their contemporaries. By following their steps in all weathers and conditions we largely escaped the crowds and discarded the regimentation and commercialism which has crept into modern Alpine mountaineering. If nought else, our 4000ers traverse has proved that real adventure in the Alps is still there for the taking.'

below: A sketch map showing the route of Moran and Jenkins, non-stop traverse of the Alpine 4,000ers in Summer 1993.

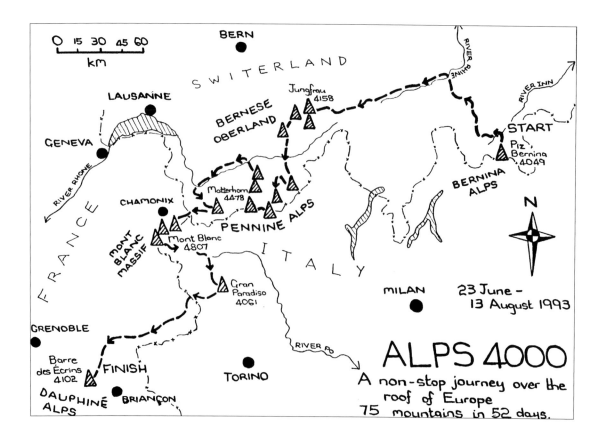

above: A small portrait of Alison Hargreaves with a big smile.

THE BIG SIX AND THE TOP THREE

Alison Hargreaves was one of the most gifted and accomplished mountaineers, not only of the Alpine Club, but of her generation. After the collapse of the climbing equipment business she ran with her husband Jim Ballard they shared responsibility for their two young children. She had to become professional and badly needed sponsorship. She could achieve this by doing a series of outstanding alpine climbs.

In March 1993, she and Jim, Tom aged five and Kate aged two, set off to the Alps. She wanted in one season to climb solo a route on each of the classic six north faces: the Piz Badile, the Cima Grande, the Dru, the Eiger, the Grandes Jorasses and the Matterhorn. She had already done three of them with partners, so there was some familiar ground. On the Jorasses, she chose the Shroud, the ice route to the left of the Walker Spur. The Matterhorn took five and a half hours climbing time, longer than she had hoped, but conditions had been more awkward and time-consuming than anticipated. The Eiger was plastered with snow and ice, so instead of retracing her previous steps up the original 1938 route, she decided on a variation of the Lauper route to the left. All it needed was a good freeze.

Their 30-year-old Land-Rover then took them to the Bregalia and a quiet campsite in the old village of Bondo. The granite slabs of the Badile's north-east face could be tackled in rock boots and she waited patiently while a German party extricated one of their number stuck with his rucksack in a deep crack. The *meteo* now promised several days of hot and sultry weather, so they returned to Chamonix for the Dru. She decided to save weight by sleeping in the valley, catching the first téléphérique and after the climb descend to the Charpoua hut for the night. On the face, she chose the Fissure Martinelli rather than the famous Fissure Allain, and reached the Charpoua as people were going to bed. But the hut was full, so she slept and shivered outside until the first of the early risers left and she could sneak into their warmed beds.

Soon they were chugging in the Land-Rover to the peaks and spires of the Dolomites for the last of the six: the Comici route on the Cima Grande. Not having climbed it before, she had some doubts about a wet and slimy corner near the top, but it proved the correct way. It began to rain as she climbed the last easy pitches, and then the downpour turned to hailstones. But it was all over and with the help of many friends, she had completed the six routes in a total climbing time of 23 hours 45 minutes, so she could call her book *A Hard Day's Summer*. Just to show it was no fluke, in November during a good weather window, she soloed the intimidating Croz Spur on the Grandes Jorasses in six hours – the first woman to do so – being dropped above the bergschrund and then lifted off the summit by helicopter! Now at year's end she could make plans for future dreams and aspirations.

Alison Hargreaves deserved to be the first British woman to climb Everest, but she was pipped to the post earlier that year, on 27 May 1993, by Rebecca

Stephens, who was then a mere aspirant member of the Alpine Club! Hargreaves wanted to do it unsupported and without using oxygen. In a casual conversation at the Club one evening, I encouraged her to try to climb the top three, Everest, K2 and Kangchenjunga, all in one year. Nobody had done this, and no woman had then even climbed Kangchenjunga. I felt the feat was within her capability. She succeeded brilliantly on Everest on 13 May 1995, and then joined American friends to try K2, in the Karakoram, where the best climbing season is in July and August. But the weather is crucial. As Roger Payne has pointed out: 'Ideally, five days is the minimum amount of good weather necessary for a summit bid: four to get to the top and back to camp 4 and then, crucially, a fifth to find the way down to camp 3.' While some others went home, Alison Hargreaves waited for a fine spell. When it came, she reached the summit on 13 August around 6 pm with five other experienced climbers. But a thick layer of cloud to the north, over China, was the harbinger of a violent storm which hit them on the descent with hurricane force; they all perished. Alison Hargreaves was literally blown off the mountain.

After the Everest success, she had achieved the publicity and the sponsorship that she needed to begin to support the family. But she was deeply hurt by some journalists who criticised her for leaving her children, as if she were failing as a mother. Her biographer, Ed Douglas, wrote that: 'In all the years she had been climbing it had not occurred to her that there might be people who thought climbing not just odd, but wrong. It made her feel she was being attacked for no other reason than being who she was. Like many who achieve fame suddenly, she could not see that so much of what was written about her was meaningless, and would quickly be forgotten.'

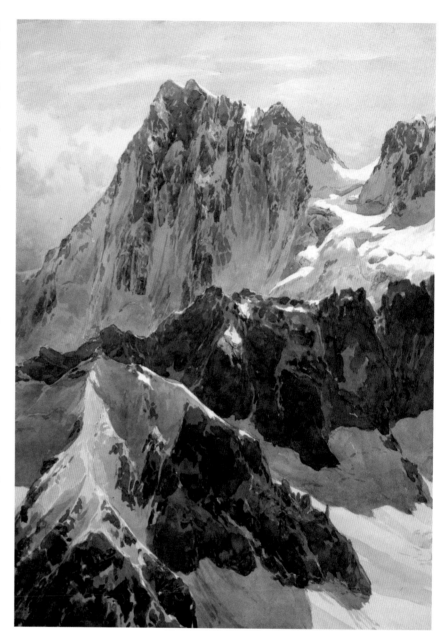

above: A superb Compton watercolour of the north face of the Grandes Jorasses, showing the Walker Spur leading to the left peak, the Point Walker, and the Croz Spur in the centre of the face.

OPPOSITE PAGE:

above right: Jonathan Pratt, a self-portrait on top of Lhotse 22 May 1996, which he climbed with Scott Darsney (USA).

right: K2, with the West Ridge in profile on the left.

THE TOP FIVE

I have admiration for the determination of two more British peak-baggers. Jonathan Pratt was not well known in British climbing circles, as he had worked for several years as a mining engineer in the USA, but since 1986 he had been climbing in North and South America, New Zealand, Africa, and taken part in many Himalayan expeditions, becoming an AC member in 1996. He has quietly logged the top five 8,000-metre peaks, throwing in Gasherbrum I (26,470 ft/8,068 m), a first British ascent, for good measure, and then given up on the highest mountains before the statistics became weighted too heavily against him. It is true that you tend to get relatively few days interesting climbing on the highest peaks in the course of an expedition which may last a month or two, and much greater enjoyment may be found in the same time at lower altitudes.

One of his more remarkable climbs was on the west ridge of K2 in 1993 with the American Dan Mazur. There were nine expeditions attempting K2 from Pakistan that year, all of them except theirs ending up on the Abruzzi ridge (or one

of its variations). British expeditions were the first to attempt the west ridge, Chris Bonington's in 1978 (when Nick Estcourt was sadly killed in an avalanche below camp 2) and Doug Scott's in 1980, but neither was successful. It was finally climbed in 1981 by a large Japanese team using high-altitude porters and oxygen. Apart from a Spanish attempt in 1982, nobody had tried it for eleven years.

Although there were five Britons in the eleven-strong party (including three Americans, a Canadian, a Frenchman and an Irishman), they failed to get any support from the Mount Everest Foundation or the British Mountaineering Council who probably did not give them much of a chance. But they started well, establishing camp 3 at 23,294 ft (7,100 metres) on 8 July within seven days. Then storms arrived and they retreated to base camp. They decided to revert to classic siege-style tactics, but only advanced 200 metres in the next 30 days. Then the Frenchman developed severe pulmonary oedema at camp 4 (24,935 ft/7,600 m), so Mazur and Pratt did extremely well to get him safely down to base, where he recovered from oedema but, suffering frostbite, eventually had to have all his toes amputated. They regrouped and tried again, getting to 26,903 feet (8,200 metres) but high winds defeated them and they retired to base once more. By now all the other expeditions had gone home (with the mountain claiming five lives), leaving just Dan Mazur and Jonathan Pratt to enjoy a period of almost perfect weather. They were well acclimatised so decided to adopt a new strategy – that of continuous climbing day and night – once they had reached their previous high point of 26,903 feet (8,200 metres).

They left at 7 am and in due course reached the south-south-west ridge, also known as the Magic Line. Here a towering rock cliff nearly defeated them, but by a great effort Mazur was able to piton up ten metres of virtually blank wall into a narrow chimney which gave easier climbing. Here they were sheltered from the tearing wind and in a brief clearance could glimpse the summit 300 metres above. They were now committed to a night out, and found some shelter under an overhanging boulder where they rested for a while, pondering whether to go for the top now, or wait for the morning. As the weather was getting worse, they decided to go for it, leaving their packs at the bivvy. They plodded relentlessly on until, suddenly, they were there, 11 pm.

'Take a photo,' gasped Mazur. 'All through the trip,' said Pratt, 'people had been complaining that I did not take enough photos. "Don't worry," I assured them, "I'll take the important one, the one on the top." I reached for my camera – it wasn't there. I had left it in my pack. Dan glared at me. "You idiot!" he said, and stumbled back down the ridge.' They had another brew at the overhanging rock and carried on down, Jonathan conscious that they had a third person with them, as if part of their team. With only a meagre 15 metres of rope, and a few pitons, they made many short abseils – about 15 in all – and eventually rejoined their small tent at 3 pm, having been away for 32 hours. In three more days, they reached base to find the tents flattened and destroyed by a huge sérac avalanche. Luckily only their liaison officer, Captain Wasim, was there, unharmed, as his tent was sheltered behind some rocks. They were the only expedition to summit without a fatality that summer and they wanted to keep it that way.

OPPOSITE PAGE:

above right: Alan Hinkes in good weather on the summit of Dhaulagiri in 2004.

middle right: The best shot I could get of Alan Hinkes near the summit of Kangchenjunga, 30 May 2005, displaying the customary portrait of his daughter Fiona, now with his grandson, Jay.

below right: Kangchenjung, upper S W face – the last 4,000 feet.

ALL FOURTEEN!

Finally, sincere congratulations to Yorkshireman Alan Hinkes on becoming the first Briton to climb all 14 8,000-metre peaks – still in possession of all his fingers and toes. He is the thirteenth person to do it. As he used to say (when the total was only ten), more people have stood on the moon than done that. Alan, a former geography teacher and Royal Marine reservist, is now 51 years old and obviously still very fit. He climbed his first eight-thousander, Shisha Pangma (26,397 ft/8,046 m), in 1987 by a new route on the north face, in a two-person lightweight push with an American, Steve Unteh. Climbing eight-thousanders is very expensive and in the UK sponsorship is hard to come by. I congratulate Alan Hinkes as much for managing to finance his 'Challenge 8000' as for the climbing achievement itself.

Early on, I remember meeting him at Plas-y-Brenin, the National Outdoor Centre close to Snowdon in North Wales. He was then a member of 'Esprit dÉquipe', a project created to climb all the eight-thousanders, and supported by the French company Bull Computers, in order to inspire their employees to greater heights. Unfortunately, after completing two or three of them, the company had some rather poor financial results and aborted the project. Thereafter, Hinkes has found support wherever he can. He has become a technical consultant to Berghaus, and his broad Yorkshire accent comes over well on Tyne Tees TV. To reduce the expensive royalty payment on 8,000-metre peaks, he usually buys a place on another expedition's permit and shares some of their base camp facilities.

It was by no means a straightforward quest. He really only worked out a master plan after he had done eight. 'In one year between July 1995 and July 1996,' he said, ' I climbed four 8000ers: K2, Everest, Gasherbrum I and II. That made eight and I decided I ought to go for all fourteen. There were only three people ever to have done them all at that point: Reinhold Messner, Jerzy Kukuczka and Erhard Loretan.' Several of Hinkes' peaks required multiple attempts. K2 took three years: first attempting the south-east (Abruzzi) ridge in 1993, then close to success on the rarely climbed north face in 1994, and finally the south-east ridge again in 1995, shortly before the ferocious storm that left seven dead, including Alison Hargreaves.

Nanga Parbat (26,660 ft/8,125 m) also required three attempts; in 1992 with Doug Scott in an attempt on the long and complex Mazeno ridge; in 1997 by the Kinshofer route on the Diamir face. This ended prematurely after his bizarre 'chapatti' incident, when he slipped a disc after sneezing from flour that had blown up his nose. He was trapped in agony before being helicoptered out to Islamabad ten days later. He came back in 1998, joining an Italian expedition but climbing separately. On 21 July, from a tent at 23,294 feet (7,100 metres), he had a 15-hour climb in tough conditions with deep snow, reaching the summit during alpenglow at 6.30 pm. The descent slopes were massively loaded by the afternoon's snowfall, presenting severe avalanche risk but, followed by two Koreans, he reached camp safely after being out 22 hours. Finally, he reached base camp where his cook, Rehman, had his favourite eggs, chips and tea ready. He felt totally burnt out, as physically and mentally tired as after K2.

Makalu (27,766 ft/8,463 m) proved another tough one. In 1988, his partner Rick Allen was avalanched and severely injured but recovered. In 1995, Hinkes fell off the path on the way to base camp and speared his thigh on a tree branch, just missing the femoral artery. In 1997, after climbing Lhotse, he was helicoptered in to Makalu base camp but weather and snow conditions stopped him. Fourth time lucky in 1999, although nearly foiled by an attack of giardiasis, he was accompanied by his Nepalese sirdar and friend, Dawa Chirring. Again in deteriorating weather, they roped up for the 60-metre stretch of knife-edged ridge between the east top and the main summit, with stupendous drops on either side.

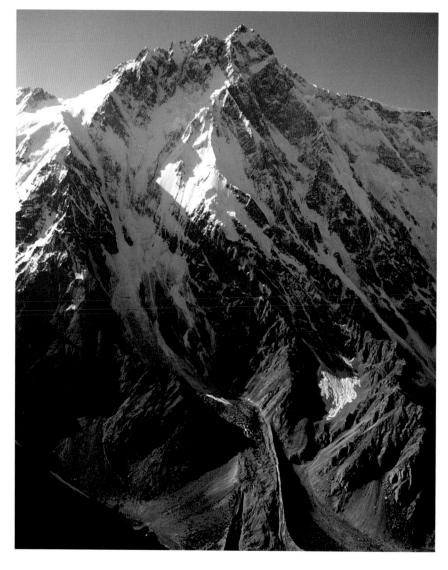

below: The Rupal Face of Nanga Parbat, which was first looked at by Mummery in 1895 and thought unclimbable. It was not until 1970 that a Herrleigkoffer expedition succeeded, on 27 June; Reinhold Messner climbing solo ahead of his brother Günther, who died on the descent in circumstances that have never been clearly resolved.

I was particularly interested in how he would find Kangchenjunga (28,169 ft/8,586 m) in comparison with the other eight-thousanders. Again it was no pushover. In 2000, trying the original 1955 ascent route, there was too much fresh snow. Turning back from above 8,000 metres, he suffered a broken arm after a snow bridge gave way on the descent. In 2003, he contracted what he believes was a dose of the sars virus and retired ill. In 2005, with Annapura, 2002, and Dhaulagiri, 2004, in the bag, Kangchenjunga became his last eight-thousander to be tried, most appropriately in the fiftieth anniversary year of the first ascent. Sharing a Swiss expedition's permit – the only one requested for Kangchenjunga that spring – they were a miscellaneous group of two Swiss, two Czechs, one Spaniard, one Mexican and Alan Hinkes with his Sherpa, Pasang Gelu.

While they were waiting at base camp for the bad weather to improve, I was escorting a trekking party to the foot of the mountain. On 9 May, we sent up fresh vegetables, paperbacks to read, and Superglue to mend his Yeti gaiters. On 21 May, the other climbers gave up and left, leaving Hinkes and Pasang Gelu on their own, waiting for a weather-window forecast in the Everest area at the end of May. Their patience paid off. From a tiny bivouac tent at 24,279 feet (7,400 metres), they set off at 1.30 am on 30 May, still with 3,890 feet to climb.

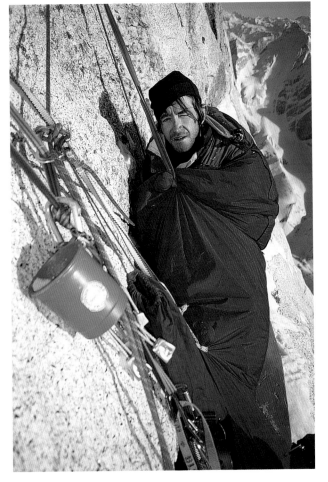

below: Andy Cave still toughing it out on Changabang, looking jaded on bivouac, morning of day eight.

'The final summit push was without a doubt the hardest climb of my life,' recalled Hinkes. 'Pasang had to stop around 15 minutes short of the summit from exhaustion. I reached it around 7 pm in driving snow and wind. Out of respect for the Sikkimese – who regard Kangchenjunga as sacred – I stopped a pace short of the very top, and looked down on the summit. I got out my new digital camera and took self-portrait photos at arm's length, then several of the summit area, just to make sure no-one could dispute I had been there.' I look forward to viewing his photographs to see what I might still be able to recognise. Hinkes continues: 'It was about 9 pm when I caught up with Pasang but with no head torch it was difficult to locate him and I honestly thought he was dead. It was with great elation that I found him, and we got back to the bivvy site around 27 hours after setting off on 31 May. Getting back to base camp was one of the best feelings of my life. I sat down in my tent and thought I've finally done it! And now I was free – finished with near-death experiences. Free just to enjoy the hills.'

Alan Hinkes' 18-year quest was ended. He was also the only person to climb Kangchenjunga in its fiftieth anniversary year. You might think that his 8,000-metre achievement would receive some recognition by the British national press. The *Daily Telegraph* gave it a good spread, but *The Times* ignored it completely. They were far more interested in chronicling Ranulph Fiennes' failure to climb Everest, after it has already had more than 2,250 ascents! But I am pleased to record that Alan Hinkes was rewarded for his efforts with an OBE in the 2006 New Year's Honours List.

WHERE ELSE IN THE WORLD?

I am running out of both space and time in trying to record the highlights of our Alpine Club members' activities over the last 20 years. I have tended to give prominence to the European Alps and to Central Asia, but their remit is worldwide – particularly in areas that are easy of access and relatively free from burdensome bureaucratic restrictions. Summer in Greenland, Baffin Island, Alaska and the Yukon has the added advantage of almost 24-hour daylight so you don't get benighted. The sheer walls of the towers of Paine and Fitzroy in Patagonia and southern Chile attract the superstars, despite ferocious winds and weather. The slightly more obscure areas such as the sandstone pinnacles of the American south-west, the jungles and geologically recent granite of Mount Kinabalu in Borneo, or the Conan Doyle 'Lost World' tepuis of Venezuela, all have their devotees. Climbers worldwide have benefited from the cross-fertilisation of concepts and techniques developed by top American rock climbers such as Warren Harding, Royal Robbins, Tom Frost, Chuck Pratt and Yvon Chouinard on the sheer walls of El Capitan, Cathedral Rock, Half Dome and other cliffs in Yosemite. After the climb, everyone would relax in the informal environment of camp 4 in the National Park at the foot of the cliffs. This campsite has been saved from redevelopment, threatened by the Park authorities, thanks to the campaigning work of Tom Frost, and by an international outcry from foreign climbers. It will now be preserved as a 'national historic site'.

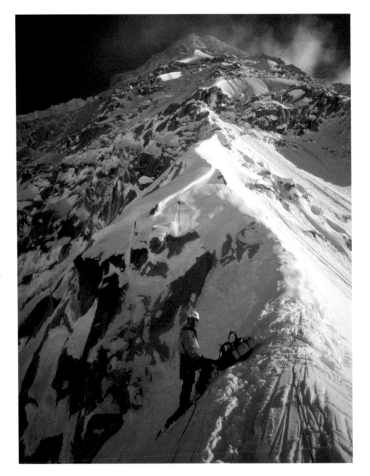

NEW TOOLS FOR ROCK AND ICE

Hard steel pitons, RURPs (realized ultimate reality pitons), hauling systems, sleeping hammocks and portaledges for bivouacking comfortably on sheer walls were all developed in Yosemite. In turn, the use of pitons is now diminishing thanks to the invention of nuts, wedges and camming devices originally invented in Britain, called Friends, or gigantic Camelots, which do not harm the rock. Firé's sticky soled rock boots from the Spanish firm Boreal were another great innovation of the early eighties, which influenced a surge in standards. The extraordinary developments in ice climbing can be traced back to the versatile and innovative Hamish MacInnes and the invention of his Terrordactyl drop-picked ice tool, rather than Chouinard's dropped pick Climaxe.

To quote Dick Turnbull: 'It was the Terror that triumphed – check out the modern Black Diamond ice tools – and led to the security, speed and increased popularity of front point or "piolet traction" as Chouinard liked to call it. The

above: Andy Cave at the third bivouac on the north buttress of Mount Kennedy, St Elias Range, Yukon, Canada, by Mick Fowler, April 2000.

right: The gear needed by Ollie Sanders for a new 2,200-ft overhanging route on the North Tower of the Torres del Paine in January 2004. The team of four was Ollie, Martin Doyle, Louise Thomas and Mike Turner, climbing in pairs. They called the route 'A fist full of dollars', precisely what the Park authorities now regrettably exact as a climbing fee.

eventual acceptance of the drop pick design by the main European hardware manufacturers and the arrival of the influential Simond Chacal reverse curve ice tool finally integrated modern ice tool design. Today, the tools most responsible for helping raising mountaineering standards world-wide can be directly related to Hamish MacInnes's original development.' Using just the front points of one's crampons on steep ice is also made so much easier and safer by the rigidity of modern plastic boots combined with secure clip-on crampons.

I have great admiration for Hamish MacInnes. The first *Alpine Journal* I received after becoming a member of the Club (Vol. LX, May 1955) included his article on the Creagh Dhu Himalayan Expedition, 1953. The party consisted of just John Cunningham and himself. They had no sponsors and very little money. Their objective was a post-monsoon ascent of Everest. When they heard of the success of Colonel Hunt's team in the spring, they switched to one of the satellite peaks, Pumori. Their trek from Kathmandu started badly. The first day they tried carrying 190 pounds each, but then capitulated and hired two porters to get them to Namche Bazar. Their sole Sherpa, Nima, followed with his small pack. At Namche, they decided to dispense with Nima, who offered to give them his knife, fork and mug. They paid him for these, as eating with pitons and tent pegs was not very hygienic …

Hamish MacInnes' Terrordactyl also had other uses. It was my pleasure to present the brilliant Polish mountaineer Andrzej Zawada with his Alpine Club tie when we made him an honorary member in 1987. In 1997, he organised the first Anglo-Polish expedition to the Hindu Kush, which involved a tiring train journey across the Soviet Union. Entering the compartment where Alex MacIntyre lay sprawled, Andrzej politely asked to 'see this new ice tool, this pterodactyl you told me about'. MacIntyre duly dug out the weapon from one of his sacks and passed it to Zawada. To everyone's amazement, Zawada then stormed down the carriage and smashed each of the six loud speakers playing Soviet 'muzak' of patriotic military tunes. 'Ah,' said Zawada 'I see this pterodactyl works perfectly. In Poland, we do not allow such tedious music.'

A NEW GOLDEN AGE?

OPPOSITE PAGE:

top left: Hamish MacInnes in his engineering workshop improving the design of ice-axes and hammers.

bottom left: Hamish winter climbing in Scotland using an early design of his Terrordactyl drop-picked ice tool.

THIS PAGE:

below: A skier dragging his pulk on the Chisel glacier, east Greenland, with the Lemon Mountains behind.

I am conscious that when any curious Alpine Club member picks up this book, he will immediately turn to the index to see whether his name, and perhaps his contribution to the Club's reputation, has been properly recognised. I will be sorry to disappoint many of you who, nevertheless, form the backbone of the Club, helping to organise its activities, run its committees, write for the *Journal*, and enjoy the annual meet in the Alps and to other ranges, or just prefer to climb with immediate friends. Let me just, therefore, close this chapter with a brief mention of a selection of the *Journal* articles over the last 20 years that I have enjoyed and would have happily incorporated at greater length if there had been the space to do so. Many are written by the brightest stars of the climbing firmament, several of whom are not yet members of the Club but who I hope will be by the time this book is published.

Chris Bonington has said recently that 'Mick Fowler and his friends are part of a New Golden Age of Climbing that is now fully underway on the world's greatest peaks, an even more exciting saga than the one played in the Alps in the nineteenth century.'

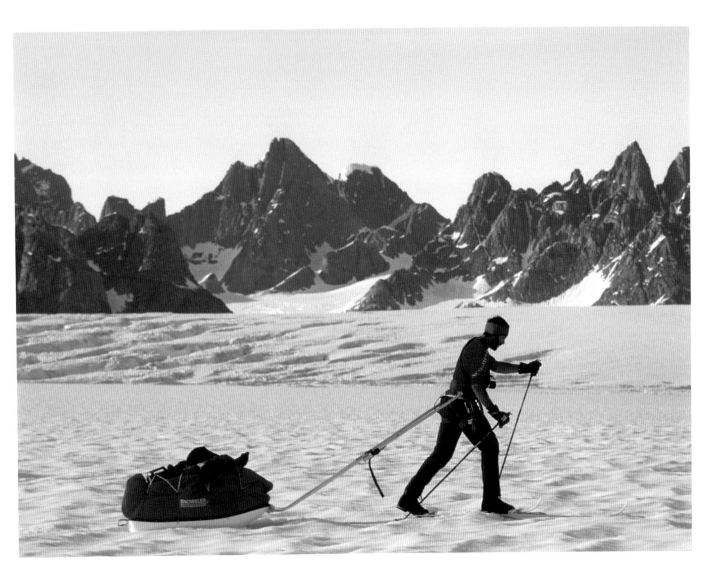

SELECTED ALPINE JOURNAL ARTICLES

year   page

1985   77   *Bojohagar* by Mick Fowler. At 7,330 m one of the Karakoram's highest unclimbed peaks. Chris Watts performs with only one boot!

1986   19   *The Siachen Indo-British Expedition* 1985 by Stephen Venables and Dave Wilkinson. Venables drops his sack on Rimo but they climbed Rimo III and seven other peaks.

1987   10   *Hunter's South Ridge* – Alpine Style by Simon Richardson. Richardson and Ed Hart alone for 20 days.

129   *The British Caucasus Expedition 1986* by A V Saunders. A new route on Ushba by the ubiquitous Saunders and Mick Fowler.

1989/90 1   *Everest Kangshung Face* – First Ascent of the Neverest Buttress by Stephen Venables. Well covered in my Everest book, 2003.

34   *The Ascent of Menlungtse West* by Andy Fanshawe. Climbed by Fanshawe and Alan Hinkes on Chris Bonington's expedition.

1991/92 8   *Ama Dablam 1990*, by Brendan Murphy. Murphy becomes the first Irishman and Kate Phillips the second Briton (after Mike Ward in 1961) to climb the peak.

1992/93 9   *Eight Days on Nanga Parbat* by Dave Walsh. Walsh and Roger Mear make the first British ascent by the Kinshofer route on the Diamir face.

22   *Kusum Kangguru* by Dick Renshaw. First ascent with Stephen Venables of the South Ridge, beside the Everest trail. Thirty abseils in descent!

1993   105   *Panch Chuli V* by Stephen Venables. A first ascent, but Venables is lucky to survive when his abseil anchor fails. A difficult helicopter rescue. Another joint Indian/British expedition led by Harish Kapadia and Chris Bonington.

125   *Mongolian Escape* by Lindsay Griffin. A Raleigh International Expedition which climbed 23 peaks. Another daring helicopter rescue after Griffin is injured in a serious rockfall accident.

1994   48   *The One That Nearly Got Away* by Mick Fowler, with Steve Sustad. The first ascent, in four days, of the 1,000-m north-west face of Cerro Kishtwar in the Haptal Nullah of the Kishtwar Himalaya.

1995   47   *Hammering the Anvil* by Paul Pritchard, one of Baffin Island's fabulous walls. The first ascent of the west face of Mount Asgard by Noel Craine, Paul Pritchard, Steve Quinlan and Jordi Tosas on 10 July 1994 after eleven days on the wall. Hyperboria is 1,000 m (19 pitches), A4+ E4 6A. There are no soul-destroying false summits on Asgard – you just slap the top and mantelshelf.

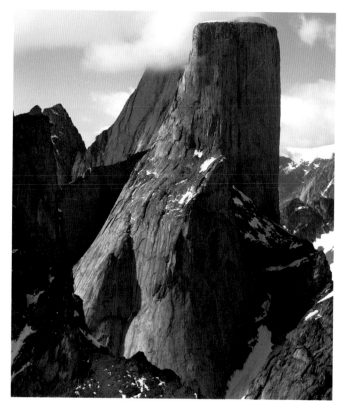

above: Mount Asgard (16,598 ft / 2,011 m) on the Arctic Circle.

85   *Crab Crawl on the Bezingi Wall* by José Luis Berm?dez, with Neil Wilson, The nearest a British party has got to a complete traverse of the Bezingi Wall in the central Caucasus – from Shkhara to East Jangi-tau.

1997   111   *Foolishly Following A F Mummery* by Roy Ruddle. An Alpine Club meet in the Caucasus organised by John Temple. Eleven people climbed eleven peaks, including the first British repeat of Mummery and Zurfluh's 1888 route on Dych-tau by Ruddle and Robert Durran.

148   *The Atlas End to End* by Hamish M Brown. A grand traverse of the Atlas Mountains from 28 March to 10 July 1995 with Charles Knowles and others.

1998   97   *Cerro Torre* by Paul Moores. The first British ascent of this Patagonian monolith in November 1995.

117   *Beatrice* by Louise Thomas. A three-woman team of Kath Pyke, Glenda Huxter and Louise Thomas climb a difficult 5,800-m rock peak in the Charakusa Basin, Pakistan, starting from a portaledge camp. Hateja ('strong-willed, determined lady') (750 m, ED+ A3+).

1999   23   *Courting the Great White Snow God* by Chris Bonington. First ascents in the eastern Nyenchen Tanglha in Central Tibet, but not quite to the top of Sepu Kangri 6,950 m.

51   *Mountaineering and War on the Siachen Glacier* by Harish Kapadia with his Bombay team. A history of exploration in this troubled area. 'The only solution to save this great wilderness is to stop the war.'

136   *Climbing and Kalashnikovs* by Chris Bedford, Derek Buckle and Gary Hill. The 1998 Alpine Club meet to the Georgian Caucasus, again organised by John Temple. Eight people climbed seven peaks, despite being robbed by armed bandits on two separate occasions.

2000   88   *When Hell Freezes Over* by Andy Kirkpatrick, with Paul Ramsden, Jim Hall and Nick Lewis. Extreme suffering while winter climbing on Fitzroy's Super Couloir in Patagonia. 'I've rationed my energy well, but now the dial has hit empty and my body has started to stall.'

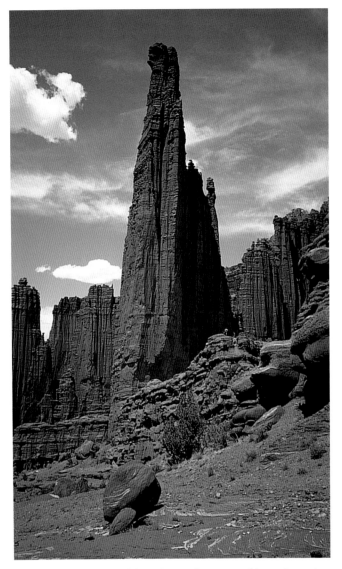

above: The Titan, made of the softest and most unstable sandstone in southern Utah.

103   *A Kind of Obsession: Climbing the Titan* by Iain Allen. The ascent of America's tallest free-standing pinnacle, in the desert south-west with Ian Howell.

278   *Charles Warren 1906–1999* by Oliver Turnbull. Brief mention of the 1933 expedition to the Gangotri glacier when Warren and Colin Kirkus made the first ascent of central Satopanth Peak (now called Bhagirathi III), alpine-style, self-supporting for six days, a remarkable achievement at that time.

2001   19   *Arwa Spire* by Ian Parnell. First ascent of the extreme 6,193-m Spire by the twins Andy and Pete Benson, followed three days later by Kenton Cool, Ian Parnell and Al Powell.

2002   **18**   *Ama Dablam* by Jules Cartwright. The first ascent of the supremely committing north-west ridge with Rich Cross in eleven days in 2001. Sadly, Jules and his client, Julie Colverd, were killed on the relatively easy approach to an alpine climb on 30 June 2004. Ian Parnell paid this tribute in AJ 2005: '[The route on Ama Dablam] had seen almost a dozen previous attempts, including a bolted siege by an eight-person Dutch team. The Brits opted for a pure and simple alpine ascent, trimming their gear to an absolute minimum; the ice rack consisted of only two ice screws and a snow-stake. I say simple ascent but the terrain was far from that, with over 4,000 m of twisting, gendarmed ridge sucking them in like a trap. One 60 m horizontal section took a full day to navigate and their eight days of already scant rations were stretched ever thinner until the food ran out with the final snow buttress still to climb. At the time, I described is as "probably the most significant British ascent in the mountains in the last decade". Since then that assessment hasn't diminished and the north-west ridge sits alongside the likes of Renshaw's and Tasker's Dunagiri climb, or the Shisha Pangma ascent by Baxter-Jones, MacIntyre and Scott, at the pinnacle of British alpine-style Himalayan climbing.'

    37   *Fathers and Sons* by Ian Parnell. The first ascent of the new route The Extraterrestrial Brothers (2,200 m ED2 Scottish VII) being the second ascent of the Fathers and Sons Wall, Denali (6,194 m), Alaska, by Ian and Kenton Cool.

    50   *El Niño* by Leo Houlding. The second ascent with Patch Hammond of El Niño on the east buttress of El Capitan, Yosemite, in October 1998, a month after its first ascent by Thomas and Alex Huber, one of the outstanding big-wall achievements by British climbers in recent years. El Niño has 30 pitches, five of 5.11, seven of 5.12 and six of 5.13. Chris Bonington comments of the 23-year-old Houlding: 'He's one of the most brilliant young climbers I've seen in a long time. He climbs at the absolute edge, but if he manages to stay alive he'll go a long, long way.'

    189   *Confessions of a Parvenu* by Dennis Gray. A potted history of the Alpine Climbing Group, and the entry of women into the Alpine Club, by the first ever paid officer of the British Mountaineering Council.

2003   **23**   *Hell to Pay: On Denali's Diamond* by Ian Parnell. The second ascent of the Denali Diamond (8,000 ft,

VIII, 8, A3) on the south-west face of Denali (Mt McKinley 6,194 m) Alaska, by Parnell and Kenton Cool over five days in late May 2002.

    57   *Citrus Delights* by Derek Buckle, Robert Durran, Roy Ruddle and Dave Wilkinson. The 2002 ACG/AC Greater Ranges meet in the Lemon Mountains, east Greenland. Eighteen peaks climbed, mostly first ascents, the best being the 1,300-m north-east face of The Spear by Wilkinson and Geoff Cohen.

    116   *A Mountaineer's New Zealand* by Paul Knott. A helpful review for those unfamiliar with the ranges.

2004   **76**   *Venezuelan Verticality* by John Arran, with Anne Arran and Alfredo Rangel. The first ascent of Acopántepúi, 600 m E6 6b (7b+), climbed on sight in six days, without pegs or bolts. The Arrans graduated as competition climbers on indoor artificial climbing walls.

151 and 161 *Peace Parks?* In the Balkans by Richard Hargreaves, and the Siachen by Harish Kapadia. Hope for troubled border regions.

187 *The Evolution of Climbing Clubs in Britain* by Derek Walker. Now some 370 clubs, 'the backbone of British Mountaineering', by a former general secretary and president of the British Mountaineering Council and of the Climbers' Club.

211 *Re-Touching the Void* by Simon Yates. Joe Simpson's climbing partner reflects on their 1985 climb and troubled descent from Suila Grande's west face in Peru, that led to Simpson's bestselling *Touching the Void* and the stunningly successful BAFTA award-winning docu-movie released in November 2003.

215 *Toward Defining the Void* by John Porter — trying to understand why it was so successful, even though it was 'not the most relaxing way to spend a Saturday evening'.

2005 **39** *The Arctic Discipline Wall* by Jon Bracey. The first complete ascent of A Pair of Jacks on the north-west face of Mount Kennedy, Yukon, Canada by Rich Cross and Jon Bracey in May 2004.

103 *Just Climbing* by Kelly Cordes. The first successful ascent of the south-west ridge of Great Trango Tower, Pakistan, in July 2004 by Josh Wharton and Kelly

Cordes. They named the 54-pitch route Azeem Ridge and graded it 5.11 R/X M6 A2.

113 *The Great Karakoram Ski Traverse* by Dave Hamilton. The first full ski traverse of the Pakistan Karakoram, a journey of 260 km from Shimshal to Hushe taking 37 days in spring 2004. A team of six led by Dave Hamilton. Includes a handy sketch map.

153 *From Dawn to Decadence* by John Harlin III. Exploring new ground on Mont Blanc's Innominata Arête, 770 m TD, 5.10+, 17/20 September 2000, with Julie-Ann Clyma and Roger Payne. Harlin is currently editor of the *American Alpine Journal*; his father died on the Eiger in 1966.

OPPOSITE PAGE:

left: A happy party on a commodious bivouac ledge, camp 5, 800 m up the 1,100-m overhanging wall of Auyántepúi beside the Angel Falls: Anne Arran (AC), Ben Heason, Miles Gibson, Ivan Calderon, Alex Klenov and Alfredo Rangel.

THIS PAGE:

below left: A map showing the route of the Great Karakoram Ski Traverse led by Dave Hamilton in spring 2004.
below right: Roger Payne and Julie-Ann Clyma below Kalanka and Changabang, 1996.

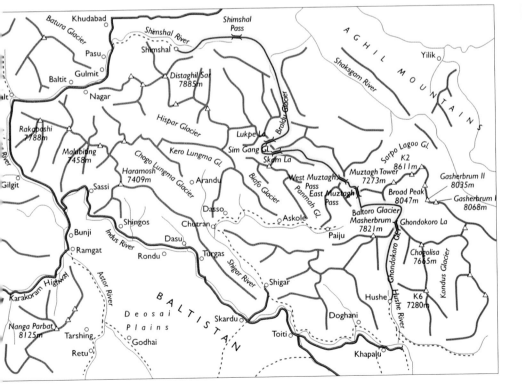

A NOTE ON GRADES

Most readers of this book will be familiar with the traditional British and Alpine grades of climbs to indicate the levels of difficulty both in a technical sense over individual pitches and for a general assessment of the whole climb. The original British general adjectival grades were Easy, Moderate, Difficult, Very Difficult, Severe and Very Severe, often further subdivided by prefixes of Mild or Hard. The tremendous advance in standards and techniques at the top end, led in the 1950s to the introduction of Extremely Severe and Exceptionally Severe. These evolved into the 'E' grades E1, E2, and, well beyond my capability, E3, E4 and so on right up to an incredible E10. At the same time Arabic numerical grades were introduced to describe short passages or pitches on rock climbs: 4a, 4b, 4c roughly equating to the range Severe to Hard Very Severe, and 5a, 5b, 5c. broadly equating with E1, E2 and E3; grades 6 and 7 equating with the higher E grades.

In the Alps, the French had a similar numerical system for pitches (originally in Roman numerals) perhaps a little more generous than the British, such that a British 5b might be considered a French VIa. For the general description of an alpine climb, the French Vallot guidebook also used an adjectival system expressed in letters: F (facile), PD (peu difficile), AD (assez difficile), D (difficile), TD (très difficile), ED (extrêmement difficile). The last three could be further subdivided with a suffix of inf. (inférieure) or sup. (supérieure).

Typical examples in the Chamonix area were:

V sup.	The Knubel Crack on the Aig du Grépon
D inf.	Traverse of the Aig du Grépon
D sup.	Ryan-Lochmatter on the Aig du Plan
TD inf.	S ridge of the Aig du Fou
TD sup.	S ridge of the Aig Noire de Peuterey
	N ridge of the Aig du Peigne
ED	W face of the Pointe Albert

In the early 1950s British climbers were tackling the TD sup. and easier ED climbs for the first time. Bourdillon and Nicol's success in 1955 on the west face of the Aiguille Noire de Peuterey and the east face of the Capucin put them well into the EDs, and Brown and Whillans' third ascent of the west face of the Dru in 1954 put them right at the top of the ED range. Such routes involved quite a lot of artificial climbing, which was further defined by A1, A2, A3, depending on difficulty. Usually the pitons were already in place.

In the United States an independent Yosemite Decimal System developed for rock climbing with 5.9 equating to a British 5a or HVS/E1. Grades 5.11 to 5.14 covered the British 6 to 7 grades.

Inventive as ever, the Americans developed further criteria to describe the seriousness of a route. I was totally flummoxed by Kelly Cordes' grading of the Azeem Ridge as 5.11 R/X M6 A2 in the *Alpine Journal* 2005 and had to refer to

Lindsay Griffin of Mountain Info for enlightenment. He kindly directed me to a summary in the *American Alpine Journal* 1999, pages 477–84, which explained all: grades for USA, UIAA, Alaskan, Russian, Scottish Winter, Canadian Winter, Mixed Grades, Water Ice and Alpine Ice. I think there was enough there to expand into a Ph.D thesis! At least it threw some further light on Kelly Cordes' climb:

R: Poor protection with potential for a long fall and injury.

X: A fall would likely result in serious injury or death.

M: These routes require considerable dry tooling (modern ice tools used on bare rock) and are climbed in crampons; actual ice is optional but some ice is usually involved. Ranges from M1 to M12, thus:

M6:   Vertical to overhanging with difficult dry tooling.

You have been warned!

In January 2006, I attended a lecture by John and Anne Arran describing their incredible ascent in 2005 of the 1,100-m overhanging wall of Auyántepúi in the jungles of Venezuela, just to the left of the famous Angel Falls, the highest waterfall in the world. The 31-pitch climb was full of E7s, which had all been climbed free during the ascent. The last pitch of the climb was given J3, J for a 'Jungle grade' from J1 to J5 depending on just how much you trusted climbing on the mixed vegetation of bromeliads, other epiphytes and creepers, or swinging on lianas! They were on the wall for 19 days in total, spending 12 nights on the wall after lift-off. The local Piaroa Indians who helped them on the river journey through the jungle to the foot of the climb were very happy to see them return to base camp. The Arrans' adventures can be followed up on **www.thefreeclimber.com**

below: John Arran grapples overhanging rock beside the 1,100-m torrent of the Angel Falls, the highest waterfall in the world.

11 THE ALPINE CLUB AT HOME

ENTRUSTED WITH A PRECIOUS HERITAGE

Ever since the Club was founded in 1857, its members have been donating to it books, paintings, photographs and memorabilia as well as more modern climbing guidebooks, expedition reports, periodicals and maps, which together cover probably better than any other library in the world the history of mountaineering and mountain exploration. The task of classifying and cataloguing some 40,000 items has been a major undertaking. In the 1970s, the Club found that managing a library of this size and variety, if its riches were to be readily accessible to readers, was beyond the resources of the voluntary effort of a Club of only 1,000 members. Thanks to the suggestion of Lord Chorley, then honorary treasurer of the Club, in 1972 a Trust was set up under the guidance of Lord Tangley (who, as Sir Edwin Herbert had been president in the 'Everest' year, 1953). The Trust has been recognised as a charity, permitting access to the general public, and the task of its council of management has been both to direct the work of the Library and to raise the funds necessary for its operation. The first chairman was Sir Douglas Busk, followed by Michael Westmacott, in the early 1980s, then myself from 1993 to 2005, succeeded by the present incumbent, Hywel Lloyd. All of us have been deeply indebted to our voluntary helpers, fellow council members, and the professional librarians, archivists and photo-librarians which we have been able to employ over the years.

left: Passage of a block of ice in a Crevasse, a visionary 1827 watercolour by John Auldjo 1805–86, best known for his *Narrative of an Ascent to the Summit of Mont Blanc,* 1828. He lived for many years in Switzerland and was British Consul in Geneva 1870–86.

below: Margaret Ecclestone, the Club's very professional librarian 1992–2003, who devoted extra hours to put the entire Library catalogue on computer.

TREASURES OF THE ALPINE CLUB

In 1982, the Library published Volume I of its new catalogue in hard copy – the first to be published since 1899 – covering all the books, climbing guides, periodicals and club journals held in the Library in March 1979. To celebrate its publication, in 1982, during the presidency of J H Emlyn Jones, a special exhibition *Treasures of the Alpine Club* was arranged at the Alpine Club's Gallery, 74 South Audley Street in London's West End. The exhibits ranged from the earliest books; including Jacques Signot's description of the ten known ways of crossing the Alps between France and Italy, published in 1518, items from the early ascents of Mont Blanc, the silver pocket compass and sundial carried by de Saussure, and a lady's fan and a parlour game based on Albert Smith's entertainment at the Egyptian Hall. On display were several original *Führerbücher* carried by famous Alpine guides, whose clients entered their comments after each series of expeditions; that of Franz Joseph Lochmatter includes entries by V J E Ryan and G W Young after climbing the south face of the Täschhorn. Paintings ranged from John Auldjo's delightful *Passage of a block of ice in a Crevasse*, dating from 1827, several water colours by John Ruskin, including his dreamlike *Lake of Lucerne and Uri Rostok*, and others by members of the Club who were active mountaineers, notably Whymper, Willink, Compton, McCormick, Loppé, Elijah Walton and Howard Somervell. In one corner was Whymper's tent, which has since been carefully repaired at the Royal School of Needlework.

THE LIBRARY APPEAL – ENTERING THE COMPUTER AGE

By 1990, the Library was in need of further funding, to help set up an endowment fund, so a special appeal was launched under the chairmanship of the Earl of Limerick which, thanks to the generosity of members and several outside supporters, raised close on £200,000. With this cushion, it could afford to move into the computer age, and it was decided not to publish Volume II of the Library catalogue in hard copy. Devoting extra hours during her eleven-year tenure, 1992–2003, our very professional librarian, Margaret Ecclestone, put the entire Library catalogue on computer.

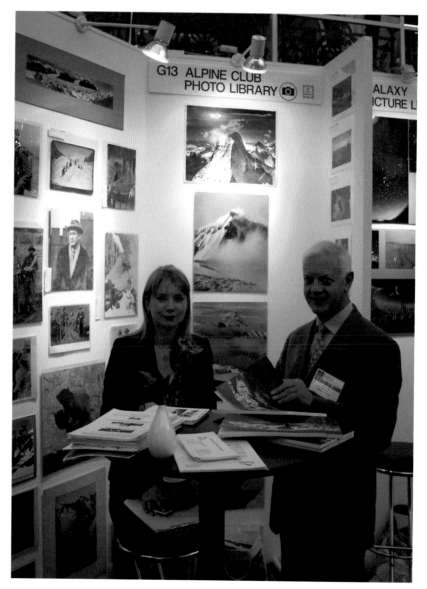

below: Rachael Swann, photo-librarian, and Hywel Lloyd, current Chairman of the Alpine Club Library Council, staff the Club's stand at the annual BAPLA Fayre, 2005. Awarded joint best stand in 2006.

With a grant from the Pilgrim Trust, a professional archivist, Susan Scott, was then engaged to do a similar job for the Club's archives. The third stage was to address the Club's photographic collection, which included some superb images going back to the earliest days of mountain photography, as can be seen from those reproduced in this book. The Club's indefatigable librarian emeritus, Bob Lawford, had already completed a traditional card index and his daughter, Anna, now gallantly undertook to set up the basis for a computerised photo-library for which professional help has been engaged, together with a volunteer from NADFAS. The work is divided between earning income from media enquiries, computerised cataloguing and scanning, and conservation work to protect the collection. The long-term aim is to be able to continue employing a photo-library manager and earn additional income for the Club and the Library.

EVEREST IMAGES

The one sad bone of contention which we hope may be resolved before the publication of this book is the ownership and copyright of the 20,000 or more images taken on the successive Everest Expeditions from 1921 through to 1953 and on Kangchenjunga in 1955. As originally agreed with the climbers who took the photographs, they belonged to the Joint Himalayan Committee (of the Alpine Club and the Royal Geographical Society) who organised the Expeditions and who duly assigned them to the Mount Everest Foundation (MEF), also jointly created by the AC and the RGS after the successful ascent in 1953. As the MEF had no premises of its own, the images were held in the archives at the RGS, as was the case in the 1920s and 1930s. In the 1970s, there was an intention to formalise this arrangement and the RGS assumed ownership and copyright, although there was no formal Deed of Assignment. When the income from marketing these unique images began to increase significantly in recent years, it was totally retained by the RGS, for their own use without any being paid over to the MEF, where, in accordance with its objectives, it would be used to support exploration and mountaineering, which was the original intention of the Everest climbers and the Joint Himalayan Committee. So both the MEF and the AC have lost out, at the expense of the RGS.

We are grateful to Alan Blackshaw (Alpine Club president 2002–04) for researching and taking up this issue again, in a personal capacity, when he realised that he had been a trustee of the MEF in the 1970s at the time the RGS assumed ownership and copyright, although he had no recollection of any formally authorised assignment as stipulated in the Copyright Acts.

below top: The indestructible Kurt Diemberger, Hon. Member, and Michael Westmacott, President 1993–95, enjoy a party at the Club. Michael has been the driving force behind the Club's unique computerised Himalayan Index.

below bottom: Lord Roger Chorley, President 1983–85, later became President of the Royal Geographical Society and Chairman of the National Trust.

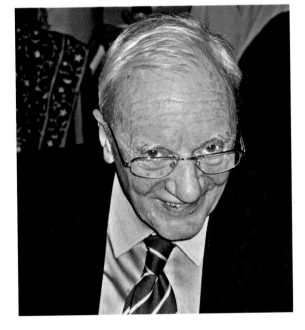

THE HIMALAYAN INDEX

Another initiative of the Alpine Club Library is its unique Himalayan Index. As more and more expeditions went to the Himalaya it became impractical to record them all in conventional reports and guidebooks. At the suggestion of the president, Lord Chorley, in 1983: 'The Himalayan Index is one way that the Club can fulfil its traditional role of providing a lead in the mountaineering world.' A computerised database seemed to be the answer. After a feasibility study endorsed the concept and some funding was achieved, it was left largely to Michael Westmacott and a small team of helpers to bring it to fruition. Now, over 20 years later, it is a monument to his dedication and perseverance. It contains records of over 6,000 ascents or attempts on 2,800 peaks over 6,000 metres in the Himalaya, Karakoram, Hindu Kush and China, and about 5,500 references to the literature. As a valuable tool for searching out new objectives, it can provide listings of peaks within a specific area, ascents of or attempts on them, and lists of journal references. It may be accessed in the Club website. The domain name was registered on 25 May 1996, and came on stream later that year. The website contains up-to-date information about the Club, its current events and news. Other pages include the Library and, in due course, the Photo Library and the Archives. The current website editor is Phil Wickens.

THE EVOLUTION OF CLIMBING CLUBS AND THE BMC

While the Alpine Club's marvellous collection was being accumulated in London over the years, and its members enjoyed their annual holiday in the Alps, the social structure of climbing in Britain was gradually changing, as recorded in Derek Walker's article in the *Alpine Journal* 2004 which I have liberally quoted. I have already mentioned in Chapter 3 the creation of local clubs at the turn of the century, based on Scotland, North Wales and the Lake District, and the cities of Liverpool and Manchester. Starting from the 1920s, some of the larger clubs had acquired huts to provide simple accommodation in mountain areas for their members, a practice that has continued ever since. The first in Britain was Helyg in the Ogwen valley, described by George Borrow in the 19th century as a 'miserable hovel', opened by the Climbers' Club in 1925. The principal universities also formed their mountaineering clubs, and when the students graduated they would often join one of the local clubs, so that they could use their huts. In 1930, Alastair Borthwick wrote that 'fresh air was still the property of moneyed men, a luxury open to few … Hiking was the hobby of an enthusiastic handful, and climbing was a rich man's sport.'

Things were soon to change, however, as recounted by Derek Walker:

By the early 1930s a new wave of working-class climbers began to emerge, helped partly by the youth hostel movement and also by widespread unemployment. New clubs such as the Sheffield Climbing Club began to explore the gritstone crags, and the Creagh Dhu lads from the Glasgow shipyards began to climb on the Cobbler and in Glencoe. The members of these new clubs had little in common with the more affluent members of the existing climbing clubs. A process of social change had begun that was to increase dramatically after the Second World War.

It was during the war that the British Mountaineering Council evolved largely due to the vision of Geoffrey Winthrop Young. Hitherto, the Alpine Club had assumed the role of representing the interests of all British mountaineers. Winthrop Young (1878–1958) was not only one of the leading rock-climbers and alpinists of his age, but also a distinguished educationalist, writer and communicator. As early as 1907 he first raised the idea of a single organisation to represent all mountaineers in Britain; and then immediately after the First

OPPOSITE PAGE:

above right: A well-nailed pair of boots? Advertising from *Alpine Journals* of the 1930s.

below right: A fine oil painting of Monte Rosa, Lyskamm, Castor and Pollux, above Zermatt, by Arthur Croft (1863–93), exhibited at the Royal Academy in 1871. It is the picture at the top left of the drawing of 23 Savile Row on p.239.

THIS PAGE:

below: Anna Lawford helping her father to move the Club out of leased premises at 74 South Audley Street, 26 December 1989.

World War in 1919, when he was president of the Climbers' Club, he suggested an advisory body of British clubs. But this idea was short-lived and it was not until the Second World War, when Young was president of the Alpine Club (1941–1943), that his vision became reality. In his valedictory address in December 1943 he persuaded the majority (but not all) of members that the AC was no longer the appropriate body to represent British mountaineers. His successor as AC president, the distinguished politician Leo Amery – whose other job was Secretary of State for India – continued Young's cause and within a year the BMC was born.

The Council initially consisted of 25 clubs. Young became first president (1945–47) and John Barford the first secretary. Within two years Barford had written a slim Pelican volume, *Climbing in Britain*, which sold a remarkable 125,000 copies, reflecting the growing interest in climbing and the outdoors. A social revolution was underway, reflected in the formation of new clubs. By 1960 there were 100 clubs in membership of the BMC, a number that was to continue to grow.

At the present time, there are over 300 affiliated clubs, the majority being small informal groups who meet at a local pub or climbing wall midweek and get together at weekends. Individual BMC membership was introduced in 1974 for the less clubbable types who nevertheless wanted to join the BMC insurance scheme or gain reciprocal rights to use Alpine huts. It was slow to catch on at first, but in the last ten years, there has been a dramatic increase, reaching 36,374 by the end of 2005, outnumbering the total club membership of some 28,378, making a grand total of 64,752. People are joining clubs at a much later age but continuing to climb for much longer. Climbing has, in fact, become a sport for life.

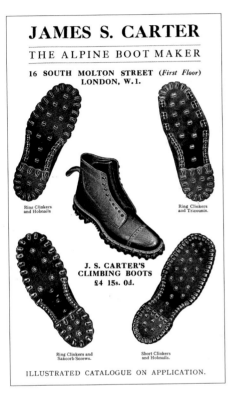

The major office-holders of the BMC have been mostly from the senior clubs, especially from the Alpine Club. Of the 22 BMC presidents listed in the BMC history, *The First 50 Years* (1997), 17 have been members of the AC. The major clubs are proven institutions and part of the fabric of British climbing society. Their membership often includes leading establishment figures and others with great expertise in the law or environment. Their standing and influence has helped to protect the freedoms of our sport over the years when officious government departments might otherwise have imposed rules and regulations on a potentially 'risky sport' such as climbing.

The BMC urges all its members to recognise that climbing, hill walking and mountaineering are adventurous activities that include the possibility of accidental injury or death. Participants should be aware of and accept these risks and be responsible for their own actions and involvement.

Like several other so-called 'governing bodies of sport', the BMC is grateful to receive some financial support from government through Sport England, both to encourage 'Sport for All' and to assist top performers. In particular, when I was president of the BMC, I felt that their matching of the relatively small grants to expeditions provided by the Mount Everest Foundation was really worthwhile, as it helped to develop a core of internationally competent young British mountaineers. Sport England's subsidy for this purpose has currently been around £40,000 per year but, in competition with other sports for limited funding, can be seen to be at risk and has continually to be justified. With the award of the Olympics to London in 2012, there may be even greater pressure to use whatever government funding is available to improve medal prospects at the expense of less competitive activities like mountaineering. It will be a great shame if the support to the BMC is not maintained.

THE ALPINE CLIMBING GROUP

To return to Derek Walker:

By the early 1950s, the Alpine Club too was beginning to feel the winds of change. Frustrated with the stuffiness, outdated rules and standards of the AC, in 1953 a group of the leading young activists formed a new organisation, the Alpine Climbing Group (ACG). This was a real landmark in the history of British climbing as the ACG broke down the class barriers that had existed previously and included in its membership the best young alpinists, no matter what social or financial background they came from. For example, although most of the original members were from among the best university climbers – the likes of Bourdillon, Nicol, Band, Chorley, Blackshaw, and McNaught-Davis – the ACG also included 22-year-old Joe Brown and 19-year-old Don Whillans. Don was flabbergasted, not only at being asked to join, but also to be invited on to the first committee. Breaking down further barriers, the ACG also had women members, notably Gwen Moffat and Denise Evans.

THIS PAGE:

above : Advertisements from the *Alpine Journal* in the 1900s. How styles have changed!

OPPOSITE PAGE:

right: Stephen Venables, President 2005–07, chatting with the internationally famous Swiss mountaineer André Roch. In 2003, the Club decided to rejoin the UIAA as an individual association.

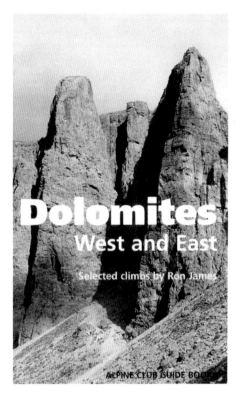

By the mid-1960s, the Alpine Climbing Group was finding that they lacked the administrative base to continue producing their *Annual Bulletin* and their excellent guidebooks of selected Alpine climbs, edited by Ted Wrangham, and there could be merit in remerging with the Alpine Club. As Dennis Gray, the first secretary of the ACG, wrote in 'Confessions of a Parvenu' (*AJ* 2002, 189), 'It began to dawn on me that most of these old chaps in the AC were not "agin us" as some of us had believed, and in fact the majority wanted us to succeed in our endeavours.' His ACG successor, John Brailsford, met with the AC representatives Emlyn Jones and Anthony Rawlinson and, after some difficult horse-trading the deed was done; the ACG merged with the AC in 1967 on a five-year trial basis; the marriage proved to be bliss, and a permanent union was sealed in 1972. The AC gained from an influx of young, dynamic mountaineers, while the ACG was provided with the administrative support it so badly needed. The guidebooks of selected Alpine climbs have proved very successful and continue to this day, under the general editorship of Les Swindin, the latest being a two-volume guide to the Dolomites by Ron James.

The ACG members were accorded full rights of AC membership, with a slightly lower subscription rate, and this remains the cheapest way into the Club if you meet the higher Alpine climbing standard.

above : The cover to the latest Alpine Club guide book of selected climbs in the Dolomites

GLOBAL MOUNTAINEERING

At an international level, the Alpine Club has provided similar support to the *Union Internationale des Associations d'Alpinisme* (UIAA), now increasingly referred to as the International Mountaineering and Climbing Federation. This was founded by representatives from 18 countries meeting in Chamonix, France, in 1932. They agreed specific tasks to encourage mountaineering for the young, develop international standards, raise awareness about safety, and protect the environment. Today the UIAA is the recognised federation for mountain sports and the acknowledged expert on all international climbing and mountaineering matters. By 2003, it had 2.5 million members in 92 member associations in 68 different countries. It works through volunteers from the member associations and is run by a general assembly, with an overall president and a council together with a series of specialist committees or commissions each headed by a president. The current BMC president invariably serves on the UIAA council, and British climbers have been well represented on the various Commissions.

The Alpine Club was involved in 1932–4 when the UIAA was being set up, but did not continue as a member because of the gathering political uncertainties in Europe at the time. After World War II, the BMC joined the UIAA as the natural representative body of British mountaineers, but in October 2003, after an absence of 70 years, the AC decided to rejoin the UIAA as an individual association to play a more visible active part in the work of the federation.

In the last 15 years, the UIAA has begun to promote, develop and regulate international competitions in climbing, ice climbing and ski mountaineering. Competition climbing is now one of the 30 sports in the World Games, and all three sports are working towards inclusion in other multi-sports events and the Olympic Games programme. Surprisingly, the links between mountaineering and the Olympic movement go back to the launch of the modern Olympic Games in the 1890s, when Baron Pierre de Coubertin insisted that there should be an Olympic prize for Alpinism. Perhaps he saw mountaineering as an example of the Olympic motto of: *Citius, Altius, Fortius* (Fast, Higher, Stronger). When the Swiss president of the UIAA died in office in 1994, Ian McNaught-Davis, as vice-president, took over and was duly elected as president for the unusually long tenure of nine years until 2004, when Alan Blackshaw succeeded him. These were the first British presidents of the UIAA. Both were AC members, former BMC presidents, and Alan also AC president 2002–04. Together, they have made an enormous contribution to the management and organisation of the sport, often in rather difficult circumstances.

below: Lady Denise Evans, the first lady president of the Club in 1986.

SHALL WE JOIN THE GENTLEMEN?

Another radical change in the Alpine Club was the admission of women despite the rearguard action of a few misogynists. At the first attempt in 1973 under the presidency of David Cox, the reformers were outgunned, not achieving the necessary two-thirds majority. Then, at a tense meeting in May 1974 under his successor, Jack Longland, the motion was discussed again. John Harding recalls that he was sitting near the front just behind Tilman, who got up, bristling, stood on his chair, and turning around spluttered, 'I don't know how anyone could have the effrontery to vote for this resolution.' But this time it was carried. According to Dennis Gray, 'Longland was worried that a schism might develop, and later alerted the committee to the news that Tilman was threatening to resign over the issue. All of us viewed Tilman with great respect, and even for climbing personalities of Jack's stature he was a legendary figure. There was only one thing to be done and that was to offer him an honorary membership. Thankfully, Tilman graciously accepted the olive branch and the matter was thus settled in a way that resulted in no broken bones.

The first ladies to be elected to the Alpine Club in their own right were two together in 1974: Sally Westmacott, the wife of the 1953 Everest climber Michael Westmacott, and Betty Seiffert, who later married Group Captain George Cubby, also a member of the Club. The ladies actually had their own club, the Ladies' Alpine Club (LAC), founded in 1907. It was logical that the Alpine Club should now invite the LAC to merge completely with the AC, on a basis of full equality, even though the entry qualifications for the LAC were not quite as rigorous. This proposal was received with mixed feelings by many ladies when they realised that the LAC would then cease to exist as a separate entity. But the majority were in favour so it was agreed in March 1975, although 37 members resigned in 1975 or soon afterwards, including such prominent climbers as Joyce Dunsheath, Monica Jackson and Miriam Underhill. The Alpine Club gained some 150 new members, but no one seems to have foreseen that, over time, the LAC and its achievements might risk being forgotten. Its monument was the series of Year-Books from 1910–75. As a labour of love, in 2000, Johanna Merz (the *Alpine Journal* editor 1992–8) produced an incredibly comprehensive and detailed Index to all these annuals, which was then published by the Alpine Club Library to ensure that indeed these great ladies' achievements would be recorded and remembered in perpetuity. It would then only be a matter of time before there was a first woman president of the Alpine Club. She was Denise Evans in 1986 (wife of Charles Evans of both Everest 1953 and Kangchenjunga 1955), although she only served for one year following the death in office of the previous president, Anthony Rawlinson, who tragically slipped and fell while traversing the Crib Goch pinnacles on his own prior to attending a Climbers' Club winter dinner.

above: Johanna Merz, the first lady editor of the *Alpine Journal* 1992–98, who is continuing in the role of Production Editor.

PREMISES! PREMISES!

In September 1991, the Alpine Club moved into its current premises at 55 Charlotte Road EC2A 3QF, on the fringe of the City. This was the Club's first freehold property in its 134-year history.

If we go back to the beginning when there were only a few members, they met in the Lincoln's Inn Chambers of T W Hinchliff, the Club's first honorary secretary. But they soon needed a place they could call their own, so in 1859 they leased rooms at 8 St Martin's Place, Trafalgar Square. By the 1890s, these were no longer adequate and in 1895 the president, Douglas Freshfield, explained that: 'Our lease was near its end, but we had ground for hope that the Geographical Society might make itself a centre for kindred bodies, and might erect new premises, with rooms and a hall available for our purposes. That hope was unfulfilled … But everything comes to those who can wait. The exact premises we wanted suddenly came into the market!'

The Club took a 15-year lease at £350 a year on 23 Savile Row and the first meeting was held there on 7 May 1895. The premises comprised a large well-lit hall, capable of seating 200 comfortably, a splendidly ornate Members' Reading Room, Secretarial/Map Room, and the Library. The lease was renewed several times and Savile Row became the Club's home for 41 years until December 1936. It was then demolished to make a through way to Conduit Street in order to relieve traffic congestion in Regent Street. So the Club was forced to move. During Colonel Strutt's presidency they found a fine building in Mayfair at 74 South Audley Street, built in the 1730s, which at one time was the Portuguese Embassy and became part of the Grosvenor Estates. The Club leased the ground floor and basement. The main room, used for lectures and exhibitions, had a particularly fine plaster ceiling, the work of a celebrated plasterer, Edward Shepherd, who gave his name to Shepherd's Market close by. R L G Irving gave the first lecture there in May 1937.

I shall never forget my first visit to this sanctum, at the invitation of Roger Chorley, to hear Eric Shipton lecture on the results of the crucial Everest Reconnaissance in 1951. In the communal entrance hall, the plaster was showing incipient cracks, in the corner a pram was covered by a dust sheet, as if the members had no immediate use for it. The lecture room was crowded. Along one side, a chaise longue was reserved for the most senior members, one of them using an ear trumpet. We sat cross-legged on the floor at the front, enthralled by Shipton's

above: A painting by Kenneth Steel of the Club's premises at the end of Savile Row from 1895 to 1936, when it was demolished to help relieve traffic congestion!

every word. I did not feel able to apply for membership until 1955 when the warm-hearted honorary secretary, Basil Goodfellow, persuaded me to do so. Years later, in 1987, I had the honour to be elected president of this venerable institution in the heart of what our renegade Committee member, Mike Banks, then called the 'fur coat and no knickers' area of Mayfair.

In an 'Opinion' article in *Climber and Hill Walker* of October 1990, entitled 'Rebellion in the Hallowed Halls', Mike queried: 'You might well ask how a club of less than a thousand members, paying only modest subscriptions, could possibly afford to live in such luxury.' The short answer was that we were indebted to the negotiating skills in the 1950s of the then honorary secretary, Emlyn Jones, who later became a judge in the Lands Tribunal. When in 1956, under a new landlord, it proved possible to have a 'surrender with grant of new lease' for some 50 years, lasting until 2011, Emlyn Jones was able to slip the 1930s terms into the new contract largely unchanged. These included rent at a fixed price of £800 per annum, with the landlord still paying the rates, heating and maintenance. By 1990, the rates alone had risen to £6,740 per annum! This new lease cost the Club £2,500. Emlyn Jones had to assure the president, Sir Edwin Herbert (later Lord Tangley), that if we subsequently wished to move, we stood a good chance of getting our money back! To complete our financial bliss, the lecture hall, which had an opening directly onto the street, served as The Alpine Club Gallery and could be rented out for picture exhibitions, earning additional income for the Club to help provide for future premises of our own. Unless we did something about it, come 2011 the Club would be out in the cold with nowhere to go.

It was just my luck to be president when this internal debate reached its climax. After much discussion, we decided to grasp the nettle while there were still 20 years of the lease to run and sell it back to the new landlord on 31 March 1990 for half a million – again negotiated thanks to Emlyn Jones – while the property market was booming.

right: The Reading Room at 23 Savile Row, from a drawing by Hanslip Fletcher. Sadly the Club no longer seems to be able to afford such a luxury.

TOWN OR COUNTRY?

We now faced a further internal debate as to where the Club should go. Should it and its Library stay in London or move to cheaper premises in the country? There was quite a strong move towards the country and to the north, where many climbers now lived within reach of the hills, but no consensus whether it should be in the Peak District, near the Lakes, or in Manchester, sharing with the BMC. This tended to overlook that the Club's remit was really to the Alps and the Greater Ranges, rather than to climbing in Britain, which was well catered for by numerous local clubs. Mike Banks was rather more outspoken in his 1990 article, published after he had resigned from the committee:

> From the outside the Alpine Club gives the appearance of Britain's finest climbing institution but things are not quite as they seem. Although most of the country's eminent climbers are members, the club as an organisation has been relegated to the sidelines of British mountaineering. The BMC is now the focal point. Despite the huge upsurge in climbing since World War Two, the club membership is, in effect, less than it was in 1912. It is in a state of slow decline; some fear its illness may be terminal.
>
> The reasons are not far to seek. Although only one quarter of the membership live in or near London this minority enjoys all the benefits: the pleasant winter lectures, the availability of sumptuous quarters and the easy accessibility of the library. The membership is elderly and overly middle class. The Club offers very little to the active country climbers and seems oblivious of the fact that the centre of gravity of British climbing has long since moved north. However, the Club has been so comfortably cushioned against reality in the financial heaven of South Audley Street that it has shrugged off these unpalatable realities …
>
> A postal poll was taken and a general Meeting was held in London. Half a dozen past presidents were trundled in, great names from climbing history. With their white hair tumbling forward like cornices ready to break, they denounced a move to the country as the death knell of the Club.
>
> The membership dutifully and predictably followed the Establishment and voted 3:1 to stay in London. The democratic decision was acclaimed. London it was. I was disappointed but not surprised. To move an organisation so conservative as the AC would, I reckoned, take at least two shoves!

above: Mike Banks after an excellent climb together on Mt Aiguille in 1987. He had outspoken views as to where the Club should relocate after giving up 74 South Audley Street.

At this same time, by chance, the Royal Geographical Society was seeking planning permission for a commercial development in its garden off Exhibition Road in Kensington. Our strong historical links with the Society, reinforced by two recent RGS presidents, Lord Hunt and Lord Chorley, who like Freshfield had also been presidents of the AC, made it natural to consider participation in this development as the preferred option. Consequently, on the Club's behalf, the committee undertook to acquire a 125-year lease on a portion of the development, to be built to our own specification. This would be some 3,500–4,000 sq ft at lower ground level, lit from above, with a mutually advantageous inter-connection with the RGS. To its detractors, and there were some, it quickly became known as the 'Kensington Bunker'. If negotiations and the construction itself proceeded smoothly and we could afford it, we would be in occupation by early 1992.

Meanwhile, we were extremely grateful to the Ski Club of Great Britain in Eaton Square for providing a temporary refuge, particularly their congenial bar, which was well patronised both before and after lectures. With hindsight, I think we were all grateful that the RGS scheme stalled when the property market dropped and the developer withdrew. It would have proved difficult to sell without significant loss if we had ever wanted to move again. After nearly a century since Douglas Freshfield's proposal in 1895, history was repeating itself!

OUR NEW HOME – CHARLOTTE ROAD

below: Bob Lawford, Librarian Emeritus, right, receives the keys from the previous owner of our new freehold premises at 55 Charlotte Road, just north of the City.

Instead we decided to look for existing properties within the London Underground's inner Circle, so as to be of reasonable access for visitors from outside London. By then, Tony Streather had succeeded me as president, so I agreed to head a working party which considered some 70 properties and

viewed half of them, finally recommending 55 Charlotte Road, EC2, near Old Street, just north of the City. This modestly converted and recently refurbished warehouse, solidly built in 1906, was currently owned by a New Zealand architect turned property developer, whose family home was just further down Remuera Road from Ed Hillary in Auckland. Was this a favourable omen? It met the essential requirements with one valuable bonus: ample space. There were 6,100 net sq ft spread over four open-plan floors and a basement, so that the top two floors could be rented out to provide income while still retaining the essential 3,500 sq ft for the Club. It did not have the Mayfair or West End image to which our members had become accustomed, but perhaps this was no bad thing. It was nevertheless on the fringe of the City, a short walk from Old Street Underground station, in a road full of character in a generally improving area.

A deal was clinched for £635,000 and the keys received by our tireless member Bob Lawford on 23 May 1991. After some £70,000 of modifications to suit our special requirements, the Club moved in during September and held the first lecture as planned on 8 October; so the working party could disband and hand over to a new house committee under Malcolm Rutherford. The move owed a great deal to numerous members of the Club giving generously of their time, resources and expertise. As I mentioned in my valedictory address in December 1989, when we

below: A drawing by the previous owner, Robert Hanson, with a brief description of what the Club had purchased.

55 Charlotte Road, London EC2A 3QF

LOCATION

On the fringe of the City, 6 mins. walk from Old Street (⊖ Northern Line, zone 1) or 15 mins. from Moorgate or Liverpool St. providing easy access from most BR main line stations. (Refer maps on reverse)

ACCOMMODATION

Solid former warehouse, simply refurbished in 1987 comprising:
1st, 2nd & 3rd floors, each 1300 sq.ft
Ground floor & Basement, each 1100 sq.ft
Total   6100 sq.ft (net)

The independent, largely open plan, floors permit flexible library / lecture space with possibility of renting out 2 floors, still leaving 3500 sq. ft for the Club.

AMENITIES
Gas central heating, 4 toilets, Ample evening car parking with 2 pubs & a wine bar in 100 yds!
TENURE
Freehold. Full business planning permission

above: The indefatigable Bob Lawford, Hon. Member and Librarian Emeritus, who has devoted himself to the benefit of the Club and Library since he became a member in 1967.

all 'chose to climb' we probably never envisaged getting quite so involved in administration, high finance and real-estate management in the name of mountaineering. However, we had to see this through in order to preserve and build on all that is best for the Club and its present and future members.

We may not have completely satisfied Mike Banks and his fellow rebels but we did manage to calm down what his article called, 'The verbal punch-ups well worthy of the Club's pugnacious Victorian founders'.

Fifteen years later, we can reflect on the pros and cons of the move (which even included some bunk beds for overnight use by members from the provinces – a particular and sensible request by Mike Banks). The extra space, in theory, gave us room to expand, but we have become so used to the income from renting out the top two floors that we are loathe to give it up and are suffering through lack of space ourselves. We also have to accept the increased responsibilities of being both freeholder and landlord, and to live within our means. An unexpected bonus in raising the tone of the neighbourhood and the capital value of its properties was when the Prince of Wales' Trust bought and refurbished the building across the street. There was even a momentary glimpse of the Club's front door on the television screens when Camilla, Duchess of Cornwall, paid her first visit there with Prince Charles.

MEMBERSHIP

The qualifications for full membership of the Club has remained the same as long as I can remember. Candidates should be competent Alpine climbers who show a continuing interest in mountaineering. The normal requirement is the completion of at least 20 respectable Alpine ascents, over at least three seasons, or their equivalent in other regions. However, in rare cases, other qualifications in the form of contributions to mountain literature, science or art may also be taken into account. The requirements for the Alpine Climbing Group are harder – at least six major routes in the Alps and Greater Ranges.

There is also a category of aspirant membership for those who have, at least, one season but currently lack the experience for full membership, but are expected to qualify in due course within, say, five years.

In 2004, an additional category of associate was added, intended for those without the necessary climbing qualifications but who had a special interest and commitment to the objectives of the Club. It is intended to appeal, for example, to writers and artists and those with an interest in the conservation of the Club's collection of books, paintings and photographs which is quite a responsibility for a numerically small Club to maintain, particularly as the more active members may prefer to spend the majority of their free time climbing.

There are some 30 honorary members, most of whom are mountaineers of great distinction. Two-thirds are from overseas; those within the UK have generally also been of great service to the Club.

The total membership has been 800 to 1,200 for the past 100 years. It is currently as high as it has ever been at 1,260, with one-sixth being foreign or overseas members. But this is just a fraction of the potential number of British climbers who meet the qualifying standard, when you consider that the membership of the BMC is now over 60,000 and has been increasing at the rate of 7 to 8 per cent per annum recently, making mountaineering, climbing and hill walking one of the UK's fastest growing sports.

A demographic survey carried out in 1997 by our member John Blacker showed the average age of Club members to be 54 and that we have a life expectancy six years more than the average elsewhere. The average age of new members is 38 and there are eleven men to every woman in the Club as a whole. 'Can we therefore conclude,' wrote Blacker, 'that provided we don't fall off, climbing mountains is good for our health and longevity? Tempting and plausible though this conclusion might seem, it sadly cannot be justified on the basis of this evidence. The causation might go the other way: only those who are pretty fit in the first place take up climbing. Or the association between longevity and membership of the AC might be because AC members tend to come from above-average socio-economic backgrounds; they smoke less, are better educated, better fed, and better cared-for medically.'

This led Chris Bonington to reflect in his valedictory address in 1998: 'We, as many committees before us, have agonised over where the Club is going and have come to a similar conclusion to that arrived at by others in the past – that we are and should remain essentially a club of like-minded people with a shared love of the mountains and reasonable competence to go amongst them, thus maintaining our modest membership qualification.'

INTO THE MILLENNIUM

One of the best activities started by the Club in recent years is the annual symposium, open to all and a great opportunity to recruit new members. Held in North Wales or the Lake District, a winter's day is devoted to one mountain area, say South America, Canada or the Caucasus. The best possible speakers are assembled both from within the Club and abroad. Over meals and across the bar, social interaction is great and who knows how many new expeditions are planned? It started on 10 March 1984 with a symposium on Lightweight Expeditions to the Greater Ranges, and has continued ever since.

Club members are also involved as individuals in the Mountain Heritage Trust. This began in a small way when I had just been elected as President of the BMC in April 1996 and Barbara James stood up and said that climbers should not discard old and outdated boots, axes and equipment, but the best should be preserved to create an exhibition or museum of mountaineering to show how the sport had evolved and developed. I barely expected the project to take off, but amazingly it did – without any funding from the National Lottery which at the time of the Millennium, was supporting many projects which subsequently fell flat on their faces. Fortunately, we met John Dunning, who was the force behind the Rheged Discovery Centre then under construction near Penrith, on the edge of the Lake District, the birthplace of climbing. A Cumbrian farmer, entrepreneur, hill walker, skier and mountain rescue team member, the idea of a National Mountaineering Exhibition incorporated within the Centre intrigued him. With a lot of hard work, fund-raising, support from Helly Hansen, imagination and skill by many dedicated individuals, the project came to fruition.

The first exhibition was planned around the history of mountaineering and the ascent of Everest in 1953, with film clips of the BBC's genial John Peel providing continuity between a succession of 'Camps' leading to the 'Summit Theatre'. We even had the prime minister, Tony Blair, to open it formally on 26 July 2001, when the livestock in the surrounding farmland was devastated by the nationwide plague of foot and mouth disease.

Now after ten years from the initial daydream the exhibition is firmly established and wholly owned by Rheged, with the Mountain Heritage Trust providing technical expertise and consultancy, and also starting to build up its own archive of

OPPOSITE PAGE:

above left: Sassolungo from Santa Cristina, a woodcut by Una Cameron, a prominent member of the Ladies Alpine Club in the 1930s.

below left: Dying Light, Drohmo, Nepal. A painting by Julian Cooper of Grasmere, where both his father and grandfather were Lakeland artists. It was the Club's Christmas card for 2005.

THIS PAGE:

right: The British Ambassador to Nepal, Keith Bloomfield, addresses the gathering of the Kangchenjunga Golden Jubilee Celebrations in Kathmandu, 25 May 2005. Seated right are the three summiteers: Norman Hardie, Tony Streather, George Band.

historic documents and artefacts. In April 2005, a further small exhibition was added, 'Kangchenjunga – the Untrodden Peak', to celebrate the fiftieth anniversary of the only other 8,000-metre peak first climbed by a British team. The first chairman of the Trust, Chris Bonington, was succeeded in mid-2005 by AC member John Innerdale, a retired architect, who fortuitously lives close to Rheged and by his professional expertise and devotion has contributed more than anybody to ensure the exhibition's success. On 3 December 2005, the Club recognised this success by hosting its annual symposium and dinner at Rheged for the first time, focusing on the mountains 'East of the Himalaya', with Tamotsu Nakamura of the Japanese Alpine Club as the guest speaker at the symposium and our honorary member Joe Brown at the dinner.

Back in London, the Club continues its regular programme of lectures held traditionally for the last 150 years on the second Tuesday of every month. These are supplemented by periodic art exhibitions organised by Peter Mallalieu, the honorary keeper of the Club's pictures. In May 2005, again celebrating Kangchenjunga, *Imaging a Himalayan Mountain* was curated by Simon Pierse, Lecturer in Art at Aberystwyth University, and was enhanced by a superbly illustrated and scholarly written catalogue.

A new modern Club logo has been devised and represented in a new tie, replacing the traditional yellow stripe on a green background dating, I was told, from the days of 1909 and the influence of Geoffrey Winthrop Young.

The periodic *Newsletter*, edited by Dick Turnbull, now appears on glossy paper in gorgeous Technicolor, starting to rival the hardback annual *Alpine Journal* in its accounts of meets and members' activities. The February 2005 number announced the creation of the AC Climbing Fund – a ring-fenced capital sum designed to produce an annual bursary with which the AC can assist its members in fulfilling their mountaineering ambitions and put climbing back at the heart of the Club. The Grépon Club subscription prize fund will help to finance the Climbing Fund. Quoting from the announcement: 'the AC was originally formed to "promote alpine climbing and exploration" across the world. For many years, it has been the Club's illustrious members that have been championing the Club by their achievements rather than the Club being in a position to facilitate the ambitions of its members. We believe that the AC should now make a major effort to promote our stated aims and give our members real support.' So the Club is in good heart and more active than ever.

I conclude with some short quotations from the valedictory addresses of the last three presidents:

Chris Bonington, 1996–8:

I believe that as a Club we're in good shape. I think our most important role is to continue to be a Club which all of us who seek adventure in the Alps and Greater Ranges will want to be part of, irrespective of the tangible benefits it might offer us. Our Club is a fellowship that is strong, through the roots we have with the beginnings of our sport and the way we look to the future. We share a love for the hills and everything they give us!

OPPOSITE PAGE:

top: Doug Scott at Everest base camp in 1979 with his well-acclimatised children, Martha, the elder, and Rosie.

bottom: Alan Blackshaw went on to be elected President of the UIAA.

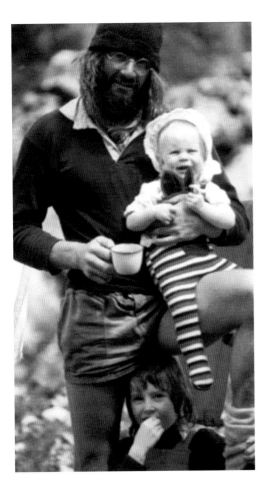

Doug Scott, 1999–2001:

> The AGM has just voted for a significant change in the rules by highlighting the need for the Club to protect the environment and to conserve the Club's heritage. Obviously 150 years ago, before the age of mass mountain tourism and before there was any heritage to speak of, such additions were unnecessary.

The Club has, of course, always taken a constructive stance on these issues but now, in these days of mass tourism and with the rapid expansion of interest in mountaineering, it is time to take on a greater responsibility and to be more proactive before such problems escalate into crisis. The Chinese ideogram for crisis is two characters, the first for danger, the other for opportunity.

Alan Blackshaw, 2002–04:

> I hope that if, at some point in the future, the BMC decides to move to larger premises and offers the Club the possibility of sharing them, then the Committee of the day will consider the issue on its merits, bearing in mind the success of the American Alpine Club's move to larger premises in Golden. We considered the possibility of combining premises with RGS some 15 years ago, so it is not really a particularly new idea.

> We have also floated with the BMC the idea of a British Mountain Heritage electronic network which might record on a common or interlinked database the contents of the Club's and other British mountain libraries, and perhaps also the locations of archives, paintings, photos, and artefacts of heritage value. Within that, I hope that there might be an enhanced role, and perhaps improved public financing, for the Club's library and other archives.
>
> It is essential also that there should be some recognised focal point in Britain for the documentary and photographic archives of key individuals, which might otherwise be lost to posterity.

Alan has gone on to be elected president of the UIAA, the International Mountaineering and Climbing Federation. He has campaigned particularly for freedom of responsible access to mountain areas. He has researched the work of James Bryce, AC president 1899–1901, providing evidence to the Scottish parliament that there is, in fact, no Scots law of trespass for harmless access to land – contrary to assertions by ministers and officials since the mid-1960s. He has argued that mankind has a fundamental human right to enjoy nature.

The Club's current president is Stephen Venables, who has a distinguished mountaineering record, including being the first Briton to summit Everest without supplementary oxygen, and by a new route to the South Col in 1988. I was fascinated to read the letter of condolence that he wrote, shortly after being elected, to the widow of Anderl Heckmair, who led the classic first ascent of the north face of the Eiger in 1938, at a time when our Colonel Strutt, president 1935–7, was pontificating in his valedictory address: 'The Eigerwand still unscaled, continued to be an obsession for the mentally deranged of almost every nation. He who first succeeds may rest assured that he has accomplished the most imbecile variant since mountaineering first began.'

February 2005
Dear Frau Heckmair

I am writing as President of the Alpine Club to offer our condolences on the death of your husband Anderl.

As I am sure you are aware, the editor of the Alpine Journal in the Thirties was very critical of the early Eiger attempts. It was a time when British alpinism had become rather lack lustre and few people here appreciated the brilliance of alpinists like your late husband. (I suspect that there was also a touch of envy at the superior skills and technique of continental climbers at that time.)

I am glad to say that things are very different now. I and many fellow Alpine Club members have had the unforgettable experience of repeating the original Eigerwand route; and I think that all of us have been overwhelmed with admiration for what Anderl achieved, leading all the way, through storms and avalanches, in 1938. It remains one of the greatest climbs in the world.

I had the pleasure of meeting you and Anderl at the Les Diablerets festival a few years ago. As usual, you were translating with patience and charm for the people like me who have failed to learn German. From what I have heard and read, it seems that you had a wonderfully content and fulfilled life together, and that until very recently Anderl enjoyed very good health. What an amazing life! And what a treasure of memories you must have. I hope that those memories sustain you in the weeks and months ahead as you adjust to the future.

With very best wishes from all of us Alpine Club members around the world.

Yours sincerely
Stephen Venables.

below: Stephen Venables, current President, 2005–07, and first Briton to summit Everest without supplementary oxygen.

Finally, re-reading the more recent chapters, I am saddened by how many of the finest climbers have not returned from their adventures. However safely they climb, there is always an element of risk from objective dangers or misjudgement of the weather, which can catch up with those at the top of the pyramid, simply because of their increased exposure to the mountains over time. Don Whillans died in his bed, but his mentor, Joe Brown, who was my climbing partner to the near-summit of Kangchenjunga, is happily still active on roadside crags (provided he doesn't have to walk far) and in the evenings, when he is at home in Llanberis, enjoying a pint and a chat or a game of pool with friends in the Royal Victoria. Long may he remain so. Here is the last verse of Tom Patey's *Joe Brown Song* portraying one who has become a legend in his lifetime:

He's like a Human Spider
Clinging to the wall
Suction, Faith and Friction
And nothing else at all
But the secret of his success
Is his most amazing knack
Of hanging from a hand-jam
In an overhanging crack.

below: Joe Brown on an early ascent of Suicide Wall, Idwal, 27 May 1957, one of the earliest climbing films specially commissioned by BBC TV.

below: Baron Brown, the Grand Old Man of the Rock and Ice. Chief guest at the Annual Dinner on 3 December 2005.

BIBLIOGRAPHY

My main historical source has been the Club's *Alpine Journal*, sub-titled *A record of mountain adventure and scientific observation*, currently published annually, and in continuous production since 1863 under a distinguished series of editors. It followed on from the Club's first publication in 1858, the three volumes of *Peaks, Passes and Glaciers*, edited by John Ball, the Club's first President and published by William Longman. For the first hundred years, I am particularly indebted to the *Alpine Centenary Journal 1857–1957* and Arnold Lunn's *A Century of Mountaineering*. The following selection of books, mostly from my own library, have been invaluable for further background reading and research.

Alvarez, Al
  Feeding the Rat, Profile of a Climber, Bloomsbury, 1988
Ament, Pat
  Royal Robbins, Spirit of the Age, Stackpole Books, 1998
Anderson, J.R.L.
  High Mountains & Cold Seas, A Biography of H.W.Tilman, Victor Gollancz Ltd., 1980
Band, George,
  Road to Rakaposhi, Hodder & Stoughton, 1956
  Everest: 50 Years on Top of the World, Harper Collins, 2003
  Everest Exposed, Harper Collins, Paperback 2005
Banks, Mike
  Rakaposhi, Secker & Warburg, 1959
Bender, Friedrich
  Classic Climbs in the Caucasus, Diadem Books, 1992
Boardman, Peter and Tasker, Joe
  The Boardman Tasker Omnibus, Hodder & Stoughton, 1995
Bonington, Chris
  I Chose to Climb, Gollancz, 1966
  Annapurna South Face, Cassell, 1971
  Mountaineer, Thirty Years of Climbing on the World's Great Peaks, Diadem Books, 1989
  The Climbers, BBC Books, Hodder & Stoughton, 1992
Braham, Trevor
  When the Alps cast their Spell, Mountaineers of the Alpine Golden Age, The In Pinn, 2004
Brown, Graham T
  Brenva, J. M Dent & Sons Ltd, 1944
Brown, Joe
  The Hard Years, An Autobiography, Victor Gollancz Ltd. 1967
Buhl, Hermann
  Nanga Parbat Pilgrimage, Hodder & Stoughton, 1956
Busk, Sir Douglas
  The Fountains of the Sun, Unfinished Journeys in Ethiopia and the Ruwenzori, Max Parrish, 1957
Cave, Andy
  Learning to Breathe, Hutchinson, 2005
Clark, Ronald
  The Victorian Mountaineers, Batsford, 1953
Clark, Simon
  The Puma's Claw, Hutchinson, 1959
Cleare, John
  Collins Guide to Mountains and Mountaineering, Collins, 1979
Clinch, Nicholas
  A Walk in the Sky: Climbing Hidden Peak, The Mountaineers, 1982
Conway, Sir William Martin
  Climbing and Exploration in the Karakoram-Himalayas, T. Fisher Unwin, 1894
  The Alps from End to End, Constable, 1895

Curran, Jim
  K2 The Story of the Savage Mountain, Hodder & Stoughton, 1995
  High Achiever The Life and Climbs of Chris Bonington, Constable, 1999
Dent C.T. and others
  The Badminton Library Mountaineering, Longmans, Green & Co., 1892
Diemberger, Kurt
  The Kurt Diemberger Omnibus: Summits and Secrets, The Endless Knot, Spirits of the Air, Bâton Wicks, 1999
Dumler, Helmut & Burkhardt, Willi P.
  The High Mountains of the Alps, Volume 1 4,000m Peaks, Diadem, 1993
Evans, Charles
  Kangchenjunga, the Untrodden Peak, Hodder & Stoughton, 1956
Finch, George Ingle
  The Making of a Mountaineer, Arrowsmith, 1924
Fowler, Mick
  Vertical Pleasure, Hodder and Stoughton, 1995
  On Thin Ice, Baton Wicks, 2005
Freshfield, Douglas W. (with illustrations by Sella, Vittorio)
  The Exploration of the Caucasus; (2 volumes) Edward Arnold, 1896
  Round Kangchenjunga, Edward Arnold, 1903
Hankinson, Alan
  Geoffrey Winthrop Young, Poet, educator, mountaineer, Hodder & Stoughton, 1995
Harding, John
  Pyrenean High Route, A Saki Mountaineering Odyssey, Tiercel, 2000
Hargreaves, Alison
  A Hard Day's Summer, Hodder and Stoughton, 1994
Haston, Dougal
  In High Places, Cassell, 1972
Herzog, Maurice
  Annapurna, Conquest of the First 8000-metre Peak, Jonathan Cape, 1952
Hillary, Sir Edmund
  View from the Summit, Doubleday, 1999
Hunt, John
  The Ascent of Everest, Hodder & Stoughton, 1953
  Life is Meeting, Hodder & Stoughton, 1978
Hunt, Sir John and Brasher, Christopher
  The Red Snows, Hutchinson, 1960
Huxley, Anthony
  Standard Encyclopaedia of the World's Mountains, Weidenfeld & Nicholson (Educational) Ltd. 1962
Jackson, John Angelo
  More than Mountains, George G. Harrap & Co. Ltd. 1955
  Adventure Travels in the Himalaya, Indus Publishing Company, New Delhi, 2005
Jones, Chris
  Climbing in North America, University of California Press, 1976
Keenlyside, Francis,
  Peaks and Pioneers, The Story of Mountaineering, Paul Elek Ltd. 1975

Longstaff, Tom
    This My Voyage, John Murray, 1950
Lunn, Arnold
    A Century of Mountaineering 1857-1957, Alan & Unwin, 1957
Mason, Kenneth
    Abode of Snow, Rupert Hart-Davis,1955
Messner, Reinhold
    All 14 Eight-Thousanders, (translated by Audrey Salkeld),
        The Crowood Press, 1988
Milner, C. Douglas
    Mountain Photography, The Focal Press, 1945
Moore, A W.
    The Alps in 1864 (3 volumes) Basil Blackwell, 1939
Mummery, A.F.
    My Climbs in the Alps and Caucasus; T Fisher Unwin, 1895
Neale, Jonathan
    Tigers of the Snow, Abacus 2003
Neate, Jill (W.R.)
    Mountaineering Literature – A Bibliography, Cicerone Press, 1986
Newby, Eric
    Great Ascents, A Narrative History of Mountaineering, David Charles, 1977
Noyce, Wilfrid
    Mountains and Men, Geoffrey Bles, 1947
    Scholar Mountaineers, Pioneers of Parnassus, Roy Publishers, 1950
    The Springs of Adventure, John Murray, 1958
    They Survived, A Study of the Will to Live, Heinemann, 1962
Patey, Tom
    One Man's Mountains, Victor Gollancz Ltd. 1972
Pierse, Simon
    Kangchenjunga, Imaging a Himalayan Mountain, School of Art, Univ. of Wales,
        Aberystwyth, 2005
Perrin, Jim
    The Villain, The Life of Don Whillans, Hutchinson, 2005
Pilley, Dorothy
    Climbing Days, G. Bell & Sons Ltd. 1935
Rey, Guido
    The Matterhorn (translated from the Italian by J. E. C. Eaton and revised and
        two additional chapters by R.L.G. Irving), Basil Blackwell, 1946
Ring, Jim
    How the English Made the Alps, John Murray, 2000
Roch, André
    Climbs of my Youth, Lindsay Drummond, 1949
Rose, David & Douglas, Ed
    Regions of the Heart, The Triumph and Tragedy of Alison Hargreaves, Michael
        Joseph, 1999
Sale, Richard and Cleare, John
    On Top of the World, Climbing the World's 14 Highest Mountains,
        HarperCollins, 2000
Salkeld, Audrey and Bermudez, José Luis,
    On the Edge of Europe, Hodder & Stoughton, 1993
Scott, Doug
    Himalayan Climber, A Lifetime's Quest to the World's Greater Ranges,
        Diadem Books 1992
Scott, Doug & MacIntyre, Alex
    Shisha Pangma, The alpine-style first ascent of the South-West Face,
        Bâton Wicks, 2000
Shipton, Eric
    That Untravelled World, An Autobiography, Hodder & Stoughton, 1969
    Eric Shipton, the six mountain–travel books, Diadem Books Ltd. 1985
Simpson, Joe
    Touching the Void, Jonathan Cape Ltd. 1998

Slesser, Malcolm
    Red Peak, Hodder & Stoughton, 1964
Smythe, Frank
    Frank Smythe, The Six Alpine / Himalayan Climbing Books, Bâton Wicks,
Steele, Peter
    Eric Shipton, Everest and Beyond, Constable, 1998
Stephen, Leslie
    The Playground of Europe, Longmans, Green, & Co., 1910
Symonds, John and Grant, Kenneth
    The Confessions of Aleister Crowley, Jonathan Cape, 1969
Tilman, H. W.
    H. W. Tilman, the seven mountain-travel books, Diadem Books Ltd. 1983
Tullis, Julie
    Clouds From Both Sides, Grafton Books, 1986
Unsworth, Walter,
    Because it is There, Victor Gollancz Ltd. 1968
    Everest, The Mountaineering History, Bâton Wicks, Third Edition, 2000
Venables, Stephen
    Painted Mountains, Two expeditions to Kashmir, Hodder & Stoughton,1986
    Everest: Kangshung Face, Hodder & Stoughton, 1989
    A Slender Thread, Escaping Disaster in the Himalaya, Hutchison, 2000
Venables, Stephen, with Fanshawe, Andy
    Himalaya Alpine Style, Hodder and Stoughton, 1995
Ward, Michael
    In this Short Span, A Mountaineering Memoir, Victor Gollancz Ltd. 1972
    Mountain Medicine, A clinical study of cold and high altitude,
        Crosby Lockwood Staples, 1975
    Everest, A Thousand Years of Exploration, The Ernest Press, 2003
Wells, Colin
    A Brief History of British Mountaineering,
        The Mountain Heritage Trust, 2001
Whymper, Edward
    Scrambles Amongst the Alps in the Years 1860–69, John Murray, 1871
Whillans, Don & Ormerod, Alick
    Don Whillans, Portrait of a Mountaineer, Heinemann, 1971
Yates, Simon
    Against the Wall, Jonathan Cape, 1997
Young, Geoffrey Winthrop
    Mountaincraft, Charles Scribner's Sons, 1920
    On High Hills, Methuen & Co. Ltd. 1927

FURTHER INFORMATION

www.alpine-club.org The Alpine Club. The world's oldest mountaineering club and the leading UK club for active Alpine and greater range climbers.

www.mef.org.uk The Mount Everest Foundation is the original UK charity devoted to the support of mountain exploration and science, financed initially from surplus funds and subsequent royalties after the successful ascent of Everest in 1953. It is a continuing initiative between the Alpine Club and the Royal Geographical Society. Since its inception, it has dispensed some £800,000 in grants to 1,400 expeditions.

www.rgs.org The Royal Geographical Society exists to advance and promote geographical knowledge and understanding of the world around us.

www.thebmc.co.uk The National Mountaineering Council has over 64,000 members and exists to promote the interests and the protect the freedoms of climbers, hill walkers and mountaineers, including ski mountaineers.

www.pyb.co.uk The National Mountain Centre, near to Snowdon, runs courses in hill walking, rock climbing and mountaineering throughout the year.

Picture Credits

All reasonable efforts have been made by the Publisher to trace the copyright holders of the photographs contained in this publication. In the event that the copyright holder of a photograph has not been traced, but comes forward after the publication of this edition, the Publishers will endeavour to rectify the position at the first possible opportunity.

If the photograph has come from a picture library or private collection, the name of the photographer has been given first where this is known.

Page numbers are in **bold** type.

Abbreviations

t – top; m – middle; b – bottom; l – left; r – right.
AC – Alpine Club; GB – George Band; CB – Chris Bonington; MB – Martin Boysen; JB – Joe Brown; RC – Roger Chorley; JC – John Cleare/Mountain Camera; KD – Kurt Diemberger; MF – Mick Fowler; BG – Basil Goodfellow; DJ – Dulcibel Jenkins Collection; HM – Hamish MacInnes; TN – Tamotsu Nakamura; RP – Roger Payne; PL – Picture Library; RGS – Royal Geographical Society; AS – Audrey Salkeld; DS – Doug Scott; SV – Stephen Venables; EW – Edward Whymper

7 R Collister **9** GB **10** GB **11** GB **12** Bisson/ACPL **13** ACPL **14** Martens/ACPL **15** t GB b ACPL **16** t Scheuchzer/ACPL b ACPL **17** EW/ACPL **18** Baxter/ACPL **19** t AS b EW/AS **20** John Wills **21** l r ACPL **22** t b ACPL **23** t EW b ACPL **24** ACPL **25** b EW/ACPL **28** JC **29** ACPL **30** t Doré/ACPL bl Calkin/ACPL br ACPL **31** Doré/ACPL **32** t ACPL b Lily

Bristow/ACPL **33** l Charnaux/ACPL r ACPL **34** Charnaux/ACPL **35** ACPL **36** l Garcin/ACPL r Donkin/ACPL **37** ACPL **38** l Milner/ACPL r EW/ACPL **39** l EW/ACPL r ACPL **40** BG/TAJ Goodfellow **41** ACPL **42** t Lee/ACPL b ACPL **43** ACPL **44** t b ACPL **45** E Gyger/ACPL **46** t G de Rham/ACPL b ACPL **47** R G W Young & J Hunt/ACPL **48** l ACPL r BG/ACPL **49** RC **50** SV/ACPL **51** t D Milner/ACPL b Donkin/ACPL **52** V Sella/ACPL **53** ACPL **54** R Ruddle **55** l Donkin/ACPL r GB **57** K Murray/ACPL **59** EW/ACPL **60** JC **61** ACPL **63** t ACPL **64** ACPL **65** lr ACPL **66** Somervell/GB **67 68** ACPL **69** AS **70** Loppé/ACPL **71** C Monteath/Hedgehog House **72 73 75** ACPL **77** Colin Monteath/Hedgehog House **78** Barnard/ACPL **79** l Morris Taylor/ACPL r BG/ACPL **80** JC **81** t b BG/ACPL **82** t J Ruskin/ACPL b ACPL **83** ACPL **84 86** JC **87** GB **88** RC **89** ACPL **90** RGS **91** t ACPL b GB **92** t GB b ACPL **93** l J Earle r GB **94** t b **95** t DJ b Schwarzgruber/DJ **96** JC **97** l AM Dowler r RC **98** t b RC **99** GB **100** J Bourdillon **101** JC **102** TD Bourdillon/ M Nicol **103** t ACPL b H MacInnes **104** t RP b GB **105** l r BG **106** t CBPL b **107** M Nicol **108** ET Compton/ACPL **109** HG Willink/ACPL **110 111** ACPL **112** SV **113** l GB r CB **114** l CB **115** t J Cunningham/HM b L Hughes/ACPL **116** SV/ACPL **117** CB **118** ACPL **119** L Hughes **120** ACPL **121** CB **122** t I Clough/CBPL b SV/ACPL **123** CBPL **124** t K Wilson b CB **126** DS **128** t GB b Somervell/ACPL **129** R Meredith-Hardy **130 131** t GB b F Smythe/ACPL **133** DS **134 135** D Molenaar **136** GB **137** Indian Air Force **138** JC **139** RGS **140** JB/RGS

141 GB/RGS **142** l r RGS **143** GB **144** JB/RGS **146 147 148** DS **149** l Peter **150** P Schoening/ American Karakoram Expedition 1958 **151** American Karakoram Expedition 1958 **152** JC **153** L Hughes/ACPL **156** S Razetti **157** GB **159** JB **160 161** l GB **162** M Banks **163 164** l **165 166 167** t b **168** CBPL **169** B Murphy/K Phillips **170** t GB b J Ward **171 172** GB **173** M Gravina/S Clark **174 175** GB **176** JB **178** J Porter **179** R Barton **180 181** J Tasker/CBPL **182** DS **184** DS/CBPL **185** l CBPL r R Barton **186 187** t b M Boysen **188 189 190** CBPL **191** R Richards/CBPL **192** t b l & r **193 194** KD **195 196** SV **197** GB **198** A McGarry/G Stainforth **200** t b **201 202 203** MF **204** t TN l MF r GB **205** MF **206** B Murphy **207 208** RP **209 210** M Moran **211** ER Allen **212** ET Compton/ACPL **213** t J Pratt b CBPL **215** t m A Hinkes b J Older **216** JC **217** B Murphy **218** MF/ACPL **219** M Doyle **220** t H MacInnes b JC **221** Luke Hughes **222** DS **223** Ian Howell **224** J Arran **225** l D Hamilton r MF **227** A Arran **228** J Auldjo/ACPL **229** GB **230** Diana Fitzpatrick **231** t ACPL b GB **232** R Lawford **233** ACPL b Croft/ACPL **234** ACPL **235 236** JC/ACPL **237** J Merz **238** K Steel/ACPL **239** H Fletcher/ACPL **240 241** GB **242** R Hanson/GB **243** GB **244** t Una Cameron/ACPL b J Cooper **245** GB **247** t DS b **248 249** GB

End Papers TN **Front Cover** M Gravina/S Clark **Rear Cover** GB **Rear Flap** N Riley

INDEX